T0289107

Dissent and Affirmation

Dissent and Affirmation:

Essays in Honor of Mulford Q. Sibley

Edited by
Arthur L. Kalleberg
J. Donald Moon
Daniel R. Sabia, Jr.

Bowling Green University Popular Press
Bowling Green, Ohio 43403

Library of Congress Catalogue Card No.: 83-71965

ISBN: 0-87927-239-8 Clothbound
      0-87972-240-1 Paperback

Cover photo by Tom Foley, University of Minnesota

for

MULFORD Q. SIBLEY

teacher, scholar, political activist, human being extraordinary

Contents

Preface

This collection has a long history. Originally conceived nearly a decade ago, a number of Professor Sibley's students, especially Michael Gargas McGrath, helped keep the idea of a *festschrift* honoring Mulford Sibley alive. Together with Don Moon, McGrath helped identify former students and other friends who might wish to participate in such a project. Somewhat later Dan Sabia, and then Art Kalleberg, became involved in the evolving process; eventually, papers were solicited and concrete plans laid; and the initial result was a two volume collection of essays—bound in red—and presented to Professor Sibley on his retirement in June of 1982. The present collection represents, therefore, but a portion of those initial essays, and but a part of the efforts and contributions made by many individuals over a long period of time.

The editors wish to thank the present contributors for their willingness to tolerate, in good spirits no less, the many demands placed upon them. They want also to express their gratitude to Marjorie Sibley for her unique and indispensable help and advice, and to Elaine Spitz for her help in editing the paper contributed by her late husband, David, whose absence is sorely felt. Finally, they want to thank the many friends, colleagues, and former students of Professor Sibley, and also Loyola University of Chicago, and the Department of Political Science at the University of Minnesota, for providing the financial support without which publication of this collection would not have been possible.

The Editors
December 1982

One

Introduction:
Reflections on the Political Thought
of Mulford Q. Sibley

Arthur L. Kalleberg
J. Donald Moon
Daniel R. Sabia, Jr.

Politics, Mulford Sibley has written, comprises "man's deliberate efforts to order, direct, and control his collective affairs and activities; to set up ends for society; and to implement those ends."[1] This conception of the political has been a central theme of Sibley's wide-ranging writings, informing and unifying his work on nonviolence, on utopia, and on the nature of political theory. As Sibley has often reminded us, it is a conception of politics that is central to classical political philosophy, a conception that arises when "the predeliberate orderings characteristic of nature and primitive human nature" break down.[2] It is also an ideal, for we often fail not only to control and direct our affairs, but even to make the attempt. In the lectures he gave annually at the University of Minnesota on the "History of Political Thought," he was fond of quoting Plato's complaint in the *Laws* "that man never legislates, but accidents of all sorts...legislate for us in all sorts of ways. The violence of war and the hard necessity of poverty are constantly overturning governments and changing laws."[3] But even if most legislation is a result of accident, Mulford Sibley holds out to us the idea of a politics that is a sphere of human freedom, in which men and women could collectively determine the conditions of their common life.

While this view of politics has ancient roots, it has not been dominant in modern, academic political science. Far more common is the identification of the political as a sphere of force and interest. From this perspective, politics becomes a struggle among people

2

who are trying to advance their own interests, and the central questions of political theory become "who gets what, when, how?". Political outcomes, on this account, reflect the balance of social forces, and we have a politics devoid of vision. What is wrong with this perspective, in Sibley's view, is that it at least implicitly denies the possibility of a different form of politics, and it does so without adequate empirical or theoretical warrant.[4] While it is certainly true that Sibley's conception of politics represents a moral ideal, he would argue that this is not a problem for political inquiry. For the primary aim of the student of politics is practical, to help us see what we ought to do, how our collective affairs ought to be arranged. We study politics scientifically because we need accurate knowledge if we are to realize our goals, or to determine if they can be realized. In projecting and analyzing moral and political ideals, the theorist "is not coming to destroy the scientific character of his task, but to fulfill it."[5]

Mulford Sibley has taught us that viewing politics as deliberate human efforts to order collective affairs leads to our asking different questions from those which are suggested by other conceptions of politics. For one thing, it keeps the practical issues of political life at the forefront of political inquiry. Towards what ends, and in accordance with what standards, do different societies organize their affairs? What groups and individuals actually participate in collective decision-making? Under what circumstances do the orderings and direction of collective life become compatible with the aspirations and commitments of individual members of society? As Sibley has often argued, 'the questions which direct scientific inquiry are never entirely internal to science, but are always in part determined by the values and preconceptions of the investigator. One of the advantages of Sibley's conception of politics is that it directs our attention to questions of real significance, and away from "the trivial questions that now so frequently concern [political science]."[6]

One of the values suggested by Sibley's conception of politics is non violence, for to the extent that politics is genuinely a sphere of collective self-determination, it excludes violence, and ideally other forms of coercion as well. This is the issue to which Sibley has devoted much of his energies as a scholar, teacher, and citizen— roles which were never really separate for him. As a conscientious objector during World War II, he was active in peace groups, and directed much of his scholarship to this problem. His *Political Theories of Modern Pacificism* and the award-winning *Conscription of Conscience* reflect his concerns in that period. He has returned again and again to these questions, in numerous articles, lectures, and books, including especially *The Quiet Battle,* and these writings constitute one of the most important contributions to the theory of nonviolence in contemporary times.

As a pacifist, Sibley holds that violence is morally wrong; all violence "undermine[s] the possibilities of deliberate ordering of human affairs and in doing so betray[s] the implicit purposes of politics."[7] Nonetheless, he recognizes that coercion cannot always be avoided. "Short of the perfect congruence of justice, legislation, and the freely developed inner convictions of individuals in a community of constant dialogue, it would seem that coercion of man by man is inevitable and, given the limitations of man in civilization, that some types of it are relatively justifiable." But he quickly adds, even if coercion is unavoidable, it "always represents a species of failure."[8] Sibley's account of pacifism, and the issues raised by the theory and practice of non violence, are discussed in the essays in section one of this book.

Pacifism and the Control of Violence

In the first essay in this section Earl Shaw analyzes Sibley's pacifism in terms of Reinhold Niebuhr's critique of Christian pacifism. Shaw describes how Sibley employs two strategies to defeat or escape Niebuhr's strictures: on the one hand, he has tried to refute directly some of Niebuhr's most telling criticisms; on the other, he has actually incorporated into his understanding and defense of pacifism many of Niebuhr's deepest convictions about human nature. Although he argues that Sibley's strategies have been in the main successful, Shaw nevertheless concludes that the two theorists remain irreducibly at odds on crucial issues, and that Sibley's defense of pacifism remains in some respects open to doubt and question.

Some of these doubts are raised by Terence Ball, who challenges Sibley's defense of pacifism in the spirit of friendly criticism. Branding Sibley's pacifism "pure" on the ground that it holds nonviolence to be an absolute duty, Ball argues that Sibley's defense is unsatisfactory in two ways. First, although Sibley appears to maintain that a consideration of consequences should not be used in defining one's moral duties, his defense of the duty of nonviolence rests at least partly on a consequentialist claim to the effect that "violence only begets violence." Second, Ball argues that an additional defense, to the effect that the duty of nonviolence is apprehended intuitively, is no (rational) defense at all since appeals to intuition or faith are nonrational. Moreover, concludes Ball, such a defense is "anti-political" since, being "deaf to argument and counterargument, reason and evidence, conjecture and refutation," it makes "public discourse and disputation" impossible, and so threatens to separate morality from politics.

Professor Sibley's rejection of violence, and his "relative" defense of certain "types of coercion," presuppose an understanding of the distinctions among violence, coercion, and related concepts. Sibley has sought to provide such an understanding and he is joined in this endeavor by Peter Sederberg in the third essay in this section. Sederberg argues that "coercion" should be used to refer only to cases of "intentional harm," and that "force" and "violence" are typically used to distinguish "acceptable" from "unacceptable" forms of coercion—"force" is acceptable, "violence" is unacceptable. After describing the difficulties raised by his suggested definitions and after explaining how these difficulties can account for disputes over the application of these terms to actions and situations, he goes on to question, as Sibley has questioned, the degree to which harm, coercion, force, and violence can be eliminated or controlled. Sederberg concludes, in substantial agreement with Sibley, that even under utopian conditions one can at best hope only for the elimination of violence, and that "an appropriate goal of utopian political action is to advocate a distinction between force and violence based on the difference between the strategy of withheld behavior and non-cooperation and that of direct attack."

The control of violence, force, and coercion is a goal that has animated a good deal of political and legal activity. In Chapter Five, Richard Hartigan describes an important historical effort to regulate the incidence and nature of war. He traces the development of rules of war to medieval times, describing the emergence of the idea of noncombatant immunity, which is now an accepted norm of international behavior and rule of international law. Hartigan offers an account of the role of the Church and of Christian ideals in the development of this and related ideas, and explores the theoretical weaknesses and limitations of these early efforts to control and humanize man's most inhumane practice.

Violence is often justified in revolutionary movements on the grounds that it is necessary for the realization of the goals of revolution: freedom, justice, and equality. Since these are goals that Sibley shares, he has had to confront this argument directly, and to show that their realization does not require violent means. In *Nature and Civilization* he describes an imaginary "utopian movement" whose members were "impressed by the futility of violence as a strategy of fundamental...change" and who consequently employed peaceful means, including nonviolent resistance, to bring about a new world order.[9] This imaginary movement experienced, however, many of the problems traditionally associated with actual revolutionary movements— and it is just such an analysis of the "dilemmas" of revolutionary action that Kathy Ferguson contributes in the fifth essay in this section. Ferguson begins with an account of the tragic dilemma described by Camus, whose rebel discovers that the struggle for good necessitates evil, and suggests that this dilemma reflects a basic "ontological dualism" in human experience. Fundamental to that experience, she believes, is the dualism between being and becoming, between order and change. This dualism is reflected in the revolutionary process, especially in the transition period in which leaders and followers must move from a preoccupation with change to a focus on the maintenance of order. "The seizure of power must be transformed into the capacity to make public decisions," and this new demand, which cannot be avoided, conflicts with and all to often undermines the ideals for which the revolution was fought. Ferguson argues that it is essentially this dilemma which accounts for the failure of most revolutions; she concludes her analysis by suggesting how revolutions might avoid this all too typical fate.

Revolutionary goals, including the control of violence, are sought also by Christian Bay who, like Professor Sibley, has in his scholarship and practical activities sought to raise the level of consciousness—and to prick the conscience—of both lay and academic audiences. In the final contribution to this section, Bay focuses primarily on the practical question, what can academics in general, and political theorists in particular, do to help bring about a more non-violent social and world order? He offers a number of proposals for reforming the structure and functions of universities and demands that political theorists work to unmask those ideologies which support domination and oppression. Political theorists should develop better strategies of political education and political resistance, and they ought to construct viable schemes detailing a more just, less violent social and world order together with an account of the means to be employed in achieving (and maintaining) that order. In offering this program for political theory Bay perfectly describes the work of Mulford Sibley.

Images of Utopia

If all politics involves the attempt deliberately to order our collective affairs, the obvious questions that must be asked are what are the conditions under which full collective self-determination is possible? What are the institutions through which a genuine politics could be achieved? These questions, with their invitation to utopian speculation, have been an important concern for Mulford Sibley for many years. His first publication was a two-part essay, "Apology for Utopia," that vigorously criticizes historicist and reductionist conceptions of politics. These views, Sibley árgues, deny the possibility of politics by denying that conscious and deliberate actions can influence the course of events. But, Sibley goes on to argue, if we suppose that humans can at least to some extent direct the course of their lives according to their purposes and beliefs, then we cannot avoid asking what purposes we should adopt, and this requires systematic reflection on our own values and political principles. It is in this context that utopian reflection has its role, for utopias enable us to represent abstract ideals in concrete terms that are intelligible and accessible to political thinkers and citizens. "Every Utopia considered as a special form for the expression of ideals is simply a coherent picture illustrating abstract principles; contrariwise, every statement of abstract principles could be converted, with imaginative and literary effort, into a Utopia."[10] Thus, utopian thinking is integral to political theory. In Part Two of this book, four of his former students address themselves to issues in utopian theory to which Sibley introduced them.

Lyman Tower Sargent presents in Chapter Eight a chronological overview of the place of the family in utopian fiction. Focusing on defenses, criticisms, and changing conceptions of the family, Sargent indicates that a perennial question for utopian thinkers has been whether this institution contributes to or undermines various political and social ideals. Particularly important are the ideals of citizenship and order or harmony, since the individual's duties and loyalties to the family unit may conflict with the former, while family structure and practices—e.g., its role in socialization and education—will substantially affect the latter.

Sargent's focus on the family reflects his belief that the study of utopian literature is most rewarding when specific themes are selected and examined historically, comparatively, and critically. In this he mirrors the practice of Professor Sibley who, in several essays and monographs, has examined such themes as religion and belief systems, democracy, and political economy. He has devoted special attention to the theme of technology in utopian thought, because complex technology seriously threatens politics. Because technology has profound effects on our society, but is seldom subjected to conscious, deliberate control, it is one of the most important "accidents" that "legislates" for us in myriad ways. In Chapter Nine, James Farr demonstrates the same concern by examining the place of science and technology in the ideas of the seventeenth-century utopian socialist Gerrad Winstanley.

Farr borrows from Professor Sibley a three-fold division of utopian views on technology—whole-hearted acceptance, radical rejection, selective implementation—and concludes that, "on balance," Winstanley embraced the third position. Although Winstanley "praised technological advance," he also recognized "the need to submit technological innovation to constant democratic scrutiny in order that it remain responsible, humane, and part of the 'common treasury for all'." Farr does not miss the fact that Winstanley, the Digger, can thus be placed in Professor Sibley's camp. Both support a socialist community, emphasizing "egalitarian participation in all areas of life and. . .an educational system which promotes virtue," in part because they believe it is only in such a system that the problem of controlling technology can be solved.

Democratic ideals, including egalitarian participation, are thus a central part of Professor Sibley's utopian vision. In *Nature and Civilization*, he envisions these ideals realized through and in a decentralized system of neighborhood direct democracies. He does not endorse an alternative version of direct democracy which Richard Dagger in Chapter Ten terms "instant direct democracy." This utopian vision employs technology—televisions, cables, and computers—to make direct democracy possible on a national scale. Explaining that this vision of national "government by electronic referendum" is or soon will be technically feasible, Dagger's thesis is that it is politically undesirable. His argument is not only that a system of this kind would likely produce less than thoughtful public policies; it would also undermine—or rather accelerate the undermining of—citizenship. True or "ethical" citizenship, expounds Dagger, is a demanding and desirable vocation that has for a variety of reasons been retarded and eroded in modern civilization. Instant direct democracy would continue, probably accelerate, this trend, in part because those political activities "which contribute to the enrichment of the individual—debate, compromise, strategy—are likely to vanish as the mechanical art of voting in the comfort of one's home, free from the frustrations of confronting other people with opposing views, becomes virtually the only connection between most individuals and public life."

Dagger's brief against instant direct democracy draws on the ancient, especially Greek, conception of citizenship. But this conception, and the ideal of self-government to which it was joined, is of course reminiscent also of Rousseau who, as Daniel Sabia makes clear in Chapter Eleven, haunts Professor Sibley's utopian vision as that vision is outlined in *Nature and Civilization*. Sibley explicitly incorporates into his utopia the "conditions for genuine community" laid down by Rousseau; and he also tries like Rousseau to reconcile individual liberty and political authority by meshing this community with the practice of local direct democracy. Sabia seeks in his contribution both to explicate and defend the theory of authority developed by Sibley (and, in the process, to describe for us at least some of the features of Sibley's utopia). By defending Sibley's theory against some important criticisms, Sabia hopes to demonstrate that the kind of normative theory of authority developed by Sibley is coherent and yet sensitive to the sometimes competing demands of individual freedom and the need for social order and collective action.

The Nature of Political Theory

Sibley's conception of politics as the deliberate ordering of collective affairs calls for political theories that address the fundamental practical questions that such a politics raises. The kinds of knowledge we require include an account of moral values and principles, as well as knowledge of the limits on human action imposed by external nature, history, and our own nature as human beings. Political theory is essential, because "thought is man's only salvation in the political realm: the gods will not provide answers for the riddle of consciously and deliberately controlling human collective destiny, and man has long ago passed the point where he can rely on instinct or rigid tradition."[11] This is the reason Sibley has defended utopian speculation, and why he has written extensively on the history of political ideas, the meaning and nature of political theory, and the relationships among empirical, normative, and philosophical questions in the study of politics.

One of the most vexing questions that political theory must address is the problems and dangers associated with moving from moral and political theories into the realm of concrete political practice. In Chapter Twelve, the late David Spitz examines these issues in the context of Karl Marx's theory of revolutionary praxis. According to Spitz, Marx never in fact connected theoretical and practical knowledge, at least not in the requisite detail. As a result, he failed to provide the moral criteria required to determine the limits on human action, he ignored the corrupting effects of violence, and he promised an altogether mythical future in the name of which his followers could commit unspeakable horrors. Having made these (and other) errors, Marx invited the uses and abuses to which his ideas were later put, and so he must, in Spitz's view, stand responsible to some extent. Rather than advancing programs of total social transformation, political theorists must develop *particular* theories of action "rooted in *specific* programmatic requirements and consequences." In this way, concludes Spitz, they may be able to have some practical effect and yet avoid the invitation to corruption that will inevitably accompany less precise and grander schemes.

Spitz's critique of Marx is motivated by an interest in a number of theoretical and practical political questions which he *shares* with Marx. That students of the history of political thought share with past thinkers and theorists a number of common concerns, and that the former can therefore (and in more than one way) learn from the latter, are two contentions that Professor Sibley has always believed and frequently defended. In Chapter Thirteen, J. Donald Moon builds upon Sibley's arguments to defend these theses. Moon argues that all human beings face an important set of common circumstances and develop what are often implicit conceptions of themselves and these circumstances. One task of political philosophy, he avers, is precisely to "articulate these underlying conceptualizations of the individual and society;" and since these conceptualizations are rooted in and related to the shared set of common circumstances, and since political philosophers articulate them at a general or theoretical level, students of the history of political thought can indeed understand and learn from these philosphers, despite their location in distant times and different cultures.

Moon's argument is embedded in, and connected to, a larger thesis about the nature of political philosophy and the study of politics. Essentially that thesis is that political philosophy involves the development of conceptualizations of the individual and society which "provide the conceptual frameworks for theories of politics" (as well as standards of evaluation for actual and potential political practices). Those who contend that political philosophy is an altogether speculative, conceptual, or "meta" activity, divorced from the empirical study of politics, are therefore mistaken. For the empirical study of politics must also presuppose or employ some conception of the person, and the success of any political theory will at least partly depend on the extent to which the model is in fact embodied in the beliefs and self-understandings of social and political actors.

Moon's discussion of conceptualizations of the individual and society may well remind one of the traditional dictum, often repeated by Professor Sibley, that all political theories contain or presuppose a conception of human nature. In Chapter Fourteen, Samuel Cook does not question this assertion, but he does question the closely related contention that particular conceptions of human nature have a significant, perhaps even decisive, impact on substantive political ideas. Cook examines several Protestant political theorists who have emphasized original sin, and asks whether these thinkers concur on the basic form of government. He finds that they have not: some advocated democratic, others authoritarian, governmental forms; still others are neutral on the issue. While Cook is aware that other explanations might account for this finding, he argues that the best explanation is that conceptions of human nature are typically "large, sweeping, ambiguous, and lacking in material content;" they are consequently incapable of driving or forcing material conclusions. "General propositions...do not decide concrete cases," and this includes propositions about humankind's nature or essence which are simply "not instructive of what kind of government is best or of which course of political action is wiser." The move from statements (and convictions) about human nature to concrete political ideas and proposals thus involves, concludes Cook, other factors which he briefly describes.

Cook's remarks about the import and character of "human nature" arguments leads to broader questions of the kind broached by Arthur Kalleberg in Chapter Fifteen. Kalleberg's intent is to sketch the "structure" of *substantive* political argument "in order to better understand how one might *do* political theory." Drawing on a number of analysts, and especially on Stephen Toulmin's reconstruction of the process of practical reasoning, Kalleberg outlines the structure of political argumentation and identifies a number of modes of argument—besides deduction and induction—that can be legitimately employed in political theorizing. Examples are drawn from Plato, Hobbes, Rousseau, and Marx to help illustrate and confirm these contentions.

Of special interest in Kalleberg's essay is his suggestion that what is most unique about, and problematic for, political theorists is that they are "always and necessarily confronted by constitutional (foundational or constitutive) and policy differences that are directly grounded in fundamentally opposed ways of life." As a result, they "cannot avoid the problem of what is meant by making a 'rational choice' *across* ways of life." Kalleberg's contention is that material arguments are crucial at this level of debate or theory—and that his identification of nonformal "conductive arguments" constitutes a first step in understanding how argument at this level can be both effective and legitimate, i.e., rational and reasonable. He thus holds open the possibility that men and women can rationally discuss and decide the direction of their common affairs. And if that is possible, we may yet hope for a politics of freedom, of collective self-determination.

I

Pacifism and the Control of Violence

Two

Christians in Conflict: Sibley and Niebuhr on the Use of Violence

L. Earl Shaw

Violence has been one of Mulford Sibley's most persistent concerns. As one of this country's most articulate defenders of modern pacifism, Sibley argues that violent coercion is *never* justifiable. Specifically, "all war, as a type of violent coercion, is morally unjustifiable, whatever its objectives."[1]

On the other hand, Reinhold Niebuhr, probably America's greatest theologian since Jonathan Edwards and often cited as the leading American political philosopher since Calhoun, has argued vigorously against pacifism or a categorical condemnation of violence. Sibley has referred to Niebuhr as modern pacifism's "most redoutable critic." Though both men are Christians, Sibley's sense of political responsibility leads him to reject all violence, while Niebuhr concludes: "A responsible relationship to the political order makes an unqualified disavowal of violence impossible."[2]

This paper examines the views of Niebuhr and Sibley on violence and pacifism. The first part of the paper summarizes Niebuhr's attack on pacifism and the theological and ethical bases for that critique. The second part of the paper attempts to ascertain the degree to which Niebuhr's general attack on pacifism is valid with reference to Sibley's position and examines Sibley's views on violence and pacifism using Niebuhr's criticisms as a reference point. The resulting analysis shows these two Christians' political philosophies are much closer than a superficial first encounter might suggest. A concluding section will highlight the similarities and differences and reflect on the contributions of each theorist.

Niebuhr's Views on Pacifism
Many do not realize that Niebuhr was once a pacifist himself.

Though a peculiar combination of American nationalism and Wilsonian liberalism led him to disavow pacifism and support the United States in World War I, subsequent revelations and events caused such a revulsion in him that he again turned to pacifism around 1923. In his diary he wrote: "I am done with the war business...I hope I can make the resolution stick."[3] In the 1920s he joined and became national head of the Fellowship of Reconciliation, a major pacifist organization.

But it is fair to say that Niebuhr was never an absolute pacifist. While he was in FOR he published an article in which he "proved the political irrelevance of absolute pacifism and revealed myself as a proponent of 'pragmatic' pacifism.'[4] Pacifism was never a position he held with confidence; almost immediately he was troubled and filled with doubts.

Niebuhr's major intellectual break with pacifism came in 1932, signified best by publication of his *Moral Man and Immoral Society*. Interestingly his break came in the context of the social and industrial strife of domestic politics and the class struggle, and not in the context of international conflict. Niebuhr, no doubt influenced by his attraction to Marxist analysis at this time of his life, would not deny the use of all violence by the underprivileged in the struggle for social change and social justice.[5] He did not formally resign from FOR until 1934. Even in the statement conveying his reasons for resigning, we see his attempt to remain a pacifist regarding international war though he had abandoned pacifism in the domestic struggle for social justice.[6] Within two years, the pragmatism issuing from his Christian realism had led him to disavow pacifism in the international arena. Not even the threat of atomic war with its attendant horrors caused him to alter his basic position again.

Soft Utopianism. Whether judged by the standards of the total gospel or the facts of human experience, modern pacifism's reinterpretation of the Christian gospel in terms of the Renaissance faith in man is a heresy, which results in naive utopianism and unjustified optimism. Pacifist political thought is one example of what Niebuhr calls "soft utopianism," whose proponents think history is a kind of process of redemption. This is rooted in the belief that "man is essentially good at some level of his being."[7] Contrary to the Christian interpretation, based on the New Testament, there is the false expectation that the ideal of love gradually will triumph and history will see the elimination of human selfishness, conflict and the need for force.

This reinterpretation is "at variance with the profoundest

insights" of the Christian faith. Niebuhr has no quarrels with the pacifist affirmation that love is the law of life; his objection centers on the pacifist tendency to equate (or reduce) the gospel to this law in which the good news becomes a challenge to try harder. Niebuhr writes: "The good news is that there is a resource of divine mercy which is able to overcome a contradiction within our souls, which we cannot ourselves overcome. This contradiction is that, though we know we ought to love our neighbor as ourself, there is a 'law in our members which wars against the law that is in our mind,' so that, in fact, we love ourselves more than our neighbor."[8] The atonement reveals God's mercy as an ultimate resource by which God *alone* (not man through his striving) overcomes the judgment which our sin deserves. The final possibility of love in history is forgiveness.

Niebuhr's rejection of pacifism is rooted in his doctrine of man. Man who stands at the juncture of nature and spirit is both finite and free, limited yet transcendent; he lives in a state of "tension." In his efforts to escape or relax that tension, through the exercise of his will he moves toward one pole or another and thus "sins." Niebuhr argues: "[E]vil in man is a consequence of his inevitable though not necessary unwillingness to acknowledge his dependence, to accept his finiteness and to admit his insecurity, an unwillingness which involves him in the vicious circle of accentuating the insecurity from which he seeks escape." In his effort to escape the tension, man claims he is more than he is, ignores his limits and dependence, and thus commits the sin of pride; or he claims he is less than he is, reducing himself to part of the natural process and thus commits the sin of sensuality. The religious dimension of sin is man's rebellion against God; man seeks to usurp God's place by refusing to accept his place in creation. More important from the standpoint of this paper is the moral and social dimension of sin which is injustice. "The ego which falsely makes itself the centre of existence in its pride and will-to-power inevitably subordinates other life to its will and thus does injustice to other life."[9] It is because all humans are sinners that justice can be achieved only by a certain degree of coercion on the one hand and resistance to coercion and oppression on the other.

Thus Niebuhr rejects the pacifist version which believes in progress because it fails to recognize the depth of man's sin and the reality of evil until the end of history, regardless of human knowledge, institutions, or efforts to "take Christ seriously." Because of man's freedom, history is both endlessly creative and endlessly destructive; each new development of life or new level of achievement presents us not only with new possibilities but also new hazards. Life in history cannot be emancipated from its contradictions and ambiguities; the inevitability of sin is a permanent fact of human history. War is not merely an "incident" in human history, it is a "final" revelation of the character of history. Man cannot live in history without sinning and history's conflicts are conflicts between sinners and sinners, not saints and sinners. Pacifists fail to recognize the gospel message that "man remains a tragic creature who needs the divine mercy at the end as much as at the beginning of his moral endeavors."[10]

Niebuhr recognizes the ethical problem of this more relativistic approach, i.e., making discriminations regarding relative virtues of competing groups and causes. "The danger of admitting this is, of course, that we make sin normative when we declare it to be inevitable."[11] But to fail to recognize the full seriousness of sin as a permanent historical fact will result in an inadequate social ethic and might lead to less real progress toward justice than is possible under conditions of sin. "Sanctification in the realm of social relations demands recognition of the impossibility of perfect sanctification."[12]

Love and Politics. Pacifism is in error in both its understanding and application of the law of love as reflected in the life and teachings of Jesus. Niebuhr admits that the pacifists are "quite right" in asserting that love is in fact the law of life. It is not some ultimate possibility which has nothing to do with human history. Niebuhr insists that the ethic of Jesus is "an absolute and uncompromising ethic": the ethic as taught in the Sermon on the Mount demands nonresistance. Nevertheless for Niebuhr this ethic is "not immediately applicable to the task of securing justice in a sinful world." There are no claims that it is "socially efficacious." In terms of social and political strategy the cross is not a success story; it stands at the edge of history, not in history.[13]

The pacifists "are just as guilty as their less absolutist brethren of diluting the ethic of Jesus for the purpose of justifying their position." Recognizing that nonresistance has "no immediate relevance," they transmute the ethic of nonresistance into one of nonviolent resistance, allowing one to resist evil if there is no destruction of life. From Niebuhr's perspective, there is "not the slightest support in scripture" for this switch.[14]

Once one makes the substitution one is moving in Niebuhr's direction toward developing a responsible political ethic. The "fateful concession" of ethics to politics is made when any coercion is accepted as a necessary instrument for social cohesion and social justice. Niebuhr asserts that there are no intrinsic moral differences or absolute distinctions between violent and nonviolent resistance. Both are coercive. "If such distinctions are made they must be justified in terms of the consequences in which they result."[15] As for social consequences of the two methods, the differences are ones "in degree rather than in kind." Therefore, the choice of appropriate means becomes more of a pragmatic and technical question whose justification depends upon their utility in achieving the morally approved ends dictated by justice. To make absolute distinctions in means used leads one to the "morally absurd position of giving moral preferences to the nonviolent power which Dr. Goebbels wielded over the type of power wielded by a general."[16]

Niebuhr's stand on love, power and coercion must be seen within the context of his understanding of love and justice, which are dialectically related. Despite the fact Niebuhr rejects the view that the law of love is directly applicable to politics (i.e., immediate possibility), he affirms love as the "primary law of man's nature; brotherhood, the fundamental requirement of his social existence." Man has an obligation to build a perfect communal life, for in his relationship to others he can become his true self by seeking self realization beyond himself. Jesus' love ethic is not useless or irrelevant to political life; in fact, it remains the "impossible possibility." Niebuhr uses this phrase to point to both the everpresent relevance as well as the difficulties of applying the law of love.[17]

Love is relevant both as a principle of indiscriminate criticism and as a principle of discriminate criticism for both motive and action. In the former sense, it judges all individuals and their actions as sinful and thereby helps them avoid self righteousness. Men are thus "prepared" for the good news of the gospel (i.e., divine grace that overcomes our contradiction and "pardons" us). The law of love not only measures our failure, it continues to have a claim on us as the ultimate criterion or goal of our achievements. It is a principle of discriminate criticism, aiding us in selecting the second best alternative or lesser of two evils. Shunning complacency, men, as convicted sinners, should humbly seek the best approximation to the ideal in society's laws, principles, structures, and concrete actions. Power and interest must be used toward ends dictated by love. Justice is love in action in the social arena under conditions of sin. Yet "love is both the fulfillment and the negation of all achievements of justice in history." While all systems and structures of justice are corrupt, love may break through and raise them to new heights. Thus justice must always be thought of in dynamic terms. Equality and liberty, though never perfectly embodied, and to some degree contradictory in their extreme literal application, are used by Niebuhr as regulative principles of justice.[18] *Individual Ethic vs. Social Ethic.* Pacifists fail to distinguish between an individual ethic and a social or political ethic (especially for statesmen or leaders of groups). This critique is rooted in Niebuhr's thesis that "a sharp distinction must be drawn between the moral and social behavior of individuals and of social groups, national, racial and economic, and that this distinction justifies and necessitates political policies which a purely individualistic ethic must always find embarrassing."[19] Whereas from the perspective of the individual the highest moral ideal is unselfishness, from the perspective of society the highest social ideal is justice. This is because individuals have the capacity and thus the possibility of acting more morally (more lovingly, less selfishly) than groups. Niebuhr has often been misunderstood on this point. He does not invoke two different ultimate norms; love remains the one true ultimate norm of life. Rather the degree to which the norm can be realized or approximated in interpersonal as distinguished from an intergroup context is different.

Pacifists are right that an individual may sacrifice (though it is not always "advisable") his life or interests rather than participate in the social struggle for justice, with all its claims and counterclaims. But they are wrong in making no distinction between individual acts of self-abnegation and a political policy of submission to injustice, whereby lives and interests of others are hurt or destroyed. Niebuhr writes: "As soon as the life and interests of others than the agent are involved in an action or policy, the sacrifice of those interests ceases to be 'self sacrifice.' It may become an unjust betrayal of their interests."[20] Thus statesmen, responsible for values, interests and lives beyond their own, do not have the option of sacrificing or committing the group to suffer injustice rather than let the conflict continue.

For Niebuhr the "very essence of politics is the achievement of justice through equilibra of power."[21] While a balance of power is not conflict, a tension between opposing forces or groups underlies it. Where there is tension there is potential conflict and where there is conflict there is always the potential for violence. Thus if one is to be responsible politically in pursuit of justice, one can not make an unqualified disavowal of violence. A sensitive conscience may find some political strategies embarrassing and offensive, but as responsible human beings we cannot "build our individual ladders to heaven" and leave the total human enterprise wallowing in social injustice and anarchy.

Connivance with Tyranny. In terms of practical politics, proponents of a pacifist political strategy, by refusing to recognize that sin introduces an inevitable element of conflict in all history, in effect give a "morally perverse" preference for tyranny over war (or other threats of anarchy) and demonstrate a callous insensitivity and disregard for the victims of tyranny. Niebuhr accuses them of proclaiming that "slavery is better than war." By refusing to see morally significant distinctions between democracy and tyranny or competing civilizations (with different values), pacifists distill moral perversity out of their moral absolutes. We live in a "tragic era." There are no pleasant alternatives; every possible policy presents "hazards and uncertainties." But to refuse to go to war (or even to "risk" war) against a tyrant, in practical terms, means complicity in that tyranny.[22]

Basically Niebuhr contends that tyranny can be as evil and destructive as war. The morally concerned person must be as sensitive to the human consequences of totalitarianism as he or she is to the human consequences of war. While tyranny is not war and it is a peace of sorts, "it is a peace which has nothing to do with the peace of the kingdom of God." It is a peace built on domination and acquiescence. Some values (e.g., equal justice) are higher than the "peace" of capitulation and submission.[23]

While recognizing there are no purely just causes, Niebuhr defended America's involvement in World War II. (The question of how and when to intervene was seen as a prudential and strategic decision.) In early 1941, Niebuhr perceived that: "Nazi tyranny intends to annihilate the Jewish race, to subject the nations of Europe to the dominion of a "master" race, to extirpate the Christian religion, to annul the liberties and standards that are the priceless heritage of ages of Christian and humanistic culture, to make truth the prostitute of political power, to seek world dominion through its satraps and allies and generally to destroy the very fabric of our Western Civilization."[24] Though one could not be certain that a new era of international peace and justice would follow defeat of the Nazis, one could perceive what a Nazi victory would mean.

Not even the advent of atomic warfare caused Niebuhr to alter his basic position on violence and war. In a 1955 comment on the Quaker publication, "Speak Truth to Power," he asserts: "Pacifism remains an irrelevance even in an atomic age." However, this "new setting" has created a new dimension of catastrophe for any future global war. The possibility and probability of incalculable destruction and death on all sides in a future war "alters" the moral problem even if it is not eliminated. That is, once again one can not draw a line in advance beyond which it would be better to yield than to resist, even by violence. But only the "most imperative demands of justice" can now have a clear sanction to justify violence or the risk of violence in today's context. Thus "the occasions to which the concept of just war can be rightly applied have become highly restricted." The claims of justice are no less, but the potentially incalculable destructive consequences of pursuing those claims is much greater. This underlines the importance of vigorously developing methods of peaceful, non-violent changes.[25]

Even though Niebuhr would not advocate a position of national defenselessness in the nuclear setting, he notes: "Yet even a nation can purchase its life too dearly. If we actually had to use this kind of destruction in order to save our lives, would we find life worth living?"[26] While nuclear weapons and the dangers of nuclear holocaust have "heightened" the moral dilemmas, the moral ambiguities and moral dilemmas have not been solved.

Isolation of the War Issue. Pacifists tend to isolate or focus on one particular moral issue (war), in which they demand the application of the uncomprising love-absolutism of Jesus' ethic (as they understand it) without seeing its broader political and social implications. He writes: "The injunction 'resist not evil' is only part and parcel of a total ethic which we violate not only in war-time, but every day of our life and that overt conflict is but a final and vivid revelation of the character of human existence."[27]

The violence problem should be seen in its broader societal setting in which the Christian lives and benefits from coercive economic and political relationships. Pacifism misunderstands the whole nature of historical reality. While worrying about Niebuhr and others "crucifying the Lord afresh" by advocating involvement in war *when necessary,* it does not recognize "that the selfishness of the best of us is constantly involved in the sin of crucifying the Lord afresh." Perfectionism in one area is accompanied with neglect in other areas where such perfectionism (if pacifists are to be consistent) might also provide a positive message of condemnation, challenge and reconstruction. Pacifists cannot "contract out" of organized society.[28]

The Validity of Religious Pacifism as a Symbol of the Kingdom. There is a kind of religious pacifism, as a version of Christian perfectionism, which is not heretical, but is in fact a "valuable asset for the Christian faith." Such pacifists have a constructive vocation in the church. Even in 1940, with war approaching, he wrote, "We who allow ourselves to become engaged in war need this testimony of the absolutist against us, lest we accept the warfare of the world as normative, lest we forget the ambiguity of our own actions and motives and the risk we run of achieving no permanent good from this momentary anarchy in which we are involved."[29] This kind of pacifism, which can probably be carried through "literally and absolutely" only upon an ascetic basis, expresses a genuine impulse in Christianity to take the law of love seriously and not to allow the "responsible" person's political strategies, which the reality of sin makes necessary, to become final norms.[30]

This religious pacifism understands the perennial paradox and moral ambiguities in man's social life. Such "goodness" knows "martyrdom to be its end." Niebuhr comments:

> If any Christian wishes to say that it is incompatible with Christianity to fool with the terrible and sinful relativities of the political world, I for one will accord him my genuine respect and admiration *if he leaves the world of politics alone* entirely and seeks simply to live by the love commandment in terms which demand an irresponsible attitude toward the problem of collective justice in international and economic terms. Let him, in other words, be a pure pacifist and remind the rest of us, who fool with politics, that we are playing a dangerous game.[31]

Sibley's Views on the Use of Violence

Sibley, who will readily confess his appreciation of Niebuhr's political thought, is intimately familiar with the theologian's critique of pacifism. Sibley admits that Niebuhr's attack on the politics of pacifism is "in some measure sustained." Part of his acceptance of the legitimacy and the limited validity of Niebuhr's attacks is no doubt due to the fact that Niebuhr's conception of pacifism is not fully identical with Christian pacifism as espoused by thinkers such as Mulford Sibley. The extremely optimistic pre-World War II pacifism which Niebuhr attacks is different from the more "realistic" pacifism of Sibley. Sibley notes that Niebuhr "fails to apprehend clearly the theological assumptions of at least non-anarchist religious pacifism. They are much closer to his own beliefs than he will admit." Sibley appears to include himself in this group of pacifists who will agree with their critics, like Niebuhr, on the "hard inner core of human nature and destiny."[32]

Sibley's assumptions regarding human nature bear a striking resemblance to Niebuhr's perception of man standing at the juncture of nature and spirit, who can "freely" choose good or evil. Furthermore both recognize the social dimensions of man's existence. Both see personhood as not only rooted in the group but transcending the group, with the ultimate locus of reponsibility for moral decision, even in a democracy, residing in the individual. In "this worldly" terms they share many of the same goals such as development of the truly human personality and justice (which finds expression in freedom, equality, and fraternity or brotherhood).[33]

While Sibley regards Niebuhr's criticisms as "in some measure sustained," he believes that, "on the whole," they are "frequently invalid."[34] Despite many similarities in views, including a common appreciation for the norm of love, there is a fundamental disagreement on the legitimacy and utility of the special "means" of violence to achieve "good ends." Though violence is reluctantly accepted by Niebuhr, with an awareness of potential dangers and implications, Sibley maintains that the use of violence, even in defensive war, is *never* morally justified and is inefficacious in the long run for attaining otherwise desirable goals.

Sibley enumerates five tenets that are held in common by modern pacifist thinkers (including himself):

1. Violence hinders the achievement of a democratic and peaceful order.
2. Modern states are built on violence and only revolution can effect a pacifist order.
3. This revolution must develop and employ a technique embodying a non-violent ethic.
4. Decentralization in politics and in the economic order is sought.
5. The ideology of non-violence has a direct relevance to politics.[35]

The meaning and implications of these tenets will become clear as Sibley's views vis-a-vis Niebuhr's specific attacks are examined. *Soft Utopianism.* Sibley explicitly rejects the validity of the heresy and utopianism critique (as intended by Niebuhr) as applicable to realistic modern pacifists like himself. "Realistic pacifists are not the 'soft utopians' so often attacked by thinkers like Reinhold Niebuhr." They do not share the naivete about human nature and illusions about politics and history Niebuhr attributes to pacifists. Sibley responds: "Contrary to Niebuhr's whole interpretation of what it holds, there is no evidence that the mainstream of religious pacifism, with the exception of Tolstoyan currents, looks forward to an easy triumph of that divine love of agape, which it seeks to infuse into politics."[36]

Sibley's view of human nature is definitely not an affirmation of the Renaissance view of goodness and perfectability of man in history. Sibley describes the paradox of man's position in the universe this way: "Hence while the limitations of language force us to describe man as both divine and natural, the commingling of the two in human existence and history can in a sense be thought of as transmuting man into a being *neither* divine nor natural. He is, as it were, a peculiar compound—not a mixture—of that which is both natural and divine and that which is neither natural nor divine."[37]

In an effort to escape this contradition in the search for security and certainty, man may stress one or the other pole. On the one hand he may deny his freedom and tell himself he is simply part of nature, dying a physical death like the beasts and flowers. Or he may seek to repudiate his ties to nature, stressing instead his divinity. In either case man tries to deny that he is in some sense *both* bestial and godlike. Yet if he faces up to this fact, he is "plagued by the disquietudes inevitably accompanying that situation." This fact of human existence—his location on the "isthmus of the middle state"—is the root of many of man's psychological, ethical and political problems.[38]

Man has certain attributes of divinity for he lives partly in a timeless dimension and he can will, can imagine and can choose; he can transform the natural world. Yet he has what Sibley calls "a kind of fatal flaw in that his judgments are limited by his frustrating position in nature or by the fact that he can and often does choose the evil." The most evil acts of human history are not "beastly," they are "human" for only humans are capable of such cruelties. For example, "only humans are capable of organizing and executing an Auschwitz or Hiroshima." Yet by the same token only humans are capable of the many dimensions of love.[39]

Thus both Sibley and Niebuhr see man as "fallen" ("mythically" speaking) with that state traceable to man's destructive use of his freedom. Sibley, in one of his earliest articles, notes that in a certain sense Christian pacifisim is "pessimistic;" it "is more nearly rooted in the idea of the unregenerate, or natural, man."[40] It is precisely because pacifism is aware of what Niebuhr terms the "demonic element" in human nature—"the tendency under all conditions to glorify force and seek power as an end in itself—that the ethical and empirical theory of pacifism is so concerned about the quality of the means used to implement ideals."[41]

Human conflict and power relations of some kind are perennial characteristics of human history. In *Nature and Civilization,* where he states his broad goals for society, Sibley says "we are not suggesting that history has within it the possibility of eliminating all forms of direct coercion."[42] The maintenance of the state is compatible with the pacifist perspective. Even in the sketches of a more preferable society, he allows for genuine policemen, restraints and sanctions, and some coercion. He has no illusions that such forms cannot lapse into violence. Pacifists do not ignore power, they try to identify and use non-violent forms of it to more realistically prevent "immoral" rule.

Sibley appears to appreciate Niebuhr's critique of the idea of inevitable and continuous progress, noting that he is "in some degree correct." Sibley wants men "released from the illusion of inevitable progress and from the equally great illusion that they can completely transcend nature and become like gods." He appears to agree with Niebuhr on the moral ambiguity of historical developments: "Every achievement of good is accompanied by the possibility of equivalent evil."[43]

Sibley correctly observes that Niebuhr in effect does not completely reject the idea of the possibility of some moral progress in history. Niebuhr speaks of the "indeterminate possibilities" for man's creative uses of freedom. Pacifists envision "the possibility of a measure of progress, in the sense that they do not believe it beyond the wit of men to make more shallow the valleys of 'decay and destruction' and to level down the peaks of power." Pacifism believes that it is not beyond human possibility to "break into what Gandhi has called this 'chain of destruction' by invoking a different political ethic that uses non-violent forms of power while remembering Niebuhr's warnings against the demonic possibilities of man."[44] The case can be made that Sibley has higher hopes for moral progress or more partial success in history than Niebuhr does.

For Sibley what progress is attained does not come easily or quickly; it often requires suffering, sacrifice, careful planning, etc. Nor are pacifists under any illusions that any new and better social and political forms attained "will remain true to their original purpose without constant vigilence and even resistance." Sibley reminds us that Christian pacifism still believes in "the fall." "The conception of a pacifist struggle is permanent on the plane of history."[45]

Love and Politics. Nowhere is the line of disagreement more clearly drawn between the two than on the issue of the relevance of the love ethic to politics. Both view the law of love as ultimately normative, but Sibley rejects Niebuhr's claim that love is not immediately applicable and argues that the ideology of nonviolence, as an expression of the law of love (and character of God) and respect for human personality, has *direct relevance* to human relations, even the realm of politics. Furthermore he argues that this point is illustrated in the life and teachings of Jesus and implicit in other parts of the New Testament.

He assumes Jesus was a "good Jew" who accepted the interweaving of ethics, politics and religion. Thus his teachings about what God's love implies were relevant to social organization and politics. Not only his teachings, but his actions reflect the relevance of the message. Sibley recognizes, as does Niebuhr, that the ethic of Jesus was primarily one of nonresistance, including passive submission to government, even foreign governments. But Sibley argues that Jesus' views on nonviolence are unmistakable. His response to the third temptation, his rebuke to a disciple who used the sword, the Sermon on the Mount, his death on the cross, and his descriptions of the nature of the Kingdom all are seen as advocating nonviolence.[46] Christian pacifism holds:

> The mission of Jesus was not to point to a "spiritual" kingdom in heaven, as contrasted with a temporal kingdom on earth; rather it was to indicate the way to conquest of power on earth by means which would not generate the will to power and hence result in a persistence of the chain of destruction maintained by man's failure to discover his own real will. It was this mission that led to the repudiation by Jesus of violence.[47]

Jesus witnessed to a basic truth. As Sibley has often noted, it is not true because Jesus said it; Jesus said it because it is true. In good Quaker fashion, Sibley subordinates scripture (which gives us our picture of Jesus) to his own conscience as the ultimate authority for decision.

In accordance with Niebuhr, Sibley clearly recognizes that the ideology of modern pacifism, perhaps partly due to its effort to be more explicitly political, has tended to eliminate the nonresistance theme of Jesus' teaching and substituted nonviolent resistance.[48] When asked about this by the author, Sibley noted that St. Paul said, "Overcome evil with good. If there is a clear conflict between Paul and Jesus, I'd prefer Paul." Thus the shift is justified in Sibley's eyes, for the nonviolent theme is retained. Furthermore, it is a more realistic response to politics.

While Sibley would agree with Niebuhr that no conduct can possibly measure up to the ideal, and that the pacifist ideal of conduct in politics represents an impossible ideal, he argues that Niebuhr draws the wrong inference from this, implying that since the ideal has not in fact been embodied in politics, the ideal should be discarded rather than used to protest actual political practices. To discard the pacifist ideal removes completely the "tension" between the "city of the world" and the "city of God"—a tension perceived by Sibley as "essential if power politics are to be controlled at all." While Niebuhr recognizes the existence and benefits of such a tension, he denies pacifism "any role in making the gulf between the ideal and real vivid and meaningful."[49]

This criticism of Niebuhr is somewhat unfair since Niebuhr commends a particular tradition of pacifism for reminding us of the compromises we are making and pointing to the law of love as the ultimate norm of our existence. Pacifism's message does make the gap vivid and meaningful. The real point of contention is that, for Niebuhr, pacifist *involvement* in politics is not going to change the character of politics, which invalidates attempts to *directly* apply the love norm.

To clarify his own ethical stance, Sibley refers to Max Weber's distinction between the "ethics of ends" and the "ethics of responsibility." The former calls for specific actions regardless of the consequences, while the latter calls for a weighing of consequences. Sibley contends that within his framework *both* ethics must be utilized. Either alone is inappropriate.

Both the statement "I shall do right though the heavens fall" and the assertion "the rightness of an act can be determined only by examing the consequences" are wrong when taken alone—the former because it seems to divorce "right" from any results for human beings, however horrible; the latter because it appears to ignore standards by which to judge consequences and also because it seems to forget that remote consequences can rarely be assessed.[50]

He does not reject the "pragmatic" element in some moral decisions.

Sibley also directs us to two other statements to clarify his position: "The end justifies the means" and "the means shape the ends." Contrary to the views of some, Sibley argues they are not incompatible; one can accept the validity of both. The means cannot be separated from the end to be achieved. The end justifies the means "only if and when the end is actually achieved, then, indeed the means selected can receive approval." The "end" is different from a "projected end" or intended goal which can "never" justify any and all means.[51]

The statement of an end often excludes certain types of means because the means used may contradict the very ends sought. He uses an analogy to make his point. If one wants a forest of oak trees, one plants acorns and only acorns. While they are not identical, the oak is embryonic in the acorn and under proper conditions it can produce an oak. Means and ends are interdependent. Sibley likens the wrong choice of means to "side effects" resulting from use of certain drugs. He also emphasizes the particular difficulty of ascertaining "long-run consequences" in the socio-political arena.[52]

Sibley rejects the view that some means may be "ethically neutral." In use, means are not neutral. To say a bomber might be used to carry freight is one thing; but when it is used to bomb, its users intend it to destroy and kill. In determination of the appropriateness of a particular means, Niebuhr's view is somewhat similar to the position being condemned here by Sibley. Yet while Niebuhr would agree that we can not determine a priori whether a particular means is good or evil, in practice all means are seen as ethically ambiguous.

Sibley's discussion of coercion as a means in politics is critical to understanding his repudiation of all violence. Coercion is inevitable but some types are more legitimate than others. He suggests a continuum with persuasion, which is always justifiable in pursuit of a just order, on the one end, and violence, which is never justified, on the other. Violent coercion is characterized by "deliberate killing, maiming, or torture of the physical body or the spirit of the human being." Not only is such violent coercion morally wrong in principle, it "negates the very purpose of social order—the enhancement of the good life for human beings—and rarely if at all can it be kept subordinate to the values embodied in the concept of justice." By its very nature violent coercion tends to become an end in itself. Sibley writes: "In fact to talk about violence in means as a way to achieve nonviolent ends is like speaking of the necessity for the production of hot ice." Pacifists such as Sibley contend that "violence is power which can never be controlled and which *always* 'corrupts' not only its user but also the end for which it is ostensibly used." Means shape the ends; the use of violence swallows up just goals.[53]

In his effort to classify morally illegitimate forms of coercion, Sibley singles out war and capital punishment as two clear examples of violence. Both deliberately take human lives, both depreciate the personality of those whose lives are to be taken. Both physical and spiritual violence are involved. Both involve the "supreme act of immorality, the destruction of human lives, itself intrinsically wrong." War like other forms of violent coercion tends to destroy the noble aims, goals or values for which wars are allegedly waged. Look not at the preferred ends; look at what war does to human beings. As war progresses the self-imposed restraints on violence diminish and the ends recede further into the background. "In the end, however, there is little to choose from a moral point of view between the two sides: Hitler burned Jews, allegedly as a war measure, and the United States incinerated thousands of Japanese women and children, also as a war measure." Short term consequences which are usually seen as bad are accepted or excused by appealing to "allegedly good long term consequences, which at the time can never be seen."[54] The same logic applies to "wars of liberation" (as opposed to imperialist wars). They too will prove counter productive or "reactionary," actually enhancing class differences and inequality."[55]

However, Sibley does not take the extreme view that war and violence have *never* accomplished anything in history. He would argue any sound pacifist philosophy of history will have to admit that war and violence may have led to "incidental goods." "But the good that was produced always flourished in a scheme of things which made it subordinate to a higher end—power." The evil produced was greatly disproportionate to the incidental good produced. "It is like burning down houses to produce roast pig."[56] Furthermore, such good might have been produced anyway without resort to violence.

Sibley's conception of violent coercion includes more than physical force such as war and capital punishment. There can be forms of non-physical violent coercion that are indiscriminate and irremediably injurious. Sibley notes: "As Niebuhr quite rightly points out, 'spiritual' force can be just as self centered, as egotistic, and therefore as violent, as physical force." As Niebuhr, Sibley would also identify Goebbels' acts as evil and forbidden. Sibley includes the utilization of the lie and unjust political and economic institutions as examples of non-physical violence.[57]

Thus Sibley's definition of violence is broader than one might see the term conventionally used. It is "all those acts, even those under the cover of positive law, which either deliberately take human life or build into the structure of society unredressable injury to human life." But Sibley also uses the term violence more narrowly than some. He does not equate the use of physical force with violence, for it is not always productive of injustice or injurious to human personalities. "To make evil co-terminous with violence is one thing; to identify violence with physical force and all physical force with violence is something entirely different."[58] Some forms of physical force may be necessary to achieve and maintain a just policy.

Between the poles of persuasion and violence, there are various forms of coercion whose moral and social justification depend on "the contingencies of the particular situation involved." This is where the Weberian ethic of responsibility comes into play. In his discussion of civil disobedience, Sibley argues he has an obligation to *both* obtain a factual background of the situation and to make some estimate of the consequences. In assessing some political actions, "the pragmatic criterion" is legitimate. Nonviolent coercion can be part of a successful social strategy. Whether an act of nonviolent coercion may be justified will depend on such factors as: "motivation and intention, improbability of serious injury to the person involved, possibility of the coercion's being subject to control, timing and direction of the coercion." One's final decision involves a judgment which attempts to consider the concrete situation, possible effects on others and the agent, and his/her hierarchy of principles (at the apex of which is non-killing).[59]

While the path of nonviolence is ethically higher and, in the long run, more efficacious in achieving things of value, a nonviolent strategy is no panacea or open sesame or sure-fire formula. Nonviolence will not always be successful or effective. Sibley notes that some pacifists do not see that individual objection to violence does not necessarily mean effective political objection. The possibility of success is partly dependent on the facts of the particular situation which should be assessed by the actor. The effective use of nonviolence depends not only on effective training and commitment by the actors, but also the "objective situation." In fact, persistence in a nonviolent campaign in the face of "unsuitable objective conditions" might actually set back the attainment of justice. "Commitment to non-violence does not mean that we can dispense with political wisdom."[60]

The capacity to distinguish between nonviolent and violent actions is critical to the Sibley argument. And on this score Sibley has dealt with two criticisms often leveled at pacifists. First, there is the critique that pacifists offer "no reliable criterion for distinguishing between violent and nonviolent action." For example, Niebuhr raises the issue about those affected in England by Gandhi's actions. Are not lives and livelihood at stake in general strikes or boycotts? Sibley's survey of pacifist thinkers suggests that they are "not satisfactory" in response to this issue. In fact he concludes, "this remains the weakest link in the whole pacifist chain." The second attack argues that not only have pacifists not adequately made the distinction, but any such distinction is *impossible* in politics. Often the critics mistakenly assume an identification of violence with coercion or nonviolence with noncoercion, which Sibley rejects. Sibley's philosophy admits the "inevitability and necessity of power," yet argues that a discrimination between types of power not only can but must be made if power is not to become the end.[61]

Sibley rejects Niebuhr's structuring of the choice. "Niebuhr apparently holds that there can be no middle ground between complete world-renunciation, on the one hand, and a willingness to see all types of power without distinction as ethically legitimate."

Sibley rejects this all or nothing approach and contends that meaningful distinctions, though difficult, can be made, particularly if one does not simple-mindedly equate all coercion with violence. One could plausibly argue that Socrates drinking the hemlock or Jesus on the cross may have been "highly coercive in compelling man, against their better judgment to act in certain ways." Or that Nehru or King in prison for civil disobedience is coercive. But surely these are ethically distinguishable from out-right physical violence like use of machine guns, bayonets, poison gas or nuclear weapons. Strikes, boycotts, mass civil disobedience, though clearly coercive in intent and fact, can be distinguished morally and in fact from war and armed revolt, even if the professed aim is to secure social justice.[62] Sibley admits there will be "gray areas" in which it is clearly difficult to draw the line. "But we should not on this ground fail to make an honest attempt to draw it."[63]

Individual Ethic vs. Social Ethic. Sibley rejects the idea that the ethic of pacifism is essentially personal without any relation to the problem of power in the collective life of human kind.[64] Sibley is not content for pacifists to play the symbolic role admired by Niebuhr admitting their irrelevance to politics but reminding us of the ultimate norm of our lives. Sibley will not leave the world of politics alone.

The following comment illustrates Sibley's view on the applicability of the same norm in the individual and "public" spheres of life.

In rare situations, it may be that we will be confronted with the choice between committing acts of violence or ourselves suffering violence. (By 'we,' we mean groups and nations, as well as individuals.) If we adhere to the standards suggested here, we should respond with Socrates' words "It is better to suffer injustice than to commit it."[65]

The juxtaposition of this quote to one by Niebuhr below clearly reveals the difference in their positions.

But only if one adopts the principle that it is better to suffer injustice than to resort to force can one wholly disavow the use of force. It is possible, though not always advisable, for individuals to suffer injustice rather than let the dispute come to an ultimate issue, but statesmen, responsible for values beyond their own lives, do not have this option. They must seek for justice by an accomodation of interests and they must protect precious values by force if necessary.[66]

In Sibley's framework, would a leader in a so-called democracy have to adopt a non-violent approach even if the citizens desired otherwise? He appears to argue one should follow one's individual conscience, especially in the principle of non-killing. But what if the individual consciences of the people collectively did not support a non-violent approach? Sibley writes that "Definitions of the common good must arise out of the group experience and be expressed through group authority."[67] As an authorized leader, am I to act contrary to the group's definition of the common good?

Sibley was a member of the Quaker committee which produced *In Place of War*. The report states: "First there must be clarity as to who can decide to use non-violent action in defending a country. As we see it, the country itself must make the decision. It can only be made by those who are legitimately responsible for setting policy and for making decisions.... The decision must be based in broad public understanding and support."[68] Sibley appears to present us (and himself) with a dilemma. One might try to "educate" the public or even resign one's position in protest. But is one to enact a non-violent approach even if the public (though morally wrong) persists in opposition?

Sibley recognizes that up to now pacifism has been largely a creed for a "rebel movement." When he speculates what if it succeeded and were called upon to furnish a handbook for governors, he observes that pacifist literature has been "amazingly vague and uncertain in the answers it gives."[69] The same evaluation might also be directed at Sibley's views on the issue.

Connivance with Tyranny. Sibley rejects outright Niebuhr's charge that in effect pacifism is guilty of connivance with tyranny. "Tyrannies arise not because men have accepted pacifism—with its stress on economic justice, absence of a psychology of subordination, repudiation of violence, and planning for non-violent resistance—but rather because they have rejected it."[70] But Sibley does recognize that tyranny must be resisted.

Sibley is not oblivious to relative moral distinctions between groups or nations, but he will condemn equally the violence used by combatants (regardless of which advocates the relatively more just cause). He can accept that in certain conflicts "it was better for the world that victory was vouchsafed to those who actually won rather than their opponents," but points out that the supposed beneficial effects "were largely negativized" because the "habit of violence itself" became more firmly established. One could say the "victory" by the Franks at Tours was "relatively better" than a triumph by the Sons of the Prophet, and yet at the same time, "and without any inconsistency" also attack the "citadel of power politics itself, and, from a position outside the presuppositions of the system deny that the outcome at Tours was good for the world."[71]

Even within Niebuhr's framework, pacifists would be guilty of "connivance with tyranny" only if it could be demonstrated that more relative good came out of the violence than would have resulted without resorting to violence. Sibley argues that a careful examination of the record does not substantiate that conclusion. Overall, violence tends to hinder moral progress. This even holds for the American Civil War and World War II (two wars Niebuhr would regard as relatively justified).[72]

Sibley has argued non-violent means can in the long run accomplish worthy objectives *better* than violence, even against totalitarian regimes. Though we really have no "direct experience" upon which to base our conclusion, for no major nation has yet followed the path of non-violence, he says "indirect experience" points to a non-violence success rate at least as great as that of military violence—and without the latter's enormous toll in physical, social, psychological and moral damage. Sibley cites numerous examples of the success of non-violence: the early Quakers in Pennsylvania, the Indian and South African struggles, King and the civil rights struggle, and Bishop Grundtvig in Denmark.[73] Thus non-violence for Sibley is "validated" in history. Pacifists cannot "connive" with tyranny if in fact their techniques are better at preventing and undermining tyranny.

Isolation of the War Issue. Sibley concedes that there is "not a little validity" in the Niebuhr argument that the pacifist thesis tends to isolate one issue and ignore "the broader social and political implications of its own philosophy." Pacifism is accused of stating it is *against* war and demands a perfectionist ethic in that area. Lacking is a statement of what pacifism would mean in *positive* terms. Sibley agrees that a genuine philosophy of nonviolence must see the problem of violence in "an extremely broad setting." Thus the "phenomena against which it is protesting cannot be exorcised by being isolated from the general problems of politics."[74] A person who begins with pacifist assumptions and has "the slightest regard for consistency and coherence" should emerge with a radical social philosophy. Once the ethical legitimacy of overt violence is challenged, logically one should question the "problem of the covert violences which stand at the very center of modern life." Every pacifist is implicitly either an anarchist or a socialist or a communist. Sibley himself is a democratic socialist who is extremely concerned about the centralization of power.[75]

Yet Sibley contends this "lop-sided" emphasis in pacifist political doctrine is "perfectly legitimate." It is because of "the very ubiquity of obvious violence, particularly war," in modern times, that the pacifist is "warranted in regarding it as the 'eruption point' where the tension between the ideal and the actual has become greatest." Different periods in history present different centers for focus. Today war is "merely the most vivid and dramatic destruction of the finer qualities of human personality and the values which all the universal religions and humanist philosophies have exalted." Other political issues are not eliminated or forgotten, they are "merely subordinated to the most contemporary question of morals and politics."[76]

Conclusion

Just before World War II, Niebuhr observed: "There is a type of Christian pacifism that does not rest upon illusions about the goodness of man. But I can find little of that type of pacifism around about me."[77] Obviously Niebuhr had not encountered Sibley's type of Christian pacifism. As Sibley himself concludes, on the "hard inner core of human nature and destiny," a large number of pacifists and their Niebuhr-like critics agree. Much of what Niebuhr wrote in opposition to pre-World War II "perfectionist" pacifism (with its political strategy of non resistance and naive trust in the power of love) is largely off target when applied to Sibley's pacifism, which recognizes that sin, conflict, struggle and power are permanent characteristics of history. Morality demands political action and the utilization of power, even non-violent coercion; disavowal of all types of power would allow the "immoral" to rule and perpetuate tyranny and injustice. This is hardly the "soft utopianism" Niebuhr deplores. There is an enormous difference between a philosophy of non-resistance to evil and a philosophy of non-violent *resistance* to evil.

Clearly Sibley, who has more appreciation of ancient Greek philosophy with its confidence in reason and a "telos" for men, sees greater possibilities for reform and movement (not irreversible nor morally unambiguous) toward a higher approximation of a social utopia which embodies justice. Niebuhr's greater emphasis on "original sin" and the indeterminate expressions of man's freedom leads him to expect and advocate a narrower scope for reform and to shy away from rather detailed articulations of what modern man should and can do. Justice is a more dynamic, less carefully defined goal in Niebuhr's political philosophy.

Sibley accepts Niebuhr's general argument that pacifists, if they are logically consistent, should see the broader social and political implications of its philosopohy of non-violence. However, Sibley feels it is legitimate to focus on war because it demonstrates in the current age the dramatic gap between the ideal and real.

Perhaps Niebuhr's most telling criticism relates to the dilemma faced by responsible leaders of groups or nations. Individuals may accept suffering, sacrifice, imprisonment or even death rather than commit an act of violence. Seldom are moral issues of war presented in such simple, unambiguous terms. "The issue often is whether or not to accept (and thus to inflict) suffering by others, as the victims of aggression.... Whose duty is it to protect the lives and liberties of others?"[78] Often the issue is lives vs. lives or present lives vs. future lives or even life as mere survival vs. quality of life. Sibley's development of a social ethic remains incomplete and somewhat vague on this issue. Christianity teaches that one is not to kill, but it also teaches one is to be responsible for our neighbors in need, who may be suffering oppression, injustice and possibly death. These obligations can and often do conflict, but Sibley offers us (especially statesmen) inadequate guidance on how to respond when we in fact have the power to do so.

Sibley thinks World War II "did little, if anything, to help and much probably to make a bad situation worse." There was "no more 'democracy' " a generation later than before.[79] But weren't there more Jews? Furthermore, the issue is not whether there was more democracy, but whether there would have been less. If Hitler had "won," we probably would have had the worst world-wide tyranny ever. Also, many might argue there is more democracy (though certainly not in Sibley's sense) today than in 1941.

Though Sibley and Niebuhr both regard love as ultimately normative, they *both* scale down the actual demand of love in politics. True, Niebuhr goes further, yet the use of non-violent techniques are also somewhat less than the agape love of Jesus. While Sibley argues nonviolence (love) is *directly relevant,* Niebuhr, though denying love's immediate or literal applicability, still finds it useful and necessary if a higher justice is to be achieved. Both see non-violent political strategies as legitimate, preferable, and potentially successful, though Niebuhr is more likely to note the limitations of that strategy. Niebuhr is willing to consider violent means; one cannot determine a priori whether a particular means is ethically acceptable or strategically appropriate. That depends on the situation. Except for the total condemnation of killing by Sibley, both actually recognize the importance of the context and pragmatic considerations in effective political strategies to realize justice.

Distinguishing violent from nonviolent means has not been done satisfactorily by modern pacifist thought. Sibley recognizes this "weak link" in pacifist thought; yet he thinks distinctions can be made. Beyond the obvious, however, we do not have clearly defined criteria to guide us. And Sibley's recognition of the potential for violence in all conflict, even nonviolent conflict, lends credence to Niebuhr's view that the distinctions are not "absolute," though they are "important."

Both claim to be realists, but there are obviously differences between the two over what is "realistic." However, efficaicousness of means is a concern for each. Sibley thinks non-violence is a better, less costly, and more fruitful means (though not always or completely successful) in securing desirable ends. In rejecting the "so-called" political realists' position, he asks: "Yet what can require a greater faith in the unseen than what the war defender asks us to believe—that out of killing and hatred will come peace and justice and love."[80] Rather than "connivance with tyranny," Sibley claims pacifism is the best and only context in which to eventually overcome tyranny. In calculating "consequences," Sibley also calls our attention to results inadequately considered by Niebuhr—the negative effects of the use of violence on the agent who uses it and the political system which sanctions it. Such use more firmly establishes the "habit of violence." In a "them" against "us" war, it is not only "they" (e.g., the tyrants) who are negatively affected, we are too.

Sibley, of course, deplores the development of nuclear weapons and the "balance of terror" on which contemporary "peace" is supposedly based. He has offered a plan for unilateral disarmament.[81] Sibley fears that men will not be able to control the historic forces that drive leaders to use these horrible weapons. In some ways Niebuhr's response on this has been inconsistent. In a 1945 article commenting on why Truman and Churchill decided to drop the bomb, he writes: "The question is whether they were not driven by historic forces more powerful than any human decision."[82] He implies they were. Yet five years later when the Soviets had the atomic bomb, he wrote: "A nation does not have the power to say that it would rather be annihilated than to produce a certain weapon. For, as the scientists have asserted, the production of that weapon may serve to guarantee that it will never be used."[83] This is obviously a somewhat optimistic view of man; Sibley would argue that Niebuhr has here forgotten his own lessons on the "demonic" element in human nature. Niebuhr was optimistic about avoiding nuclear war because of his confidence in the effectiveness of deterrence. Until his death in 1971, he never adequately dealt with the question of how much risk of involvement in a nuclear war we should take in any real confrontation with an "enemy." He appeared to imply that it would be immoral to actually use such weapons. "[P] hysical survival seemed now to mean our moral annihilation."[84]

In conclusion, we have two Christians who share a great deal in theological beliefs, desirable social goals, the ultimate norm of love, and recognition of the basic character of history. Yet these two equally conscientious men take diametrically opposed positions on the possible use of violence in pursuit of morally laudable ends. Sibley would have Niebuhr follow his conscience, wherever it may lead. "For if the individual does not regard his own deepest convictions as obligatory, he surrenders his soul." Sibley's conscience leads him elsewhere. At this point we reach an impasse. As Sibley writes: "The final moral judgment...must be left to God."[85]

Three

A Critique of Pure Pacifism

Terence Ball

The allusion to Kant in my title is scarcely accidental. For the "pure" pacifist is inclined to view the political sphere precisely as Kant viewed the moral realm: as a realm of absolute freedom, of acausal "will," unsullied by considerations of contingency, or of cause and effect.[1] The pure pacifist has, as he believes, an absolute duty to act always in nonviolent ways, regardless of the costs incurred in or consequences produced by one's so acting. The ethics of pure pacifism can best be characterized as deontological (as distinguished from consequentialist). Right and wrong, moral and immoral, are on this view to be measured against the absolute standard of pure duty, not against the shifting standard of costs and consequences. But however noble its intentions, I believe pure pacifism to be untenable, largely because its purity proves elusive if not illusory.

My defense of this view proceeds as follows. I shall begin by defending the very possibility of the enterprise in which Professor Sibley and I are both engaged. Then I shall, in the section following, briefly delineate several schools of pacifist theory and practice, showing how and why a pure pacifist cannot accept consequentialist or utilitarian arguments as definitive or conclusive. I then go on to argue that Professor Sibley, despite his disclaimers, does in fact subscribe to the pure pacifist position. Finally, I shall advance an argument which, if successful, should show pure pacifism to be highly problematic if not utterly untenable.

The arguments which follow are meant to be a contribution to, and a continuation of, a friendly dispute of long standing between Professor Sibley and myself. Although it is often said that imitation is the sincerest form of flattery, I do not believe it. Criticism, not imitation, is the sincerest form of flattery. It is in this spirit that I shall criticize a perspective and a position that is, I trust, a reasonable, if necessarily somewhat simplified, approximation of the one that Mulford Sibley has long held and eloquently defended. But before stressing our differences I should like to emphasize several points of profound agreement.

I

Political theory is predicated upon the presumption that moral and political argument is, or can be, rational. By "rational" I mean only that it is justifiable by recourse to reasons, which may in their turn be adjudged good or bad (or better or worse) according to criteria of coherence, consistency, cogency, and evidence.[2] The principles and precepts which serve to guide and justify our conduct are open to rational criticism though not, perhaps, to decisive refutation.[3] My aim here is to criticize, not to refute, the deontological doctrine of pure pacifism.

Not so very long ago it was widely believed that moral principles and political convictions were not the sorts of things that one could rationally and meaningfully *argue* about. The emotivist theory of ethics, attached to positivism to which American political science is still largely attached, held that "normative" utterances are quite literally meaningless; lacking any sort of cognitive status, they are merely exclamations or "ejaculations" (as A.J. Ayer once termed them)[4] through which irredeemably subjective tastes or preferences are expressed, emotions vented, and actions guided. To say "lying is wrong" is, on this view, to say only that one disapproves of lying: which is of course to say something about the attitudes of the speaker but nothing at all about lying. Duly extended to "normative" political theory, the emotivist theory of ethics threatened to put an end to twenty-five centuries of political discourse and disputation. For if to call one mode of political organization or way of life "good" means only that one approves of it, then political theory from Plato to the present is a purely subjective enterprise; it can yield only statements of taste or preference, not rationally grounded or cognitively meaningful knowledge claims. It was in these philosophical environs that it could be said that "for the moment anyway, political theory is dead."[5]

Yet, like the mistaken reports about the death of Mark Twain, this one proved to be greatly exaggerated. Much has changed in the two decades since political theory was pronounced dead. One of the more significant developments concerns the demise, indeed perhaps the death, of positivism itself and, with it, of the emotivist theory of ethics. Even the pioneers of that philosophical movement have recanted. When asked what, in retrospect, were the principal defects of logical positivism, Professor Ayer, with characteristic candor, replied, "Well, I suppose the most important of the defects was that nearly all of it was false."[6]

The few remaining positivists are to be found nowadays, not among philosophers but in departments of political science. Always the last to hear the war news from the philosophical front, political scientists continue to espouse the tenets of dead philosophical doctrines without knowing that they do so. The verifiability principle, the fact/value dichotomy, the covering-law model of explanation, the subjectivist-emotivist view of ethical discourse—these and other tenets of classical positivism live on, long after their timely deaths, in political science texts and classrooms. If one requires proof that there is indeed life after death, at least for philosophers' dogmas, this is surely it.

Not one to let sleeping dogmas lie, Professor Sibley, for his part, never doubted that moral questions could be meaningfully discussed and debated. Disregarding the once-fashionable philosophical prohibitions laid down by positivism, he has shown, more by personal example than by philosophical precept, how such argument is possible—and why it is vitally necessary.[7] It is necessary because debate and argument are the very stuff, the *sine qua non,* of politics itself. Politics is a *communicatively constituted* activity. As John Dewey remarked:

Society not only continues to exist...*by* communication, but it may be fairly said to exist *in*...communication. There is more than a verbal tie between the words common, community, and communication. Men live in a community in virtue of the things which they have in common; and communication is the way in which they come to possess things in common.[8]

Putting the same idea in a different way, Bertrand de Jouvenel writes:

The elementary political process is the action of mind upon mind through speech.... Even as people belong to the same culture by the use of the same language, so they belong to the same society by the understanding of the same moral language. As this common moral language extends, so does society; as it breaks up, so does society.[9]

This common moral language, like any other, will die out and disappear unless it is spoken, not just by the concerned few but by the many. Political discourse must be couched in the fraternal "tone of expostulation" of which Pericles spoke, and which he contrasted with the coercive tone of command;[10] it must, as Habermas insists,

be undistorted by inequalities of power, position, or manipulation;[11]-
or—to translate this into the Quaker idiom in which Professor
Sibley sometimes speaks—moral and political discourse is aimed at
friendly persuasion. So too are the remarks which follow.[12]

II

Briefly, pure pacifism is the doctrine that one has a
noncontingent or absolute duty to refrain from the use of violence
against other human beings, regardless of circumstances, costs, or
consequences. Pure pacifism, that is to say, is a deontological
doctrine about the inviolable rights and absolute duties of human
beings. The pure pacifist does not doubt that he has an
unconditional duty to act justly, cost what it may. His view is best
summarized by Cicero's maxim, *Fiat justitia ruat caelum,* which
Professor Sibley generally paraphrases as, "I must do my duty,
though the heavens fall." And one's duty to refrain from violence is
absolute, admitting of no exceptions. Thus, for example, a Jew could
not forcibly resist the S.S. guard who leads him to the gas-chamber;
nor could one justifiably join in a plot to kill Hitler, even if one could
somehow know for certain that millions of innocent lives would
thereby be saved. Other ostensibly moral duties, e.g. to tell the truth,
are subordinate to a single overriding moral duty to refrain
unconditionally from the use of violence against any human being.
The pure pacifist presumably could, for example, lie to the Gestapo
regarding the whereabouts of his Jewish neighbors; he could, with
equal justification, hide them in his attic, in violation of Nazi law;
but he could not resort to violent means to save them from falling
into the hands of the Gestapo, who will certainly torture and
eventually kill them. Pure pacifism is a demanding doctrine. It is
also, as I shall suggest presently, an internally contradictory one.
But before making this argument, I want first to distinguish pure
pacifism from other varieties of pacifist thought.

Professor Sibley defines "pacifism" quite broadly, to include
"all those ideas, attitudes, and movements which repudiate the use
of violence, particularly war, under any circumstances." Thus war,
or indeed any form of violence, "whether defensive or aggressive, is
always ethically illegitimate and, in the long run, inefficacious for
the attainment of desirable goals."[13] This definition, of course,
lumps together deontological and consequentialist positions, and so
requires further refinement. In the consequentialist camp Professor
Sibley places "utilitarian" and "just-war" pacifists. The utilitarian
school "maintains that war and violence, on the whole and in the
long run, work against the implementation of desirable social and

political values, whatever the short-run effects appear to be and whatever the claimed objectives of the struggle."[14]

If I understand him correctly, Professor Sibley is loath to join the ranks of utilitarian pacifists for at least two reasons. The first is that utilitarian pacifism, like utilitarianism generally, makes the morality of an act depend upon calculations of cost, weighing these against possible or probable benefits. Morality thus becomes a matter of expediency and efficiency; calculation replaces conscience as the arbiter of morality. And this, he believes, is to dangerously diminish the very notion of morality and moral action. Here he is in good company: Thoreau objected to the Reverend William Paley's pre-Benthamite version of utilitarianism for exactly the same reason. Indeed, though it generally goes unnoticed by readers of *Civil Disobedience,* that essay is a passionate and sustained critique of utilitarian justifications of resistance.[15] "Paley, a common authority with many on moral questions," Thoreau wrote, "resolves all civil obligation into expediency."[16] The consequentialist criterion, which Bentham called the principle of utility, Thoreau preferred to call "the principle of expediency." But to be a conscientious moral agent, he maintained, often requires that one act in inconvenient and inexpedient ways. Expediency—the weighing and counting of costs and consequences—means "choosing that course which offers the slightest obstacles . . ., that is, a down-hill one." But, he adds, "there is no such thing as sliding up-hill. In morals the only sliders are back-sliders."[17] Paley, he complains,

appears never to have contemplated those cases to which the rule of expediency does not apply, in which a people, as well as an individual, must do justice, *cost what it may.* If I have unjustly wrested a plank from a drowning man, I must restore it to him though I drown myself. This according to Paley, would be "inconvenient." But he that would save his life, in such a case, shall lose it.[18]

Thoreau's critique of utilitarianism, and his deontological defense of civil disobedience, are not far removed from Professor Sibley's views.[19] But here the agreement ends. For Thoreau was no pacifist: he greatly admired John Brown, particularly for his armed raid on Harper's Ferry (in which the mayor was killed); and he vowed to fight, by force of arms if need be, for "a free state, and a court truly of justice."[20] These, I hardly need add, are assuredly not the professions of a pure pacifist.

If Professor Sibley's first objection to utilitarian pacifism is that it diminishes morality, his second is that it is delusory. For utilitarian pacifism, like utilitarianism generally, is predicated upon the premise that one can foresee or predict all the consequences of one's actions. In fact, however, we cannot. Our actions have a way of going awry; purposive actions yield, more often than not, unintended or unanticipated consequences. Utilitarian pacifism thus holds out a hope that it cannot possibly realize, namely that we can accurately and unerringly calculate all the costs and consequences of our actions. This, Professor Sibley maintains, is factually false. It is the empirical worm in the utilitarian apple. Biting into that apple we find, not the knowledge of good and evil, but a delusory claim to knowledge that we cannot possibly possess.[21]

According to Professor Sibley, then, consequentialist accounts of morality—including pacifist morality—are doubly defective: they diminish morality, and they rest upon a factually faulty premise. Utilitarian pacifism, it appears, is plainly proscribed. Where, then, does this leave the would-be pacifist? Far from leaving him high and dry, this eliminative critique points to the desirability—perhaps indeed the necessity—of subscribing to a deontological defense of pacifism. It leads, in short, to pure pacifism.

The foregoing is, I hope, a fair rendering of Mulford Sibley's critique of ethical consequentialism, at least as it pertains to pacifism. Having briefly characterized his position and summarized his supporting arguments, I now propose to present a possible objection, followed by a reply.

III

It might be objected, with some justification, that Professor Sibley is not a pure pacifist, after all. To be sure, he is critical of utilitarianism and, *pro tanto,* of utilitarian pacifism. But this scarcely suffices to place him in the pure pacifist camp. For he holds that means and ends are inseparable; the failure of deontological and consequentialist arguments alike lies in their both being oblivious to this central and inescapable feature of our moral and political existence. The utilitarian mistakenly believes that the achievement of highly desirable ends may sometimes conceivably justify the use of otherwise repugnant means. Good consequences are all that matter. The duty-bound deontologist is equally mistaken in insisting upon doing his duty, utterly oblivious of the consequences of his doing so. Good intentions are all that matter.

Professor Sibley wishes to steer a middle course between the Scylla of deontology and the Charybdis of consequentialism. Citing Max Weber's distinction between a deontological "ethic of ultimate ends" and a consequentialist "ethic of responsibility," he denies the

moral supremacy, or even sufficiency, of either; for neither, morally
speaking, represents the whole truth. Thus he says that "the means
shape the ends" and that ends and means "should be examined
together; each is valid, but only when seen in the context of the
other." Equating "moral" with ultimate ends, and "technical" with
available means, he holds that "the moral and the technical must be
married."[22] And this, he further insists, is no mere marriage of
convenience; rather it is, for moral agents, a marriage of moral
necessity. Given the way of the world, in which means and ends are
inextricably intertwined, we have no choice except to sanction this
union. Both of Weber's "ethics," he writes,

must be used within the context of our framework. Both the statement "I shall do
right though the heavens fall" and the asseverátion "The rightness of the act can be
determined only by examining its consequences" are wrong when taken alone—the
former because it seems to divorce "right" from any results for human beings,
however horrible; the latter because it...seems to forget that remote consequences
can but rarely be assessed.[23]

It thus appears that Professor Sibley agrees, not with Kant but
with Hegel. Criticizing both Kant's "moral view of the world" and
the Utilitarians, Hegel wrote:

The maxim, "Ignore the consequences of actions" and the other: "Judge actions by
their consequences and make these the criterion of right and good" are both alike
maxims of the abstract Understanding.[24]

The "abstract Understanding" fails to understand that ethical life
is lived on earth, above the mud but far below the heaven of
perfection. But perhaps the most prescient paraphrase of Professor
Sibley's insight was provided by Lassalle:

> Show us not the aim without the way.
> For ends and means on earth are so entangled
> That changing one, you change the other too;
> Each different path brings other ends in view.[25]

Professor Sibley has much in common with Hegel and Lassalle.
He is neither Benthamite nor Kantian. Hence—my critic will say—I
am quite mistaken in thinking Professor Sibley a pure pacifist. This
is a weighty objection. It must be met or my previous
characterization is revealed as caricature and my argument falls to
the ground.

I take Professor Sibley's remark that "the means shape the
ends" to be an empirical statement. This of course introduces an

element of contingency—and even, I daresay, of causality—into his argument. Such contingency being unacceptable to a duty-oriented deontologist, Professor Sibley cannot belong to that class; hence my critic is right and I am wrong. Or am I?

One of the defining differences between contingent-empirical statements and analytic ones is that the former are only probably true (hence potentially false), while the latter are logically, conceptually or necessarily true. It is my contention that Professor Sibley's ostensibly synthetic-empirical claims about the relation between (non-)violent ends and (non-)violent means are in fact analytic claims expressing what he takes to be a logically necessary *a priori* truth.

Consider again the statement, "the means shape the ends." The truth of this statement is not in question. What is in question here is the *sort* of truth it expresses. If it expresses a contingent empirical truth, then Professor Sibley's pacifism is at least partially and importantly consequentialist. That is, considerations of cause and effect *do*, as he says, come in for consideration. If so, his position does not correspond to that of the pure pacifist, who eschews all considerations of contingency and consequence. If, however, his characterization of the relation of means and ends can be shown to be a noncontingent analytic truth, then considerations of context and contingency, cause and consequence, have—despite his disclaimers—nothing whatever to do with his version of pacifist theory and practice. He can then be shown to espouse what I have called "pure" pacifism.

Professor Sibley claims to give consequentialism its due. But he then undermines this by claiming—categorically and without qualification—that "free and open persuasion is *always* legitimate," while "violent coercion is *never* justifiable." Thus what had at first appeared to be an argument involving empirical contingencies and probabilities is now translated, or rather transmuted, into a noncontingent and absolute prohibition against violence, framed as an *a priori analytic* truth: "[T]o talk about violence in means as a way to achieve nonviolent ends is like speaking...of hot ice."[26] One could just as sensibly speak of married bachelors and two-horned unicorns. The upshot is that the relationship between ends and means is not an empirical-contingent relationship, but a logical-conceptual one. This runs counter to his earlier, ostensibly empirical claims that the means "shape" the ends and that we cannot foresee all the consequences of our actions (about which more later).

Having argued that Professor Sibley's version of pacifism

pretty closely approximates that of pure pacifism, I now propose to construct a critique of pure pacifism. My counterargument, if successful, will show pure pacifism to be an exceedingly problematic position. Its proponents' protestations notwithstanding, pure pacifism is, I want to suggest, covertly consequentialist—with all the difficulties that this entails—and is so, moreover, in a way that renders it impure and hence, by its own lights, untenable.

IV

Pure pacifism, as we have seen, purports to be a deontological doctrine. Unlike consequentialists (e.g., utilitarians), the pure pacifist does not rely upon calculations of costs and consequences because, firstly, this would be to degrade and diminish morality itself, and, secondly, because such calculations cannot be reliably made anyway. The pure pacifist has, as he believes, an absolute duty to act always in non-violent ways, regardless of the possible or probable consequences of so acting. This is not to say that he is utterly indifferent to all the consequences of all his actions; it is merely to say that consideration of the consequences are, or ought to be, irrelevant in deciding what constitutes a genuinely *moral* course of action in morally difficult or problematic situations. In moral matters, duty should be one's only guide. The pure pacifist's moral stance is predicated upon his peculiar view of the relation (or lack of it) between actions and their consequences. This position can be more systematically summarized, and somewhat simplified, in three propositions and their proscriptive corollaries:

(1) In moral matters, consequences don't count.
(1a) Don't count the consequences of your actions.
(2) You can't predict all possible consequences of your actions anyway.
(2a) Don't (attempt to) predict the consequences.
(3) Violence only begets violence.
(3a) Never act in violent ways.

A number of difficulties become immediately apparent. Firstly, if (1) is true, (2) is clearly irrelevant; for if consequences don't count for or against the moral worth of an act, it hardly matters whether one can or cannot predict the consequences. Indeed, even if one could always foresee all the outcomes of all acts, it would scarcely matter. A second difficulty is of much greater moment. It is clearly evident that (3) is at odds with (2); for (3) is a *prediction*—specifically, a prediction about the consequences of acting in violent ways. It is this third proposition, indeed, that is invoked as grounds for proscribing a certain class of acts, namely violent ones. This proscription is moreover, absolute: one must *never* act in violent ways. Why this should be so is not, however, entirely clear. One is told that one must act in certain (nonviolent) ways, and never in other (violent) ways; but why should one do so? One should do so, it appears, *out of a due regard for the consequences of acting in those ways.* Violent acts produce violent consequences. But to accept the truth of this third proposition entails the falsity of (1) and (2). For clearly, *contra* (1), consequences *do* count; and, *contra* (2), one can predict at least *some* of the consequences of some actions. Indeed, we can not only predict—we can *logically guarantee*—the outcome of at least one class of human actions, viz. all violent ones.

These considerations lead me to conclude that a deontologically grounded, or "pure" pacifism is untenable because it is internally inconsistent. One must, despite all the very real difficulties entailed by consequentialism, be a consequentialist. For otherwise one cannot, paradoxical though it may seem, be a pacifist.

The pure pacifist nevertheless has one last line of defense to which he can, if he wishes, fall back. This last line of defense is faith, religious or otherwise. One can always say, with Tertullian, that one believes in something despite, or even because of, its being impossible or contradictory. But this is to pay a heavy price. For it is to assume a stance and a position corresponding to the positivist's caricature: one's moral principles and political convictions are, after all, admitted to be rationally indefensible; they stand revealed as matters of purely personal taste or subjective preference. Although one might "convert" others to one's own view, one cannot hope to persuade them by rational argument. By one's actions one can set an example for others to follow or not, as they see fit; one can, in the Christian sense, bear witness by one's example. Such a stance is not without its attractions—I am tempted to say, its temptations—but these should, I think, be resisted. For this last line of defense is profoundly anti-political. It is deaf to argument and counterargument, reason and evidence, conjecture and refutation. Faith is private; discourse and disputation are public, that is, political. To rely upon faith is, in the end, to separate morality from politics. For those—pacifists, preeminently—who wish to make *moral* questions of paramount *political* concern, this recourse to purely private conviction is surely unacceptable. It involves nothing less than translating metaethical emotivism into political practice.[27]

V

My rendering of positions and arguments has, of necessity, been somewhat simplified. I can only hope that they were not over-simplified or, worse still, simplistic. My pure pacifist is, to be sure, an ideal type, though not, I hope, a straw man. Even so, he bears scant resemblance to his flesh-and-blood counterpart. I claim only to have scratched the surface, not to have plumbed the depths, of Professor Sibley's subtle and complex version of the doctrine that I have summarily—and, I fear, sometimes simplistically—described and brashly criticized. If I have mischaracterized, or misunderstood, what he is driving at, that is surely my own fault—a shortcoming due, no doubt, to age or inexperience or simple ignorance. If so, I take some comfort in the hope that all these faults are, in one way or another, remediable. And I should like to think that despite our differences, we are, to borrow John Stuart Mill's apt simile, two men climbing the same hill from different sides.[28]

Four

Coercion, Force, Violence, and Utopia*

Peter C. Sederberg

"And covenants without swords are but words..."

Hobbes

Coercion

Definitions are tools, not Truths; their value is determined in use, not in terms of their approximation of some transcendent ideal.[1] Political science, unfortunately, often possesses a surfeit of tools ostensibly designed for the same purpose. Such unwelcome plentitude characterizes the concept of coercion. Multiple meanings for the same term produce at least two negative side effects: analytical confusion and conflicting conclusions. The two effects are related, for if scholars identify different things when they examine the role of "coercion" in social relations, they are likely to reach differing conclusions as to its occurrence, necessity, and desirability.

Two strategies can be followed in combating polysemantic concepts. First, a term can be construed so broadly as to cover almost every conceivable variation. This seems to be the case when Samuel Dubois Cook says "to coerce is to compel or restrain the human will by an outside agent."[2] He then elaborates:

Coercion may be physical or nonphysical (psychological, spiritual, intellectual, aesthetic), violent or non-violent, public (official) or private, individual or collective, overt or covert, legitimate or illegitimate, positive (rewards or promise of benefits) or negative (punishment, or threat of deprivation), formal or informal, etc.[3]

The breadth of Cook's definition contrasts sharply with the narrower focus of Christian Bay who limits coercion to acts involving "physical violence" or sanctions strong enough to deter

*I wish to thank Professors M. Glen Abernathy, William P. Kreml, and Dan Sabia whose comments on an earlier draft greatly assisted me.

an individual from a strongly desired course of action.[4] Bay thinks that coercion is "the supreme political evil."[5] Given the breadth of his definition, if Cook had concluded the same thing, he would condemn the vast preponderance of human behavior. Consequently, he argues that coercion is "ethically neutral," its moral quality being determined by "its purposes, forms, processes, consequences, and alternative possibilities inherent in the objective situation."[6]

The strategy of definitional inclusiveness, of course, manages polysemy by incorporating it. Once accepted, discussion inevitably focuses upon the multitude of different "forms" of coercion and their respective implications. The second approach reverses this bias by attempting to split off meanings believed unessential in an effort to hone the concept and make it into a sharper tool of inquiry. This is the strategy I follow in distinguishing coercion first from what it is not and then attempting to establish what it is. No ultimate claim to truth is made for this approach; rather, the definitional exercise serves as a preamble, albeit somewhat lengthy, to an examination of the extent to which it is possible, or even desirable, to minimize coercion in utopia.

In defining coercion, the associations which are better accounted for by other concepts need to be bracketed in order to concentrate on those elements that appear more essential.

Coercion is not simply a matter of harm. Human beings can be harmed by many events, including natural conditions as well as the activities of others. Natural events certainly do *constrain* human activities, but to say that a flood or a hurricane coerces people seems inappropriate.[7] The concept of coercion is better confined to something human beings do to one another.

Coercion, however, needs to be distinguished from humanly imposed constraints. Coercive actions, to be sure, *may* constrain behavior, but they need not, and, in any case, constraints also emerge from other sources such as habit or conscience. Moreover, people are continually constrained by the accidental or incidental side effects of the activities of others. Similarly, a parent who constrains a child from running into a busy street is protecting, not coercing, him. To equate coercion with constraint, then, seems unjustifiably broad and misleading.[8]

Likewise, those commentators who suggest the possibility of "coercive bribes" construe the concept too imprecisely.[9] People may be induced to act in ways they would not otherwise consider through a variety of means, some of which are coercive. Enticements, however, if accepted, leave an individual better off *in his own judgment,* a rather odd consequence to term coercive.[10] The concept of "power" seems sufficiently broad to embrace both positive and negative inducements without stretching coercion in the same fashion.

Finally, the definition of coercion should not be made dependent upon the behavior of the coerced. Michael Bayles, for example, argues that coercion "is an achievement word; it denotes success."[11] Accordingly, if a person refuses to comply with the wishes of the coercer and absorbs the consequences, then coercion has not taken place, although it has been attempted. This rather interesting distinction, however, unduly emphasizes the behavior of the victim at the expense of that of the perpetrator. Moreover, it asserts that the intention of the coercer is to change the behavior of the victim. This *may* be the case when a coercive sanction is threatened, but when it is actually imposed, the coercer may be less concerned with the victim's subsequent behavior than with other matters like redressing a perceived wrong or deterring similar behavior on the part of others. To construe coercion as necessarily changing the behavior of the coerced seems again to be identifying it with the more diffuse concepts of constraint or power.

Coercion, then, is a human, not a natural, activity; it can constrain, but it might not; it is a form of power, but not the only one; coercive threats are different from coercive acts, and both threats and acts may have multiple consequences, intended and unintended. None of these factors, however, identifies any essential, distinguishing characteristic of coercion.

Many definitions of coercion, consequently, tend to conflate the concept with others that are more broadly construed. After bracketing these associated ideas, one irreducible monad remains: coercion harms a person. Coercion, therefore, belongs to that class of human activities that harm people. Coercion must be further distinguished from those actions that harm others either accidently or incidently. From this perspective, coercion is a form of human action where the perpetrator intends to harm the victim. Secondary intentions may accompany this primary purpose, but the distinguishing characteristic of coercion is intentional harm.

Organizations may be considered externally coercive if their primary purpose, like that of the military, is to inflict harm on others. All institutional arrangements constrain the activities of those who take part in them, and coercion may be one of the means used to control the behavior of the members of an organization. However, unless coercion or its threat is the major method of controlling behavior, as perhaps it is in a prison, it would be inaccurate to describe the institution as internally coercive. Admittedly, observers of different ideological persuasions might interpret the same set of social arrangements differently. A laissez faire economist would see the condition of workers in a capitalist economy as the consequence of impersonal market forces, while a Marxist would consider the workers' plight as the result of deliberate exploitation.

"Force" and "violence" can be considered the two basic types of coercion—the difference between them depends upon what constitutes "acceptable" coercion within social relations. Violence consists of those acts of coercion that violate the boundaries defining the "acceptable" use of coercion, whereas force denotes those acts that lie within the boundaries of acceptability. Unfortunately, the analytical clarity of such semantic term splitting is undercut by considerable operational obscurity. Indeed, an examination of the ambiguities attendant on each of these distinctions reveals some of the dimensions of coercion in social relations.

Meaning is a possession of human communities. Whether we believe that meaning is discovered (as would a Platonist) or imposed (as I do), it has no "meaningful" existence, no impact on human response, until immanent in a human community.[12] An undiscovered Platonic ideal is just that—undiscovered. We cannot talk about it at all. Although the imposition (or discovery) of meaning is something that humans do in human communities, this task seldom proceeds with confidence-inspiring clarity or consensus. Human beings invest enormous energy into efforts to determine meaning, but with varying degrees of success. Politics, indeed, may be defined as the process through which shared meanings are established, altered, or abandoned within communities.

Consequently, the existential meanings of the distinctions between harmful and harmless actions, intentional and accidental harm, and unacceptable and acceptable coercion are established essentially through political action and are, therefore, inherently dynamic and conflictual. Yet, conflict and dynamism need not imply total chaos; in fact, they seldom do. How the meanings of these distinctions are established, challenged, and changed within communities is central to our understanding of coercion in social relations.

HARM: Reason, Locke asserts, teaches that "no one ought to harm another in his Life, Health, Liberty, or Possessions."[13] Reason, unfortunately, teaches no such thing; indeed, it often instructs the opposite. Locke's assertion, however, does reflect what is conventionally, if not universally, perceived as a "hierarchy of harm" descending roughly from loss of life, through loss of limb or health, then liberty, and finally to loss of possessions. Of course, even this rough hierarchy founders upon the reef of individual and cultural variance. A person may well prefer death to torture or loss of a limb to the confiscation of all of his possessions. No transpersonal Benthamite calculus exists for definitively establishing degrees of comparative harm. Most of us would probably agree, however, that the loss of any or all of these four constitutes harm, and many would add other violations as well.

What, though, does "loss" mean? Presumably, a person cannot lose what was not previously possessed. John Donne aside, each man's death does not diminish me, at least not in the same way that it diminishes the deceased. If my neighbor is robbed, he suffers the loss, not me, except possibly through the decline in my sense of personal security, but this latter loss differs from his.

Previous possession alone, though, is insufficient to establish a loss. If my neighbor takes back what was stolen from him by the thief, he does not thereby harm the thief, for the thief was not entitled to the goods, and my neighbor was. Pure restitution, if it could be determined, is not harmful; only if some additional penalty is imposed would harm be done to the thief. Only when a person suffers the loss of something to which he was previously entitled has he been harmed.

Entitlements to possessions, like other meanings, are established in human communities, and, like other forms of meaning, questions of entitlement may be shrouded by ambiguity and dispute. In a situation where entitlement is unclear, it becomes debatable whether harm has been done. The hierarchy of harm noted earlier may reflect not so much the recognition of "inter-subjectively transmissible" degrees of harm, as the clarity of title. Thus, titles to life and limb seem fairly well founded, whereas those to liberty and property are somewhat more nebulous.

Even in areas where title seems well established, it still may not be absolute, unambiguous, or universal; debates over meaning can still occur. The abortion controversy aptly illustrates this point. Those who advocate abortion on demand hold that the fetus possesses no independent title to life; therefore, the termination of the pregnancy cannot constitute a harmful act. Indeed, to prevent a woman from doing so if she wishes is viewed as harmful in that she suffers a loss of liberty and, perhaps, other possessions. Those who oppose abortion adopt a quite different perspective. They see the fetus as possessing a title to life from the moment of conception, and believe ending that life is an act of murder. A third, intermediate, position is also possible. A fetus could be conceded to have a claim to life, and abortion, therefore, harms it. Nevertheless, abortions may be accepted under certain specified circumstances, such as to save the mother's life. Such an intervention would then be a case of "justifiable homicide."

Harm, then, even in terms of the deprivation of something apparently so fundamental as life, does not have any social reality until so recognized by a community. Animals who die for human purposes suffer no harm in this sense except insofar as they have been bestowed with certain entitlements by the community. Those who empathize with the sufferings of animals butchered for food or used in medical experiments probably think not at all about the millions of microbes slaughtered when they take antibiotics. Microbes are rather remote from our consciousness, whereas chimps and other "higher" life forms partake more closely of our humanity and thus are granted, at least by some people, certain entitlements of which they may be deprived. Man is the measure of all things in the sense that all entitlements within human communities can only be derived from human communities.

If the meaning of harm is derivative from the community even in an area apparently as absolute as the "right to life," the concept becomes progressively more disputable when other Lockean rights are considered. Title to limb and health relates quite closely to questions of life but with some additional ambiguity. A person, after all, can have part of his body removed for the benefit of the whole. Surgical removal of a diseased organ could be calculated as the acceptance of a lesser harm to avoid a greater evil. Yet, it appears equally plausible to focus only on the benefit gained. Most people do not view doctors as harming them to prevent greater harm but simply as helping them to preserve their health. This is not to say that they cannot or should not recognize the harm done to them, merely that they need not and probably do not see harm in this situation.[14]

When the presumed benefits of medical treatments are challenged, however, questions of harm do arise. Recently, doubts have been raised about certain forms of elective surgery, chemotherapy, and radiology, and people are more inclined to consider questions of harm in these areas where none existed before. Nevertheless, the harm, if so defined, is still perceived as incidental or accidental, regrettable but not coercive.

Another related consequence of the divisibility of limbs is that harm to a person's health can be a matter of degree. One cannot, in any socially significant sense, be more or less dead; one can be more or less tortured. Losses suffered to liberty and property are also questions of degree. Problems of establishing and comparing the extent of the losses to various persons' health, liberty, and property add yet another ambiguity to culturally derivative notions of harm. Debates develop over what point of change in an individual's health, liberty, or property harm actually occurs.

Determination of harm to liberty and property are further complicated beyond questions of degree. Concepts of life and limb have at least one foot, so to speak, in a biological reality independent of culture; however, notions of liberty and property appear to be completely culturally dependent. A person's title to liberty or property and the degree to which this title may have been violated are impossible to determine until some common agreement as to the meaning of these terms has been reached. Granted that some debates do occur over clinical definitions of death or health, these disputes lack the breadth or significance of the arguments over the nature of liberty or property.

Generally, liberty seems to imply some idea of space, most basically, a literal space within which to move, more figuratively, space to express a range of opinions or engage in a variety of behaviors.[15] Positively, liberty may suggest the possession of resources necessary to utilize available space. In no community are either liberties or the resources needed to realize them unlimited. Harm to a person's liberty, therefore, involves the imposition of restriction *beyond* those that have been conventionally established. Of course, the definition of the conventional limits on liberty, and thus where harm begins, is often what is in dispute.

The concept of property is also culturally dependent, and questions of harm to property relate to how property is construed. The range of this particular problem extends from Proudhon's dictum that private property is theft, to Robert Nozick's assertion that taxes are theft. In contexts where private title is established, harm is relatively easy to identify, but in the case of community property or so-called "free goods," just who is harming whom, or whether anyone is being harmed at all, is more difficult to determine. People tend to exploit and pollute resources held in common because of the difficulty in establishing individual reponsibility. The concept of harm is further attenuated when stretched to cover damage to the collective in the absence of demonstrable damage to specific individuals.

One final complication seems worth mentioning: the

interconnectedness of the human enterprise and the resultant possibilities for indirectly affecting others. Interdependency could be used to argue that no title is absolute, not even to life, for a person's actions necessarily affect others. To take one's own life, to exploit one's own property, to abuse one's own body, therefore, may indirectly harm others, and this indirect harm could justify limiting entitlements.

The concept of harm, then, emerges somewhat unsteadily from the ongoing efforts of human beings to establish meanings within communities. Whether a harm is perceived as being done depends on whether an entitlement exists at all, and if it does, to what extent. In relatively stable communities, a widely shared consensus may exist, but the consensus will seldom go unchallenged or unchanged for very long.

INTENTION: Harm, once its occurrence has been established, must be "intentional" to be considered coercive. This condition adds the next layer of ambiguity to the concept, for not only is intention difficult to assess, but also intent itself is commonly conceived as a concept of degree, with the "coerciveness" of the harmful act partly dependent upon the level of premeditation. Somewhat arbitrarily, five levels of premeditation may be distinguished.

Accidental Harm: An accident occurs when the harmful event is unforeseen, essentially random, and unavoidable. A child darting in front of a car whose driver is in conformance with all rules and norms of safe operation of his vehicle is killed accidentally. The child has been harmed (according to communally accepted titles), but he has hardly been coerced.

Incidental Harm: Related to accidental harm, but worth distinguishing from it, are harmful consequences that may occur as a secondary concomitant to an action. The harm is not the intention of the action, but it is recognized beforehand as a possible outcome. An example would be a patient who dies on the operating table. All surgery involves risk, but normally the medical staff would not be judged as coercing the deceased.

Negligent Harm: Harmful consequences are sometimes judged to be avoidable, even though they were not specifically intended by the perpetrator. For example, if the driver of the automobile had not been speeding or if the surgeon had not been intoxicated, the deaths of the victims *might* have been avoided. Avoidability, to be sure, is a question of probability and introduces another area of judgment. Negligence implies a degree of culpability; nonetheless, it seems dubious to consider negligent harm coercive.

Diminished Capacity Harm: In one sense, negligence

contributes to a diminished capacity to *avoid* doing harm. At this level a desire to harm is present, but that desire is mitigated by some factor which diminishes the capacity of the perpetrator to recognize the implications of his actions. Insanity and passion are two arguments from diminished capacity. The idea of diminished capacity, admittedly, implies some notion of "full" capacity, and thus is a matter of degree. This level of intentional harm seems plausibly labeled as coercive, although culpability would be lessened.

Full Capacity Harm: "Premeditation" is the concept most commonly associated with the highest level of intentionality, but this presumes the premeditation is done with the person exercising his full mental capacity. Harm that is the intention of full capacity premeditation, however that might be ascertained, implies the greatest degree of culpability and is the clearest form of coercion defined as intentional harm.

Another's intent, especially given the complexity suggested above, is impossible to know directly. Nevertheless, people cannot avoid assessing intent in responding to the social world. This paradoxical plight injects an additional element of instability into social relations generally and, in particular, into the interpretation of harmful acts. "Appropriate" response depends upon the interpretation of intent which is not directly accessible. Indirectly established intent, however, need not be based upon haphazard and essentially subjective guesswork. Without developing the intricacies of the hermeneutical approach to social relations, let me simply assert that a motivational construct can be formulated by drawing upon a careful (and intersubjectively transmissible) analysis of the cultural matrix within which the act occurs.[16] Such analysis permits a plausible narrowing of the intentional range, which even if it does not establish definitive truth, at least sets forth "probable" intent. Such reasoning proceeds overtly in a court of law and more or less consciously whenever human beings try to interpret one another's motives. Yet no matter how carefully they conduct their analyses, there will always remain a gap between the interpreted and the actual intent. This, in turn, suggests the possibility that any two people may assess intent differently and, therefore, may differ as to whether the action should be termed coercive.

ACCEPTABILITY: Intentionally harmful acts range from the essentially trivial (e.g., mild forms of parental discipline) to the devastatingly destructive. Moreover, desirable or not, coercion suffuses social relations. A distinction between "force" and "violence" may be based upon whether or not a particular coercive act is considered to be "acceptable." Such a definition explicitly recognizes that the meanings of force and violence are socially established and admits the possibility that two people may evaluate the same coercive act differently.

Despite, or perhaps because of, the possibility for disagreement, one function of politics generally and of the modern state in particular is to determine the boundaries defining the acceptable use of coercion. The state does not so much claim a monopoly on the "legitimate" use of coercion as the ultimate responsibility for demarking the boundaries governing the use of coercion.[17]

In a relatively stable social order, commonly agreed upon definitions of acceptable coercion, whether set through custom or law, are usually biased in favor of the status quo. Acts of greater harm will be tolerated if perceived as essentially defending the established distribution of resources and values. Alternatively, ceorcive acts that are seen as undermining the established order will tend to violate the boundaries. This does not necessarily mean that anything goes as long as it is defensive, or that all redistributive coercive acts will necessarily be deemed violent. The definition of force may be biased, but the extent of that bias may vary. In fact, one possible definition of an "open" society is one where "establishment" coercion (e.g., police powers) is strictly regulated, while certain forms of redistributive coercion (e.g., industrial strikes) are tolerated.

The distinction between force and violence requires four further clarifications. First, "acceptable" does not imply conformance with a universally agreeable standard of the good. The word was chosen, instead of possible alternatives such as legitimate or justifiable, in order to emphasize its situational character; that is, acceptability is determined by the dominant systems of meaning in a culture. One may argue, therefore, that the use of force in a tyranny is evil and unjustifiable, while the use of violence against tyranny is justifiable and good. Acceptability in any particular social order, therefore, is determined empirically, albeit with inevitable interpretational ambiguity.

Second, the boundary between force and violence, even in a relatively stable social order, is not always clear cut. Inevitably, disputes will arise over the acceptability of certain acts of coercion, and, in modern systems, a major purpose of adjudication is to make such determinations.

Third, the boundary, based as it is on conventionally established criteria, can change over time and vary from place to place. The increasingly stringent restrictions placed on parental discipline of their children illustrates this process of change in the United States over the past century.

Fourth, if the consensus over the definition of the boundary disintegrates, then the distinction between force and violence collapses. The complete dissolution of shared meaning in this critical area casts the community back into a Hobbesian state of nature, where each individual is his or her own judge as to what is acceptable. This Hobbesian extremity, however, is probably only of hypothetical interest, as people will still share meaning within groups even while contending over the carcass of the wider community.

To regard an act of coercion as acceptable may also be viewed as involving the suspension of a conventionally recognized entitlement. Within limits, parents may suspend certain entitlements of their children, ones derived primarily from the children's participation in the small community of the family. Other entitlements, such as that to life, are generally recognized as deriving from the children's membership in a wider community of shared meaning, a community in which the intentional killing of a child would be an act of violence. Acceptable coercion or force, then, is determined by what entitlements exist within a community and the circumstances under which they may be suspended. These conditions are both variable and open to dispute.

Coercion, force, and violence have no meaning outside of a community; in fact, to establish their meaning, or any other meaning, takes a continuous political act of considerable complexity. To be coerced means to be harmed, but harm can occur only with the loss of an entitlement, and entitlements exist only within communities. Harm is also a concept of degree, but the degree of harm is at least partially rooted in nontransmissible perceptions. Coercion presumes that the harm was intended, but intention, too, is a question of degree and can only be indirectly assessed. The distinction between force and violence depends upon the concept of acceptability, which itself may be more or less consensually established and will fluctuate over time and space. Finally, all these meanings are open to challenge and change.

One might wonder, given this complexity, how any consensus at all is established. Without belaboring the issue, two paradoxically related answers may be suggested: People do not think very much about what they are doing, yet they invest enormous energies in their efforts to do it. Human beings tend not to recognize the extent to which they are responsible for the meaning of the world, even though the point of all social behavior is precisely to impose such meaning.

Coercion and Utopia

The threat and practice of coercion pervade human relations, a condition that stimulates a variety of responses. Hobbes was so frightened by his vision of unrestrained, reciprocal coercion that he was willing to submit to a highly coercive bondage to escape it. The Leviathan, in the terms developed previously, acquires legitimacy to the extent to which it establishes and effectively defends a restrictive distinction between force and violence; it uses force to contain violence.

Other theorists judge coercion in terms of the ends for which it is used beyond the coercive control of coercion. Samuel Cook argues that:

Illegitimately lodged and used, [coercion] is a deadly weapon of human enslavement, oppression, and exploitation. Legitimately institutionalized and utilized, it is a unique agent of human freedom and the enlargement and enrichment of human experience. It can be a tool for the exploitation of the weak by the strong, but it can equally serve both for the protection of the weak against the strong and for the humbling and weakening of the strong and the strengthening and elevation of the weak.[18]

Finally, some see at least extreme forms of coercion, whether defined as force or violence, as an absolute evil. Mulford Sibley, for example, argues that "violent coercion" (that which takes or severely harms life) is so inherently evil that it necessarily corrupts the ends for which it is used, whatever their merits.[19]

Yet, as Robert Paul Wolff notes, even those who argue that coercion can be justified, still view it as an evil that needs to be minimized and not as ethically neutral.[20] Harm, however defined, is unpleasant, at least for the victim. Consequently, a place where people do not harm, or if they harm, they do not coerce, or if they coerce, they do not violate one another holds considerable allure.

Utopianism, at its best, attempts to raise the level of critical consciousness, introduce new meanings, and move the political community in some specific direction (either toward a eutopian or away from a dystopian projection). Such speculation, it must be emphasized, takes place within some community of meaning. No "metacommunal" position exists from which to criticize and expound, for critics can move from one community of meaning only to another more or less closely related to the first.

Before considering the dimensions of a place free from coercion, two misleading antinomies may be usefully abandoned: Coercion is not the direct antithesis of either reason or freedom in social relations. Reason reflects the drive to order, explain, and ultimately control the world, and coercion is the resort of reason when other means fail. The imposition of reason upon a recalcitrant "reality," whether the physical universe or the social world, can be enormously destructive. As Richard Rubenstein argues with respect to the Holocaust, we cannot understand the resort to coercion of even genocidal scope until we recognize the extent to which it may be a reasonable solution to a difficult problem.[21]

Nor should coercion be considered the simple antithesis of freedom, at least freedom defined as the absence of restraint. The relation of coercion and freedom so defined is somewhat more complex. Coercion may be used to restrain, but it is neither the only nor necessarily the most effective form of restraint. Other mechanisms for channeling behavior, whether external inducements or internalized habits of obedience, may be far more successful, especially since they are less likely to be recognized as restraints. Whatever its other demerits, at least when coercion is used to control behavior, there is little likelihood of mistaking what is going on.

Coercion, then, is not the best, but merely the last, resort of someone attempting to control the behavior of others. Its absence from a social relation does not necessarily signify the presence of freedom; ironically, the reverse may be true. A social arrangement that tolerates a fair degree of freedom of action from its participants may have to accept a certain amount of coercion as a concomitant for loosening the bonds of other restraints.

THE ABSENCE OF HARM: A "harmless" place is either a horror or a dream, either a society without entitlements or without flaw. Where there are no entitlements there can be no harm. Such a condition may appear so pathologically extreme as to merit little consideration, but this conclusion would be dangerous. For although the full realization of such an arrangement seems unlikely, its partial incorporation is a fact of social existence: Not all the elements of the environment are granted entitlements within the community. Harm may be limited by limiting the coverage of the concept of harm.

Given the debates concerning the rights of the unborn or of animals, it might appear that the concept of harm is being extended to incorporate wider circles of existence. The history of the 20th century, however, confounds such optimism. If entitlements have a meaningful existence only within communities organized to defend them, then it is possible to eliminate entitlements through expulsion from the community. The German Jews, for example, were first cast out of the community and only later destroyed. Perhaps the initial act harmed them, but the full enormity of the Nazi innovation is that the extermination of the Jews did not involve any harm within the Nazi community of meaning. Of course, harm may have been done in terms of the wider world community ("crimes against humanity") and certainly in terms of the Jewish community. While the holocaust was proceeding, however, the behavior of the "world community" suggests that the Jews were considered outcasts by more than the Germans. The participation of the Jews in their own destruction, moreover, suggests they accepted, at least to some extent, the meanings of their exterminators.[22]

If limiting entitlements, in some sense, simplifies the task of limiting harm, then expanding entitlements may increase the probability of harmful events. Even assuming complete knowledge and perfect benevolence (two truly utopian assumptions), harm could still occur due to scarcity. Thus, a doctor might still be faced with a situation where either the mother or infant must die. Only by eliminating scarcity as well would the possibility of tragic harm be avoided. A society of limitless knowledge, benevolence, and resources is, of course, heaven. No harm is done, therefore, in either heaven (the realm of no limits) or hell (the realm of no rights).

ABSENCE OF COERCION: Assuming a world of both entitlements and limits, some harm is inevitable, but it need not be coercive harm. To be coercive the harm must be intended, which assumes that people can "intend" at all and that they will at times intend harm.

To intend anything implies that one *could* have intended to do something else. If people are merely the instruments of forces beyond their control or even conception, then their sensation of intention is an illusion. Such a determined condition resembles, but is not identical with, having one's behavior structured through the manipulation of external constraints. Placing choice in chains does not deny that the individual still retains the capacity to intend otherwise, or even to act otherwise, if he is willing to accept the costs of defiance. Complete determinism denies precisely this capacity, and human behavior becomes essentially similar to events in the physical universe; therefore, any harm humans inflict upon one another has the same cognitive status as other harmful events in nature. It would be as inappropriate to term harmful human behavior "coercive" as it would earthquakes.

Such a world is envisioned by B.F. Skinner. A society where

behavior is perfectly determined through conditioning is not only "beyond freedom and dignity" but beyond coercion as well.[23] Harm could still be inflicted and punishments meted out, but notions of coercion, force and violence would exist only as convenient fictions useful to the process of operant conditioning. In theory, harm resulting from "breakdowns" in conditioning, as opposed to that arising accidentally, incidentally, or as a consequence of scarcity, could be minimized in a completely deterministic community. "Walden Two" is a happy place for Skinner in part because harm is minimized and coercion impossible. His utopia is rightly considered a perfect totalitarian order.

In order to coerce, in the sense used here, people must have the capacity to choose to do or avoid doing harm. Assuming the capacity to choose, to intend anything, could a world be imagined where people would freely choose not to harm one another? The answer depends on the function of coercion in social relations as much as upon whether one believes human beings to be inherently "evil" or flawed. Coercion, as noted earlier, is one way, perhaps the ultimate way, of imposing an order on the world. As Morse Peckham rather cynically notes:

> The only final way to prove that [a person] is indeed mistaken is to kill him. Throughout human history it has been a very popular way of defeating an opponent in arguments about meaning. Certainly it has an almost irresistible charm.[24]

Whether a parent is disciplining a child during toilet training or armies are slaughtering each other in the mud of a battle field, human beings coerce each other primarily over meaning. In order to minimize or eliminate coercion, meaning would have to be definitively established to the satisfaction of all concerned parties through ways short of coercion. This is what politics is all about— the effort to determine meanings. Political "success" is achieved when meanings are satisfactorily established through devices other than coercion such as argument and bargaining. Once established, though, meaning will be undermined by inadequacy. Unless the explanation is correct, now and forever, no meaning can ever be final. The temptation to resort to coercion will therefore be continuous, especially as the frustration over the failure of the other devices grows.

A second reason for the continued possibility of coercion in a free society relates to an earlier point. As the restraints on behavior are relaxed, the range of behavior spreads.[25] No guarantee insures that all aspects of this behavioral variation will be tolerable within a social interaction. In the absence of other prior restraints, coercion may be necessary to protect the community from ultimate dissolution.

ABSENCE OF VIOLENCE: If coercion cannot be eliminated, can it be contained? This objective is fundamental to the distinction made between force and violence: to limit coercion to "acceptable" forms. For example, coercion might be effectively contained in a system of "imperfect" totalitarianism, that is, a system that defines all, or nearly all, forms of state-directed coercion as being acceptable. Assuming the state possesses extensive coercion capabilities, it may well be able to enforce such a boundary. The totalitarian control is imperfect, however, because the state's reliance upon force is a sign that other means of controlling behavior have failed. The use of regime terror is a tribute to the continued presence of freedom.

Unlimited state coercion is not a definition of acceptability that most political theorists would find desirable. Sibley, for example, condemns capital punishment as an intrinsic evil regardless of what justifications the regime provides or what legal niceties have been followed.[26] Acceptable coercion for Sibley would proscribe certain extremely harmful acts no matter who, regime or citizens, perpetrates them. Such a limitation, though, seems to presume an absolute entitlement—e.g., the right to life—that cannot be suspended under any circumstances. An absolute entitlement can only exist if recognized by and incorporated in a community. Once established, the temptation will always exist to qualify it (e.g., self defense), and the debates over meaning would continue.

Apart from a notion of an absolute entitlement, arguments for limiting state coercion could be based upon principles of proportionality, due process, or pragmatism (i.e., unlimited state coercion causes destruction far in excess of any presumed benefits). These arguments are more judgmental than that from an absolute entitlement, which at least possesses surface clarity. Consequently, they are subject to continual dispute. Questions of proportionality can never be definitively resolved for, as Walter Kaufman notes, a person's "just deserts" can never be determined.[27] Concepts of due process are clearly rooted in culturally relative conditions. Arguments from pragmatism can be more or less well defended, but their truth or falsity can never be demonstrated, for following one policy negates the possibility of ever knowing the consequences of alternatives.

A second question, beyond the methods of limiting state coercion, concerns whether certain forms of coercion directed against the state should be accepted. The dominant distribution of values and resources, after all, also reflects an explanation or related set of explanations, and as such confronts the problem of adequacy. If the established order is necessarily imperfect, then the need for change must be recognized. Coercion is one means at the disposal of those disputing over explanations. Granting the use of this means (however limited) to the side of the status quo, while denying it to the advocates of change presumes that the status quo is more adequate than the alternatives. Such is the position of the conservative—not to deny the possibility of change altogether so much as to tip the scale in favor of what is.

Not surprisingly, those less convinced by the relative merits of the established order tend to favor equalizing the "debate." If the system does not accept some forms of "innovative" coercion, then the more radically inclined may well advocate violence. In the United States, and other reasonably open societies, certain forms of strikes and boycotts are tolerated even though their intent is clearly redistributive.

Interestingly, the major forms of redistributive coercion that appear to be accepted tend to be those that use the strategy of withheld behavior rather than direct attack. A refusal to cooperate, like a general strike, can be tremendously coercive, but the harm is done indirectly. Theorists of the strategy of noncooperation argue that such coercion is less destructive of the warp and woof of social relations and is less likely to corrupt otherwise noble ends than direct attack.

Consequently, although the elimination of harm and coercion seems a highly improbable, and even dubious, objective, perhaps an appropriate goal of utopian political action is to advocate a distinction between force and violence based on the difference between the strategy of withheld behavior and noncooperation and that of direct attack. As Gene Sharp notes, the credibility of such "indirect" coercive techniques suffers from the myth of efficacy that surrounds strategies of direct attack.[28] To be effective, admittedly, noncooperation must involve something of value being withheld. The value of an individual's or group's contribution to a wider community is partially a function of the degree of interdependence characterizing that community. The more interdependent a social relationship, the more effective a strategy of withheld behavior becomes, and, for the same reason, strategies of direct attack grow more self destructive. It is against those who are independent of us that the strategy of direct attack holds out its greatest promise.

Noncooperation is not inherently good, for it may be used for purposes as evil as the worst of conventional violence. But in an increasingly complex and interdependent world, it may be the coercive alternative that becomes not only increasingly possible but also more conducive to the survival of the species.

Conclusion: On Human Responsibility

The concepts of political philosophy tend to be dry, dead things—"mummies," as Nietzsche once called them.[29] The formal definitions of coercion, force, and violence offered here are really no more lively than most. In order to vivify them, I have argued that the formal meanings take on life only in communities through a process filled, like life itself, with flux, cônflict, and uncertainty. The refusal to recognize that meanings can exist only within communities is a denial of life. The quest for transcendent certainty is fulfilled solely by the grave.

Definitive assertions of absolute entitlements, unambiguous intentions, and clear-cut distinctions between force and violence are, at best, "noble lies" and, at worst, an evasion of responsibility.[30] We produce the meanings; we endow the rights; we formulate the norms. Yet, ironically, we do not completely control our fate, for the human "we" are communities of meaning extending over space and through time. What we as individuals can do is limited by the communities within which we dwell.

Though we can never free ourselves from the shackles of humanly imposed meaning, we can reforge them, link by link, through a process appropriately called political. The Greeks recognized that politics was central to the life of their communities, for through politics meanings can either be preserved or transformed, even if they can never be transcended. To accept responsibility for the communities of meaning of which we are a part is to embrace politics. To recognize the paramountcy of the political is, ultimately, to accept life over death.

Five

The "Peace of God," Chivalry, and the Emergence of the Civilian

Richard Shelly Hartigan

We command also that priests, clerics, monks, travelers, merchants, country people going and returning, and those engaged in agriculture, as well as the animals with which they till the soil...shall at all times be secure.

Canon XX, *Second Lateran Council*

In the waning years of the 20th century, mankind is faced with a series of inescapable truths: war has been his constant historic companion; war will probably continue as a future human exercise; another major war, waged with nuclear weapons, would effectively eliminate man as a successful species.

It is not determined, however, that man must wage war or that if he does, that it must be conducted in slavish conformance to the weapons which he has contrived. The choice remains his to settle his differences without recourse to violence, or if this proves impossible, to limit his violence at some point short of total, mutual destruction.

To the 20th century, the nations of the world had come to a tentative acceptance of a principle which placed warfare in a fairly proper perspective: it was a means to achieve a political end. Another notion had also been ingrained in the consciousness of those nations which subscribed to international law: civilians ought not to be intentionally killed—to the extent to which they were uninvolved, non-supportive, passive spectators to conflict. In effect, there had developed within a substantial portion of the world community, a certain sensitivity that war, if it must come, should not involve and ravage all.

The norm upon which this institution was based is the notion of innocence; the law which flows from it is expressed in the Hague and Geneva Conventions.[1] Simply stated, the law holds that civilians should not be subject to intended deprivation and death in war.

The origins and development of both the norm and the law

67

require a larger study.[2] However, some of the origins of both the norm and law stand out in isolated historical periods and deserve scrutiny in their own right. Such is the case with the medieval institutions of 'Peace of God' and chivalry.

I

The early Middle Ages were not totally devoid of illumination but they were deeply shadowed. The most casual reading of Europe's history at this time starkly reveals a society nearly bereft of order and at the mercy of rampant violence. Little imagination is needed to appreciate the devastation which early medieval society must have suffered at the hands of warriors who maintained the right to settle their private disputes by force. Most writers consider the Middle Ages as a period of "limited war" from the standpoint of the number of warriors involved. No one, however, could consider the period, from the fall of the Western Roman Empire to the twelfth century, as an era of limited warfare in any but this most special sense.

It is true that the wars were for the most part short, that small portions of the population actually engaged in the fighting, and that for the warriors themselves the lure of ransom often prevented death in battle. But these facts in no way diminished the effects of feudal violence on the non-fighting population—the vast unarmed and unwarlike masses of clergy, peasants, pilgrims and merchants. That these people must have suffered terribly from feudal war—monasteries and churches sacked, farms stripped of buildings and products, villages burned and plundered—is evident from the fact that the peace movements which originated in the 10th century sprang from the nonwarrior class. When medieval warfare is described as limited it must be understood in reference to the warfare of the High Middle Ages, and that in large measure the mitigation of violence in that period was due directly to the influence of the 10th and 11th century peace movements.

In the last years of the 10th century a wave of popular and clerical protest against the unrestrained violence of private feudal war was channeled into a series of canonical decrees to which historians have variously given the names *Pax Dei, Truega Dei, Paix de Dieu* and *Treve de Dieu,* or simply the Peace and Truce of God. Though there were two separate movements involved, the Peace of God and the Truce of God are usually referred to in their later combined form as the Truce of God.[3] The basic difference between the two movements, aside from the times of their respective beginnings, lies in that which they specifically intended to accomplish. Though the general intent of both movements was to limit private feudal wars, the one limited war with respect to persons and things, while the other attempted to limit war's duration. The Peace of God was designed specifically to protect certain classes in society, along with their buildings and possessions, thus severely limiting or reducing legitimate objects of military attack. The Truce of God, on the other hand, sought to limit the incidence of war itself, not by prohibiting it entirely but by restricting to a specified number of days and seasons in the year the times when war might be conducted. The Peace of God, as a formal movement, antedated the Truce of God, though its prescriptions were tacitly assumed to be included in the Truce. Hence the formal distinction tended to disappear as time went on. Of interest here are the formal prescriptions of the Peace of God and its later influence on custom and practice.

Until the last century, historians believed that the Peace of God had its genesis as a formal instrument, i.e., as a declared body of canons (or pronouncements) about the year 1031. Peace movements were known to exist for some time before this date, but it was generally supposed that no formal enunciation of rules was previously made. In the mid-19th century, however, Ernest Semichon published his definitive work on the Peace and Truce of God in which he maintained that the Peace of God must be seen as dating from the year 988. Fully substantiated by later authorities, this date is now accepted as the true beginning of this movement.[4]

In 988, at the monastery of Charroux in Poitou, a Church council was held, attended by numerous clerics and laymen. One of the objects of the council was to discuss the problems caused by incessant private war. The assembled members hoped to find some means of exerting their influence on the bellicose feudal nobility. Canon I declared that those who violated churches shall be anathema; Canon II pronounced the same sanction on those who pillaged the poor; and Canon III condemned those who attacked an unarmed priest or cleric.[5] With this single statement, signed by the Archbishop of Bordeaux and the Bishops of Poitiers, Limoges, Perigeux, Saintes and Angouleme, that which had previously been an unarticulated desire on the part of so many of the clergy and laity became a sharply defined rule and guiding principle. The peace movement had begun, and under the leadership and authority of the Church it was to spread rapidly. As one writer has observed, "The Council of Charroux marks the emergence of a vague collective consciousness that was to soon crystallize in a widespread public movement of unusual social idealism. It definitely introduced the first wave of popular enthusiasm for peace in pre-crusading France."[6]

The object of the Council of Charroux, and other local French Councils to be cited shortly, was not to outlaw war or even to restrict its duration. Rather, the aim was to limit the effects of war on the nonwarrior segment of the population. Hence, though representative of a degree of social idealism long foreign to European society, the Peace of God was nevertheless realistic in its goals: it was simply an attempt to formalize in rules the shared moral intuition that certain members of society ought not to suffer in wartime. The attempt to actualize this feeling by using the authority of the Church was perfectly reasonable, not only because it was the interpretative custodian of what was moral, but also because the Church was the single organization powerful enough to enforce such rules of conduct.

It was understandable that the populace would look to the Church for leadership, and that in turn the Church would be willing to furnish that leadership. Though the Church's desire to alleviate or mitigate war's ravages was based upon humanitarian motives, there were other equally compelling reasons why it was interested in promoting peace. It was the greatest property owner in Christendom yet it did not possess the physical resources to defend its properties from depredations or seizure. By fostering a peace policy, and by throwing the weight of its moral influence into the balance, the Church protected itself while helping to protect the defenseless.

Under the influence of the Church, the spark that was struck at Charroux began to burn brightly in the south of France. In 990, a council was held at Narbonne, the first of several which were to affirm and define the status of noncombatants in war. This council declared against nobles who confiscated the goods of ecclesiastics and attacked their persons. The sanctions for transgressing these prescriptions were excommunication of the individual and interdict for his community, if it was determined that his immoral actions enjoyed the consent of his subjects. Under the auspices of Widon, Bishop of Prey, and of Theobald, Archbishop of Vienne, a written pact was signed between the nobles and bishops in 998 called "The Pact of Peace." Its provisions demanded protection of the weak (*faibles*), of laborers and of merchants.[7] The South of France had given the signal for reform.

From its beginnings in local synods in the south and middle of France, the peace campaign spread north, including all France, and eventually parts of Germany; then it swept south into Catalonia, where the civil authorities would later incorporate and enforce its rules.[8] In the second quarter of the 11th century the Peace of God reached its climax as an independent movement, as the French people for the first time exerted themselves collectively in support of the public cause. The next step in the advancement of the peace movement was marked by its formal incorporation into the Truce of God, which itself had been proclaimed at the Council of Elna in 1027. In this Council it was forbidden to attack or slay unarmed monks and clerics, men going to or coming from Church councils, and men escorting women. The penalty for such actions was excommunication.[9] Two peace councils were held at Narbonne, in 1043, and again in 1045. The canons of these councils are not extant but the evidence indicates that they reaffirmed allegiance by all concerned to the principles of the Peace and Truce. The importance of these councils lies not only in the nature of the decrees passed, but also in the machinery which was gradually being developed to deal with violation of the rules already established.

By far one of the most important local French synods was again convened at Narbonne in 1054. At this time, the distinction between the Peace and Truce was still made. Canons I through X refer specifically to the Truce, Canons XI through XXIX to the Peace of God. In addition to the rules and prohibitions that the person and property of unarmed clerics, monks, nuns and their companions shall be immune from attack, the canons also prescribed that serfs and their property should have equal protection. An adjunct to previous statements on the Peace is the discussion in six canons of the equal obligations of women to obey the terms of the Peace. Olive groves were also to be immune from attack but not for their agricultural value; rather the olive was the sign of peace and its oil to be used for holy chrism.[10]

It was in this Council that an important statement was made which at once raises the peace movement, and the Church councils which were its expression, to a level above that of the mere pragmatic desire to safeguard life and property. Canon I contains the phrase "...quit Christianum occidit, sine dubio Christi sanguinem fundit" (He who kills a Christian, without doubt sheds the blood of Christ.).[11] Though implicit in the intentions of many who had fostered and subscribed to the peace movement since its inception, here finally was a definite and explicit expression of the fact that the Christian must hold Christian life sacred, for Christ's sake. Even though this intuition that the defenseless should be spared was still limited to Christians, the importance of its expression at the Council of Narbonne cannot be overestimated.

A further step in the direction of extending the category of those people or things which should be immune from attack was marked by the Second Council of Elna in 1065. In this Council's canons protection was extended to all domestic animals and beasts of burden, and homicide of any sort was forbidden whether there was good reason for it or not.

By this time, the influence of the French peace movement had thoroughly permeated Catalonia to the south and Germany to the north. All that was required now was Papal approval in order to consolidate the gains already made. Such approval was not long in coming. In 1059, Pope Nicholas II sent a Bull to all the bishops of Gaul stating that henceforth pilgrims would be immune from attack. Already at the Council of Rheims in 1049, Pope Leo IX had declared that clerics in holy orders and poor people should be immune from attack. Finally, at Clermont in 1095, Pope Urban II's plea for subscription to the Truce of God threw the whole weight of the Church's authority behind these rules to limit war. Semichon has correctly called Clermont not only the most important council of its own century for the propagation of the Peace and Truce of God, but also the most important in its effect on the next century.

The three appropriate canons from this council are the 1st, 30th, and 31st. Canon I confirms immunity for clerics, monks, and women, while the other canons proscribe violence against the Church, and prescribe anathema against those who kill clerics or steal their goods. Of far greater importance are the twelve "peace decrees" of Urban II. The first seven decrees deal specifically with the principles of the Peace, while the last five pertain to the Truce. For the most part these decrees are a re-statement of the ideas already found in earlier conciliar canons, but these same ideas were elaborately presented in great detail and over the signature of a Pope. Herein lies their importance.[12]

After Clermont there could be no doubt that the Peace and Truce of God had become a medieval institution of surpassing significance. By now a thoroughly popular movement, with clerical direction and papal approval, the principles embodied in the Peace and Truce had become part of the public consciousness. A commentator states that the chief gain for society was the development of an active public opinion. "The peace movement fostered the development of public opinion in eleventh century France, and actually brought forth a distinctly new public conscience on matters concerned with law and order."[13]

A litany of later councils which reaffirmed the principles of the Peace of God is not necessary. It should be noted however, that the Truce of God—and by common understanding now the Peace of

God—was declared still operative and binding in 1123 when it was affirmed without detailed comment at the First Lateran Council. The Truce was henceforth reaffirmed at the Second and Third Lateran Councils in 1139 and 1179 respectively. Thus, three Ecumenical or general Councils saw fit to incorporate the peace principles of the Truce in their decrees. It is a comment on the times however that as late as 1179 it was still necessary to affirm these principles at all.

The Church had taken the initiative in promoting the peace movement for various reasons. One, as already noted, was that the secular political authority was incapable of enforcing limitations on private war. Hence, by default, the Church assumed this responsibility. It is probable too that Churchmen felt it their duty to aid in promoting the protection of certain classes of the population. It is understandable why the Church was concerned with the condition of pilgrims: pilgrimages were a common religious practice in the Middle Ages, frequently prescribed as a penance. Hence, the Church could be expected to exert its pressure to protect Christians who embarked on a pilgrimage at its direction.

Yet, in those places where a modicum of civil authority did exist, rulers were quick to make the principles of the peace movement into formal law. An example of this can be found as early as 1061. From 1061 to 1063 Count Ramon Herenguer promulgated the *Ustages de Barcelona.* His code was derived from an earlier one of the Emperor Lothair II and attempted to reconcile the practice of the old alloidial system of property with the newer system of benefices and *honores.*[14] Among other provisions were those which set punishments for breaches of the Peace and Truce of God, and of various ecclesiastical pronouncements, one of which had decreed protection for the Jews. A later code, *Las Siete Partidas,* prepared between 1256-1263, but coming into force only in 1348, included several chapters devoted to military rules and discipline. But this was already in a period of greater humanization of war when the results of the efforts exerted in the 10th and 11th centuries had become evident.

II

Finally, no overview of the ways in which medieval society sought to limit war would be complete without mention of the chivalric code. Though a great deal has been written about chivalry, it is well to note particularly the Church's influence on the development of this knightly code.

In citing the origins of the chivalric code it is necessary to point out again a fact which has already been made with regard to the Peace of God, namely that at its base there was an almost inextricable admixture of religious idealism and pragmatic intent: A desire on the one hand to Christianize the near-pagan warrior in order to save his soul, combined with a desire to tame his turbulence in order to save the lives and property of the rest of the population.

In feudal society, in which the aristocratic knight enjoyed tremendous prestige, it is easy to understand how the virtues of military prowess—courage, skill, and above all loyalty to one's feudal obligations—would come to be admired. When these purely military virtues were channeled and directed to the service of the Church, or at least restrained by an ethical ideal so that they were not used against the Church, the feudal warrior became the Christian knight. The primary function of the feudal aristocracy was to fight; its secondary function was to provide some form of temporal government. Hence, the extent to which the church exerted a civilizing influence on this feudal governing class cannot be overestimated.

It should first be observed how the very factors which accounted for the knight's predominance as a military fighting man also contributed to the development of a knightly code of action between knights. The armored knight enjoyed supremacy in his society for several reasons—noble birth, wealth, long training and leisure. Yet, a "class which makes war both its vocation and avocation is bound to develop rules to alleviate its unpleasant features."[15] Since knightly armor was heavy and hot, the knight declined to wear it except when necessary. When he travelled, he carried it on a pack horse. Hence, a custom developed which required that a knight give his enemy time to put on his armor before an attack. Eventually, a knight trusted his fellow knight's word to such an extent that parole was commonly given for the defeated knight to raise his ransom.[16]

Though this code of military honor served the warrior well in his relations with his peers, it did little of itself to alleviate the lot of the rest of the population, whose lower social status necessarily placed it beyond the pale of knightly ethics. Only when the ethics of feudal chivalry were infused with a religious idealism did a truly Christian ethic of knighthood appear. This fusion of ideals did not exist in any systematic form before the 12th century, though the theoretical base of religious chivalry went back a century earlier.

The basic idea of religious chivalry held that a Christian knight, because of his power and privileged position, had obligations to defend the Church, its property and its flock, and to fulfill these obligations in accordance with ecclesiastical direction.

This notion took root in the early crusades and was shaped into a definitive system by John of Salisbury. What is of importance here is not the completed view of the Christian knight as the temporal protector of Christian society so much as the specific influence of the Church in developing this ideal.

In this sense the Peace of God must be seen, not as a set of prohibitions, but rather as an appeal to the warrior to become fully Christian, to assume the responsibility to aid and protect those less privileged than himself. By ennobling the warrior, by elevating his military virtues instead of disparaging them, the Church was able to hope with some chance of success that its injunctions to limit war would be obeyed. Hence the code of the Christian warrior acted as a greater deterrent to the knight's lawless behavior than the threat of excommunication or exile. It became the duty of the knight *as a knight,* rather than just as a Christian, to obey the rules of the Peace. One who broke the Peace or ignored the immunities of persons or property was automatically not only excluded from Christian society, but more significantly, he was considered outside the brotherhood of his fellow knights. He was in fact in the opinion of his peers, no knight at all.

The Church's success in infusing this attitude is exemplified by two restrictions, apart from those of the Peace of God, which it attempted to impose on feudal war. In both areas it was unsuccessful, but the fact that the Church would even make the effort demonstrated the degree to which its influence had permeated the realm of knightly ethics before the end of the 12th century. These restrictions applied first to medieval tournaments and secondly to the use of missile weapons.

By the 12th century, the tournament was flourishing in northern France, where it had originated, and in England and Germany. The tournaments of the 12th century differed very little from actual battles. If life grew dull through too long a period of peace, a noble might arrange to hold a tourney. He selected a site and sent out heralds to announce to all neighboring knights the time and place. On the appointed day, the knights assembled, chose sides and put on their armor in safety-zones. Then the two lines of heavy cavalry would charge at each other. When lances were broken, the combat would continue with swords and axes. Though the intent was not to kill but to force an opponent to yield in order to collect ransom, it is easy to see why the Church would frown on such dangerous sport.

The first ordinance directed against tournaments was Canon IX of the Synod of Clermont in 1130 of which the following canon from the Second Lateran Council (1139) is a repetition. It is worth citing in full.

> We condemn absolutely those detestable jousts or tournaments in which the knights usually come together by agreement and, to make a show of their strength and boldness, rashly engage in contests which are frequently the cause of death to men and of danger to souls. If anyone taking part in them should meet his death, though penance and the Viaticum shall not be denied him if he asks for them, he shall, however, be deprived of Christian burial.[17]

Even though stronger measures were urged against them at, for example, the Fourth Lateran Council and the Council of Lyons, tournaments continued to increase in popularity until the middle of the 16th century, though by this time they were a pale shadow of their former ferocity.

The other effort of the Church was an attempt to limit specifically the way in which feudal war was waged. In this same Lateran Council, a canon was directed against the use of a new and deadly weapon, the arbalest or crossbow. The canon decreed that it was "a deadly and God detested" weapon and that those who used it against Christians and Catholics should be anathema.[18]

The immediate impression which one has from this is that it was an attempt on the part of the Church to "humanize" the weapons of war. But there were many weapons which inflicted much greater suffering on a combatant than a bolt from a crossbow. More probably the Church's intent in banning it was to restrain the use of weapons of this sort which would have the effect of destroying the military monopoly of the knight. Once military commanders discovered that a disciplined and efficient body of low-born footmen, armed with a weapon considerably less expensive than a knight's panoply, could in fact inflict heavy losses on feudal cavalry, war could no longer be confined to the minority. War would increase in the number of its participants to the degree to which more persons could be employed efficiently in its prosecution. If the knight and his code suffered eclipse the effect would be felt by both the Church and the civil population, at this time not actively engaged in fighting, and enjoying a period of relative security unknown since the days of the *Pax Romana*.

Unfortunately, the Church was as unsuccessful in halting the general adoption of the crossbow as it had been in abolishing tournaments. Yet, these instances of specific restrictions are noteworthy not so much for what they failed to accomplish, but for what they attempted. Basically, they show to what extent the code of chivalry had permeated medieval society in that the Church should address itself to all Christendom in an ecumenical council on a matter pertaining to the knightly code, and expect to be heeded. The condemnation of the crossbow was not an effort to ban a weapon nearly so much as it was a plea for the continuation of an ethical code which offered some hope of limiting formal violence to those whose business it was to fight, while leaving the rest of society undisturbed.

If there is a common characteristic which can be perceived in all of these institutions, it might be that they were all spontaneous products of the Christian society within which they originated and flourished. As an illustration, the most influential of them, the Peace of God, was not the result of a carefully blueprinted theological or philosophical doctrine; rather, it arose spontaneously, in response to felt social needs, and quickly obtained formal sanction and direction from the magnates of the society. Here it is clear how institution, necessity and moral sensitivity can provide for the lacunnae left by formal reasoning.

With all due praise to those who developed the various rules surveyed, one should not attribute to these rules, nor to their sponsors, a sophistication which they did not possess. For example, it should be remembered that these rules were constantly invoked for "Christians" and "Christian men." Though the official decrees were obviously intended to apply only to Christians, it does not necessarily mean that Jews and Saracens were considered fair game for war's excesses. The *Capitularies* of Charlemagne and various Spanish codes of civil legislation specifically extended protection to these groups. Yet in the whole period of the Middle Ages there was often a peculiar blindness to the universal applicability of humanitarian principles. The best description of this might be "moral parochialism." Nowhere is this fact more evident than in warfare between Christians and Saracens. In such cases, no rules of fair play or mercy were particularly applicable or expected.[19]

This raises another point. The intent of the prescriptions of the Peace of God was to ameliorate suffering for certain classes in private feudal wars. In medieval warfare, to destroy a man's cattle meant more than merely destroying his property. In an agricultural society wherein the primary means of exchange was goods in kind, to destroy a man's property meant his starvation. Thus when immunity was extended to cattle and draught animals, the intent of the rule was to safeguard the life of the beast's owner. This no doubt accounts for the disproportionate immunity for property. Since the purpose of private feudal wars was invariably to acquire booty rather than to simply destroy an enemy, it was reasonable to emphasize the immunity of those objects most prized as ends of these wars.

III

We also perceive that those who established the categories of immune classes were still ambivalent as to *why* those classes should be immune. Here we must return to that "parochialism" mentioned above. The first peace decrees on immunity applied to ecclesiastics and the property but not the persons, of the poor; only later were all women and other defenseless classes such as merchants and pilgrims included; later still, serfs and their property were declared immune from attack, at which point the reason was given for the first time that homicide of these classes of Christians was wrong because it was equivalent to shedding the blood of Christ. The progressive inclusion of more and more categories under the protection of immunity from attack can be explained as resulting from an increasing awareness of those who both theoretically should and practically could be protected. It does indicate however, that the formulators of these rules were not acting upon a clear-cut set of theological or philosophical principles which accorded a fundamental right of immunity to all defenseless persons, regardless of religious belief, as in the case of Saracens. As a result, with all the humanitarian and charitable impulses which actuated the medieval peacemakers, they still did not recognize, much less accept, the principle that an "enemy" possessed "rights."

The only persons who could really fit the category of "enemy" in the Middle Ages were non-Christians. According to the Augustinian-Thomistic notion of war, few of the private quarrels which feudal nobles engaged in could have qualified as "just wars," and even less would the serfs, pilgrims, merchants and ecclesiastics have fitted the category of an "enemy population." These were simply the victims of unjustified violence. As they were Christians who suffered victimization at the hands of other Christians, it was easy to deduce the necessity of sparing them from this violence in Christ's name. In fact, such a notion needed only formal proclamation to receive ready acceptance from Christians of all classes.

A true "enemy," however, the Moslem was looked upon as being unworthy of merciful treatment. There are numerous sources which detail the unchivalrous conduct of the Crusaders in their relations with the "infidel." The nature of the war itself being what today might be called an "ideological" struggle, the absoluteness of the objectives, the release of frustrations which soldiers experienced when a besieged city was finally taken—all of these factors tended to loosen restraints on the conduct of Christian-non-Christian conflict. Granted that these elements were contributing causes to the inhumane conduct of the Crusaders, the point is that in this case of medieval Christian Europe facing an external enemy, the restraints on war's conduct which had thus far evolved were not considered applicable.[20]

It is true that acts of chivalry and mercy may be found in the histories of the Crusades, most often to the credit of the Saracens. But these were exceptions to the general rule, and the probability is that Richard Coeur de Lion felt more restrained by his warrior's code of fair-fight than by any commitment to Christian mercy. Acts of chivalry between participating warriors is beside the point. The issue is the attitude of the warrior towards the defenseless, and here the conclusion can only be that to the Christian crusader the enemy was morally guilty and vengeful destruction was his due.

This attitude could hardly be other when the Christian theology of war at this time, and through the time of Thomas Aquinas, is recalled. But this in no way diminishes the contribution which the medieval peace-movements made to the developing notion of immunity for noncombatants. Many of the categories of the population which are accepted today as immune from attack in time of war were first designated by the Peace of God, passing then into the chivalric code, and finally becoming ingrained in the consciousness of European culture. Though much evolution was still required before a developed ethical principle of noncombatant immunity was enunciated, at least the customary acceptance of some such principle was established. The most important change in Christian just war theory in the late Middle Ages was a modification of the Augustinian-Thomistic view of war as punishment, and of the enemy as subjectively guilty. Such a change, when it did come, made it possible to apply the principles of Christian mercy to all men, even non-Christian enemies.

Six

Ontological Dualisms and the Dilemma of Revolutionary Action

Kathy E. Ferguson

A man does not show his greatness by being at one extremity, but
rather by touching both at once.

Pascal

The dualistic quality of human existence has repeatedly been the
focus of inquiry for philosophers of many diverse eras and
traditions. The search for a satisfactory ontology, whether of the
One or of the Many, has inevitably led to a confrontation with the
fragmentation of experience as it is lived by ordinary human beings.
The pre-Socratics struggled with the split between permanence and
flux, between a sought-after stable unity and an observed
diversified movement. The same problem has been handed down to
us in the paradox of Zeno, whose "proof" that motion is impossible
rests upon his inability to reconcile stable space, which is static and
object-like, with motion, which is ever coming-to-be and passing-
away. Plato, of course, wrestled with the dualism between mind and
body, as well as the split that his cave metaphor illustrates between
appearance and reality. St. Augustine and his fellow Christians
defined the fragmentation they perceived as the split between the
City of God and the City of Man. Marx's class war echoes the
dialectic of the more profound Hegelian dualism between freedom
and necessity. Modern conceptions of the opposites that divide our
experience are myriad: reason versus passion, subject versus object,
culture versus nature. The tension here, which is revealed in
perhaps its most acute form in the dilemmas of revolutionary
thought and action, has permeated both Western political thought
and Western political experience.

Thus most systems of thought seem to have conceptualized the
polarity of human experience in terms of the dualisms that the
women and men of that era experienced. In the twentieth century,
with the paradigm of Einstein central to the intellectual community,

and with the emergence of phenomenology and process philosophy, it is perhaps not unexpected that one might conceptualize the fragmentation of our experience in terms of space and time. We are simultaneously both spatial and temporal creatures; our experience is both a "being" and a "becoming." The spatial aspect of experience is perhaps the most easily perceived, because it is literally spread out around us and can be directly observed. Sight, sound, touch, taste and smell all put us in touch with the reality of the spatial dimension. Objects have an unyielding facticity, as do the needs that are connected with these objects: hunger is as real as food, cold as real as clothing, exposure as real as shelter. The spatial axis of experience confronts us with what *is*, with the immediacy of present pressures and requirements. It is the realm of necessity and actuality.

But at the same time we are also temporal creatures; time is also a directly experienced phenomenon. The going-on-ness of experience, Bergson's duration, is surely one of its most fundamental aspects; the present has "a disappearing edge and an appearing edge," and our experience of it demonstrates the reality of *process*.[1] Human beings do not simply exist; they *emerge;* in James' words, "We humans are incurably rooted in the temporal point of view."[2] Bergson describes duration as "succession without distinction," an intuition of the process of experience as "a succession of qualitative changes, which melt into and permeate one another, without precise outlines, without any tendency to externalize themselves in relation to one another, without any affiliation with number."[3] Duration is the experience of *becoming*, a gathering up of the multiplicity of experiences as they flow into one another. The temporal dimension of experience confronts us with the reality of change. In phenomenological terms: "What we, in fact, experience in duration is not a being that is discrete and well-defined but a constant transition from a now-thus to a new now-thus. The stream of consciousness by its very nature has not yet been caught up in the net of reflection."[4] The temporal axis of experience allows us to project ourselves into an imagined future and to construct alternative modes of existence; it is the realm of possibility.

These two dimensions of experience, spatial and temporal, stand facing each other in an ontological tension. "Being" and "becoming" are equally real; we are both tied up in what is, and able to imagine what could be. Metaphorically, time carries us forward while space holds us back; and this original fragmentation of experience persists despite conceptual efforts to eradicate it in the name of a higher unity. The requirements of order versus the vision of change, the lure of possibility versus the risk of loss, the beckoning of imagination versus the pressure of necessity—in both our private and our public lives we experience the persistent brokenness of experience.

The fragmentation of experience into spatial and temporal dimensions is so ubiquitous that it has come to the attention even of such a philosopher of unification as William James. James, like Whitehead, rejects most dualistic analyses of experience, claiming that they fall into the "fallacy of misplaced concreteness" by mistaking a conceptual distinction for concrete reality. Yet even James recognizes an underlying split in experience that does not originate in classifications of it: "Experience is only a collective name for all these sensible natures, and save for time and space (and, if you like, for 'being,') there appears no universal element of which all things are made." But these particular universals are crucial, and the opposition between them is more than linguistic in origin: it is *experienced*. James, true to his radical empiricism, recognizes that such an experience cannot be erased by any conceptual slight-of-hand: "whatever separateness is actually experienced is not overcome, it stays and counts as separateness to the end."[5]

An indication of the tension involved in the opposition of these two dimensions is the common practice of reducing time to a form of space. This reduction, convenient for scientific purposes, entails defining time as an homogenous medium of identical units moving along in evenly-spaced intervals; duration is thus abandoned. In so doing, we are "falling back upon space and giving up time." By collapsing the two dimensions into one another, the experience of process is lost. Time, thus conceived, is "nothing but the ghost of space haunting the reflective consciousness."[6] Time as we experience it in duration must be rescued from this reduction and reinstated in order to make proper sense of the experience of "becoming."

To pose time and space as ontological opposites is not to claim that there is no relation between them. Einstein used the concept "space-time" to indicate such a relation in the physical world, and he defined such basic concepts as "simultaneity" and "interval" in terms of the relation.[7] In the social world, concerted human effort can sometimes bring together being and becoming, transforming what is into what could be. But such effort is mammoth, and the unity achieved is fragile, because the dialectical tension between the two dimensions continually reasserts itself. In phenomenological terms, the fundamental opposition re-emerges "between the constitution of the lived experience in pure duration, on the one hand, and the being of the constituted objectification of the spaciotemporal world, on the other."[8] Attempts at political and social change bear the mark of this endemic split, because politics reflects ontology. Changes in the constitution of collective life cannot be made through purely conceptual means; rather, they reflect the structures and boundaries of lived experience. This being the case, an analysis of revolutionary action must take into account the persistence of fragmentation as well as the search for unity. If we take seriously the notion that the task of political theory is to distinguish between possibility and madness—between humanly liveable visions of social alternatives and self-destructive schemes—then it is crucial that we search out the limitations that ontology places on revolutionary politics.[9]

The Rebel's Dilemma. In his classic study of political radicalism, Albert Camus presents an image of the act of rebellion as an attempt to reconstitute an illusive unity of thought and action. The rebel, like the artist, is a "fabricator of universes;" she or he attempts to overcome the fragmentation of experience while maintaining its full complexity. But the rebel is not willing to take refuse in simplicity, to embrace one dimension of experience and dispense with others, so this sought-for unity is in fact a balancing of opposites in a condition of acute tension. The rebel acts in the name of both freedom and justice, not just against masters, but against the world of masters and slaves. She/he wishes not to become a master, but rather to abolish domination. "He is not only the slave against the master, but also man against the world of master and slave." The rebel demands justice in the name of the "community of men," and to seek this goal he must confront the masters. To oppose injustice and affirm life he must destroy the oppressor, who is also a man.

He cannot, therefore, absolutely claim not to kill or lie, without renouncing his rebellion and accepting, once and for all, evil and murder. But no more can he agree to kill and lie, since the inverse reasoning which would justify murder and violence would also destroy the reasons for his insurrection. Thus the rebel can never find peace. He knows what is good, and, despite himself, does evil.[10]

Thus the rebel is faced with an agonizing contradiction: to achieve what could be, he must destroy what is; but such destruction undermines the creative vision that a commitment to rebellion affirms. The rebel commits murder for the same reason that she or he is unable to justify it. Numerous ideological gymnastics have been performed in an attempt to supercede this tragic vision—for example, by defining the oppressors as less than human or by dwelling on the vision of a just future so as to eliminate the spector of present violation—but the rebel must reject the lure of such false solutions. Even though, in weariness, the rebel might sometimes "imagine some barbarous state where truth would be effortless," he or she clings to the realization that action, to be lucid, must be integrated into the *Angst* of experience.[11]

The rebel, then, is one who is torn between the vision of good and the need for evil; he is guilty for what he admits he *must* do. His will toward morality is thwarted by the evil it leads him to do toward others. Thus in Camus we find a conceptualization of split experience that is formulated on moral grounds.[12] His solution, of course, is for the rebel to seek consistency through self-sacrifice. He urges us to sacrifice our own lives when we take that of the oppressor, so that the higher value of life is affirmed: "The Rebel has only one way of reconciling himself with his act of murder if he allows himself to be led into performing it: to accept his own death and sacrifice. He kills and dies so that it shall be clear that murder is impossible."[13] In his admiration of the fastidious assassins, who combine regicide and suicide, Camus indicates his willingness to replace effective public action with martyrdom. The rebel's principles remain intact, even though his life is not.

The contradiction lived by Camus' rebel is, then, primarily moral and not ontological in form. He ultimately sacrifices his life to his principles, embracing a moral perfectionism that limits him to demanding change rather than effecting it. The ontological dualism between the spatial and temporal realms of experience is presented here as a moral split. In this way Camus can be seen as the twentieth century heir of Augustine; his world is divided into good and evil, and the City of God and the City of Man can be united only through martyrdom. The fastidious assassins take the place of Jesus and we are urged to die in the name of principles larger than life.

The difficulty, indeed the tragedy, is that moral and ontological categories do not coincide. Temporality, the on-goingness of experience, cannot be equated with good; the realm of possibility may offer some options at the expense of others, leading us to a freedom filled with sacrifice. Spatial experience, similarly, cannot be equated with evil; the web of necessity offers much that is comfortable and secure. One need not accept the entire conservative argument to see that the familiar often recommends itself; space, indeed, has its own virtues.[14] To be torn, ontologically, between possibility and necessity is not the same as being torn, morally, between good and evil. If it were, the dilemmas of revolutionary action would be simplified immensely. But the realms of possibility and necessity are equally riddled with moral conflicts. Thus Camus' rebel, whose rejection of revolution in favor of insurrection is an attempt at moral purity, does not provide an adequate explanation of the dualisms in revolutionary action. To adequately understand the tensions in revolutionary action we must go further, looking at the contradictions within revolution that are ontological in nature. *Dualisms in Revolutionary Action.* There is considerable debate among scholars over the proper definition of revolution.[15] Yet, while there is no consensus concerning an exact definition, it seems that "all analysts share a somewhat vague conception of revolutions as structural changes in a society."[16] The origin of the word is a subject of some dispute; its beginnings have been located alternately in the political explosions in Italy in the 15th-17th centuries, in early French literary criticism, and in the conversation between Louis XVI and his Duke at the storming of the Bastile: "C'est une revolte;" "non, Sire, c'est une revolution."[17] At any rate, there was a point in time at which the ancient astrological reference was replaced by a secular abstraction referring to a particular human drama. For present purposes revolution can be defined as a process by which the major institutions of the existing social order are challenged at their roots, and a new social order, built upon the principles of an ideology of liberation, is created. This definition includes several important features: revolution is a process, an on-going set of actions and relations, rather than a single event. It is a radical action, challenging the *status quo* at its roots, rather than settling for cosmetic reforms. It is social in direction and scope, focusing on the institutionalized power relations in society, as opposed to isolated anti-*status quo* actions. And it is a creative endeavor, involving purposive public action aimed at constructing a new social order.

The structure of revolutionary action reflects the spatial/temporal split on several related levels. Any social action, including revolution, requires both initiation and maintenance. In a very suggestive analysis of Rosa Luxemburg's theory of revolution, Ernst Volbrath has traced the dualisms of beginning and continuing through the history of Western thought, with particular emphasis on the writings of Plato, Aristotle and Cicero:

The structure of action involves (at least) two moments: the start and the continuance, both essentially linked.... Founding start (*condere*) and continuing maintenance (*conservare*) are the two structural moments of human action in general and of political action in particular.[18]

In a revolutionary context, the initiation of revolutionary action requires a break with the past and a new beginning. Even in those contexts in which there is a long-established tradition of radicalism, such as that among the Spanish anarchists before the Civil War or among the Russian intelligentsia before 1917, there still must come a time when a decisive beginning is made: villages are turned into communes, or factories seized. The initiation of radical action calls for the projection of an alternative vision, one that transcends the existing spatial context. New beginnings are made by shifting the emphasis in human action to the realm of temporal possibility.

Such action requires a particular kind of leadership, one which can focus popular discontent around the vision of a qualitatively different social order. The sparks which ignite such spontaneous mass uprisings as the February Revolution in Russia or the student/worker strikes in Paris in May, 1968, find their source in imagination, through which one projects oneself forward and conceives of new possibilities for freedom. The dialogue of revolutionaries at this phase, at its best, is such as to crystallize the popular imagination around a common vision. Revolutionary leaders speak the language of time, not of space.

Similarly, the post-revolutionary situation requires a shift to considerations of space and context. A foundation must be laid for the new social order; workers' councils must be initiated, communes organized, food and commodity cooperatives established. The shift is made from beginning to maintaining; post-revolutionary organizers speak the language of space. The seizure of political power must be transformed into the capacity to make public decisions, and the revolutionaries must develop the more mundane skills of overseeing, administering, coordinating.

While the entire revolutionary process involves multiple risks and perils, it is this transition from demanding change to creating order that poses the greatest danger to revolutionary goals. It is incumbent that such a transition be made; the consequences of not doing so also endanger revolutionary aims. For example, the enthusiasm of the people in the Algerian revolution soon changed to confusion and apathy because there was no viable structure established for post-revolutionary rule.[19] But more often than not the demise of the revolution occurs here, as the revolutionaries-turned-administrators abandon the vision of freedom in the name of order. Lenin and the Bolsheviks eliminated the soviets almost immediately after their seizure of power, and moved quickly to eradicate any vestiges of revolutionary participation. Defenders of Lenin are quick to point to the pressures of the international situation, the threat of counter revolution, and the inefficiency of workers' control as justifications of such actions. But it is reasonable to suppose that the execution of anarchists, the massacre of the Kronstadt sailors, and the systemic elimination of citizen participation in favor of party control went far beyond the needs of the situation. It is commonly claimed by the apologists for Leninism that it was Stalin who caused the downfall of the Russian Revolution; Stalin may have buried the revolution, but Lenin and the Bolsheviks strangled it, and helped to dig the grave. As Camus points out, the revolutionaries can all too easily metamorphose into a new ruling elite, with only the facade of radical rhetoric to distinguish them from their predecessors:

The revolutionary is simultaneously a rebel or he is not a revolutionary, but a policeman and a bureaucrat who turns against rebellion. But if he is a rebel, he ends by taking sides against the revolution.... Every revolutionary ends by becoming either an oppressor or an heretic.[20]

The space/time dualism can thus take a wicked turn in this shift from the initiation of change to the maintenance of order. Many contemporary studies of revolution have focused on this shift and attempted to account for it by reference to personality or socialization differences. For example, E.V. Wolfenstein applies a Freudian analysis to the biographies of Lenin, Trotsky, and Gandhi, and concludes that an unresolved Oedipal complex is at the root of revolutionary behavior.[21] Eric Hoffer's famous study of fanaticism ultimately reduces revolutionary action to the same level as malicious gossip and snooping; he sees revolutionary leaders as individuals harboring negative self-images and compensating for a lack of confidence in themselves by putting their faith in the revolution.[22] Lucian Pye, in his study of Malay guerrilla fighters in the 1950s, concludes, on the basis of interviews with Malay Communist Party members who either surrendered to the British or agreed to cooperate with the government after capture, that the major concern of the revolutionary is personal gain and self-interest.[23] Such studies, which are either absurdly reductionist or else based on an insufficient and self-selected sample, tell us little about the real basis of revolutionary motivation. While personality and childhood experience may have an influence on revolutionary behavior, to focus exclusively on such variables is to neglect the effect that context has on action.[24] The initial stages of revolution encourage the actors to explore the possibilities of future freedom; the latter stages confront them starkly with the requirements of present necessity. The shift from creation to maintenance focuses the energies of the actors in opposing directions, as temporal options give way to spatial requirements.

Two more recent studies have dealt more adequately with the connections between situation and action in the revolutionary context. In one study of "revolutions and the men [sic] who made them," William Daly surveys the literature on "types" of revolutionaries and suggests that the common patterns of behavior observed among them might be seen as "a rational response to the shared and distinctive situation which confronts all revolutionaries." He argues that the revolutionary often retreats into dogmatism because she or he secretly harbors doubts about the revolutionary project which, if voiced, would be paralyzing. The attacks on the beliefs and values of the Old Regime, and upon those who hold them, engenders self-doubt as well. But the revolutionary leader cannot afford the hesitation that serious moral ambiguity brings, so she/he retreats into militancy, embracing a dogmatic ideology that reassures both the leaders and the followers of ultimate victory.[25]

A second study focuses on the relationship between stages of revolutionary action and the level of "conceptual complexity" at which a leader functions, as judged by his or her speeches, writings and communications. The authors go beyond the common focus on personality and analyze the constraints that changing situations impose on action. Their hypothesis, confirmed by their data, is that

individuals who showed themselves to be successful both before and after the success of the revolutionary movement should demonstrate a low level of conceptual complexity before the movement takes power and a high level of complexity after its success... leaders who did not show such changes would be unable to remain successful in the long run.

They thus differentiate between the agitator and the administrator by pointing to the skills necessary for each, as determined by "the changing demands of the environment as one progresses from rebel to ruler, and on the necessity for different problem solving characteristics to meet those changing demands."[26] The notion of low conceptual complexity should not be taken to mean that the agitators are stupid, while the administrators are intelligent; rather, it means that the agitators deal with the rhetoric of possibility, where grand vision takes precedence over practical detail, while the administrators must cope with the nitty-gritty of social organization.

The neutrality of the language used to describe revolutionary leadership in social scientific studies such as those described above should not be allowed to blur the basic human passions that are at stake. As human beings we exist simultaneously in two dimensions; we are both wedded to the constraints of the spatial dimension, and able to construct possibilities for an as-yet-undefined future. The tension between these two modes of existence, between being and becoming, reaches an acute pitch in the lives of those who pursue their dreams through political action. The vision of the projected future is no less compelling than the pressure of the present and the weight of the past, yet they pull the revolutionary in different directions.

In the revolutions of the past, those individuals who perceived the tensions inherent in political action, and who refused to become either fanatics or compromisers, have often met with a tragic fate. To live with dualism rather than attempting to abolish it, to recognize the conflicting pull of opposites and not fall into a false unity—such perception has been the exception rather than the rule among revolutionary leaders. Those who cling to the vision of freedom while dealing with the realm of necessity are likely to end up as either the enemies of the revolution or its victims. The administrators react harshly to continued agitation, even within their own ranks. The Kronstadt sailors' record of revolutionary heroism did not save them from the Red Army when they rebelled against the Party in defense of the workers' and soldiers' soviets.[27] Rosa Luxemburg's revolutionary valor and theoretical brillance made her even more of a threat to the German Social Democrats in 1919, whose ambitions for power far surpassed their commitment to change.[28] The initial enthusiasm that Emma Goldman and Alexander Berkman felt for the Russian Revolution changed quickly to bitter disillusionment when they discovered that the Bolshevik administrators had ended the revolution almost before it had begun.[29]

The commitment to freedom and justice that these individuals maintained, which brought them their death and exile, reflected not naiveté but a willingness to live with tensions rather than evade them. The Kronstadt sailors had set up a successful council among themselves; Luxemburg was thoroughly familiar with the nuts-and-bolts of socialist party politics; and Goldman had spent a lifetime involved in anarchist organizations. These were not irresponsible agitators, but committed revolutionaries, and their fate at the hands of the "successful" revolutionary parties illustrates the truth of Lamartine's oft-quoted remark: revolutions do seem to consume their children.

What Is To Be Done? Given this persistent fragmentation of our experience, both personal and collective, into opposing dimensions, it is crucial that we explore the consequences of this dualism for unified public action. What are the conditions for bringing together the constraints of "being" with the options of temporal projection? Can we, as Pascal urges, stand between the two poles, touching both at once? Revolutionaries ultimately seem condemned to the pursuit of unity in a fragmented world. Given the constraints that a dualistic ontology imposes, what are the possibilities offered by revolution?

Revolutions have historically been caught up in a search for some absolute standard by which to justify the new order and guarantee its validity. Melvin Lasky argues that this reflects the consequences of revolutionary intrusion into the existing order;

once it is established that change is possible, the revolutionaries must erect some barrier against continued change or else face the possibility of their own demise:

> Every revolution needs a theory of its own permanence, for even in its finest moments of triumphant consolidation it is beseiged by its own niggling fears that this too might pass away, that its own watchwords of mutability and change could be turned against itself.[30]

Hannah Arendt, too, notes this pattern, which has been "inherent in the revolutionary event itself."[31] This can be partially explained by reference to the form of the Old Regime against which revolutionaries often rebelled; as is often recognized, centralized and authoritarian Old Regimes tend to beget similar post-revolutionary governments.[32] But Arendt maintains that there is a more basic and constant need behind this search for an absolute; it is needed to legitimate the "very task of foundation" by bestowing an external legality on what would otherwise obviously be a human construction.[33] The Old Regimes had claimed legitimacy by reference to the antiquity of custom, or the station of the monarch, or the authority of religious belief. But the fruits of revolutionary change seemed clearly to be an invention rather than a discovery; thus there ensued the search for a source of authority that could claim an origin beyond human action. As long as law, as seen from the lingering medieval view, was defined as a commandment from a higher authority, then revolutionary authority also required an ultimate sanction. Thus the revolutionaries who were inspired by Rousseau appealed to his notion of the General Will, the Marxists have looked to history, the Leninists to the Party, and even the American liberal tradition to "the laws of nature and Nature's God."

The seductiveness of this view is thus readily seen; in a world of absolutes, it is understandable that the advocates of change would construct their own. But its dangers to the radical project must be even clearer. For those who wish to rebel in the name of autonomy and freedom, the replacement of one absolute source of authority with another is anathema. As Camus notes, "To ensure the adoration of a theorem for any length of time, faith is not enough; a police force is needed as well."[34] Any viable revolutionary action must create some form of new government; the requirements of human community demand some institutionalized channels for the making and enforcing of decisions. But it must avoid, in the process, enshrining a new absolute and enforcing it with guns. The alternative virtually guarantees that the post-revolutionary society will use its police force, not to enforce rules collectively arrived at, but to ensure mental and spiritual conformity.

In contemporary western industrial societies, the established ideological justifications are more pluralist in form than absolutist; thus, if Arendt's argument holds, one might expect that revolutionary groups emerging out of this context would also be pluralist in form. To some extent this is the case; for example, the sentiment behind the Paris uprisings in 1968 was definitely plural in form, consisting more of a celebration of liberation than of a specific ideological line. Similarly, the liberation movements that flourished during the 1960s presented a diverse array of theoretical views. However, the continued existence of different varieties of "Old Left" organizations indicates that the problem of absolutism remains. Such groups personify the danger that William Daly described with respect to revolutionary leadership; when the Party claims moral certainty for its actions, it both rationalizes central control and encourages the leaders to dogmatism, since there is no legitimate arena for the active interchange of truly diversified ideas. Thus I believe that the whole concept of revolutionary consciousness must be reformulated in such a way as to avoid (or at least try to avoid) the re-emergence of an Absolute.

The problem of revolutionary consciousness, and especially of false consciousness, plagues non-Marxist radicals because it seems to be both necessary and unacceptable. The category of false consciousness is necessary in order to account for the gross manipulation of minds that we know is possible, especially by those who have power. Coercive institutions of various sorts—churches, schools, bureaucracies, mental hospitals, armies, bosses, sometimes families—frequently are able to restrict the environment and distort the consciousness of their inmates, even to the point of convincing the oppressed to acquiesce in their oppression. Without the concept of false consciousness, there seems to be no adequate way of accounting for those individuals and groups whose view of themselves and their society has been manufactured for them to serve the interests of others. While no individual ever formulates his or her understanding of the political world in isolation, it still makes sense to distinguish between relatively autonomous versus relatively manipulated modes of thought. At the same time, the category of false consciousness is unacceptable in that the claim that some consciousness is false seemingly implies that some other consciousness is true, thus elevating one perspective on the world above all others and claiming for it a unique metaphysical status. This claim is at best pompous, and arguments made in its behalf usually abandon the diversity of temporality and change in favor of a static view of experience.

Perhaps, however, there is a solution to this difficulty; it may be that there are many "false consciousnesses" but no one "true consciousness." In other words, there are many ways that an individual's ideas can be manipulated, and many barriers that can be erected to independent analysis. But there is no one truth that constitutes correct consciousness; rather, there are a variety of perspectives generated out of the particular experience of different individuals and groups. A search for clarity must necessarily result in a diversity of points of view.

It seems on the surface illogical to claim that false consciousness exists but true consciousness does not, because the structure of Western logic tells us that the boundaries of any phenomena are defined by its opposite: A cannot be non-A; further, A is defined by reference to non-A. Accordingly, it would seem that, in order for the category of "false" to have meaning it must be defined by comparison to that which is "true." Thus, to oppose the false consciousness of those who have uncritically adopted the official view of reality, the revolutionary has historically claimed to have a monopoly on true consciousness and thus be in possession of the standard by which false consciousness is judged.

But logical categories do not always coincide with experience. False consciousness definitely exists; sociologists can point to ample evidence of the comparative ease with which individuals can be manipulated to adopt a perspective not of their own design. But "true consciousness" belongs to the pretentious realm of those who claim access to timeless metaphysical certainties. Consequently, the initial logic of the position must be re-examined. In the realm of human values and choices, the opposite of falsehood may be clarity, and the opposite of truth, a silencing of the mind. A truly revolutionary consciousness, then, would be one that replaces allegiance to absolutes with a critical and creative apprehension of oneself and the world. It would demand that individuals continually confront the dilemmas and contradictions in their experience, rejecting simplicity in favor of a lived complexity of possibility and risk.

Marxists historically have despaired of making a revolution with individuals such as this, who have cultivated the ability to view a question from different perspectives. It may be that the ability to see an issue from multiple perspectives simultaneously is the key to knowledge, but it serves less well as a guide to action. A revolutionary consciousness such as I am describing here, which recognizes the paradox in experience and confronts the inconsistencies, is not meant to serve as a justification for hypocrisy or a shield for shoddy thinking, nor is it intended to postpone action indefinitely. It is, rather, a plea for the retention of the complexity and multi-dimensionality of experience into theory as well. A dialectical, critical perspective on experience is required, not to resolve the contradictions but to approximate them in thought.

The definition of revolution proposed above specifies that revolution be a creative act, an on-going process in which intentional collective action creates a new social order. The latter stage of revolution, in which order is established, must be an approximation of the initial phases in which possibility is imagined. To return to Volbrath's argument: the structure of all social action, including revolution, involves both initiation and maintenance. The post-revolutionary society must be structured in such a way as to allow for the continued pursuit of revolutionary goals. This requires that the revolutionaries create a viable public space where all interested parties can participate in the making of collective decisions. The transition from a temporal to a spatial emphasis will still be necessary, because no human community can live on dreams alone. But, on the other hand, no revolution can live long without them, and the only way that people can attempt to achieve a fragile unity in their collective lives, bringing together an approximation of what could be with what is, is through meaningful participation in public life. The soviets that sprang up in 1917 out of the tsarist collapse had many limitations, but they were evidence of the authentic desire for self-rule. They could have been nurtured, and made into the foundation for a genuinely democratic society. Instead, they were destroyed; the requirements of participation gave way to the cult of efficiency.

The Russian experience demonstrates that when public decisions are monopolized by a small and self-selected elite, there is indeed a danger that possibility will degenerate into madness, because there is no open forum within which to investigate the limits of the possible. When opposition is equated with treason, the powerful leave themselves with the choice between abdication and barbarism. The only way that revolution can avoid tragedy is through the creation of a viable public space. Of course the classic Marxist demands for economic justice are important, but without meaningful institutionalized channels for the making of collective decisions, any economic redistributions effected by an elite will be gifts, not achievements. They are what Max Stirner has called "donated freedoms," and they are a pallid substitute for self-government.[35]

The revolutionary consciousness described above, in which autonomous individuals critically confront the tensions in their experience, and attempt through participation to bring together possibility and necessity, can never be achieved by police tactics. At most, a few participants might be forced into abnegation, as the appalling spector of the Stalinist purge confessions testifies. Barbarism has prevailed when men and women can be made to embrace their own destruction in the name of liberation; in such a case, the revolution not only devoured its children, but the children were made to acknowledge that, "after all, the revolution was hungry."[36]

It might be asserted that to encourage individuals to demystify their experience and confront it authentically would be to paralyze them in fear, guilt, or simple confusion. Perhaps this is so. The confrontation with personal contradiction can be agonizing, as both the nihilist and the vitalist traditions of political thought attest. But it can also be liberating, in that it frees the individual to create new meaning rather than to merely mourn the loss of the old. If we are ever to entertain a revolution that nurtures its children rather than devouring them, we must start with a pedagogy of revolutionary consciousness in which it is preferable to live a liberating contradiction than capitulate to a consistency that is oppressive.

Seven

Toward A Non-Violent Social Order: What Academics Can Do

Christian Bay

"Respect for human personality" would be one of the central characteristics of a non-violent society, writes Mulford Sibley; "this would be reflected in a non-authoritarian educational system..."[1] What does this mean? And is it possible to have a non-authoritarian educational system in an authoritarian society based on violence and oppression?

In these brief reflections I shall discuss (I) the violent, authoritarian nature of allegedly democratic North American society and its imprint on today's world; and then argue (II) that we can nonetheless struggle for a non-authoritarian educational system and thereby hope to improve the chances for a less violent society and world. I conclude (III) by reflecting on the contributions that political theorists ought to make toward building a non-violent world of optimal human rights.

I

Our society, like every other political order, is basically authoritarian, based on a massive concentration of power. For purposes of comparative political analysis there are important differences in degree of authoritarianism among states, and they are not to be slighted. But for purposes of analysis of the prospects in our society for democracy, for respect for personality, and for non-violence, we must begin by stressing the facts of oppression.

We have come some way from the jungle, to be sure. The physically strong are nowadays not free to kill the weak, not with impunity at any rate, under most circumstances. Nowadays it is the technologically, organizationally, and financially strong who oppress and kill people who are in their way, but not visibly or directly. The multinational and other large corporations, in collusion with the largest states, maintain an armed international order that protects the freedom of corporate enterprise. The best lands the world over are acquired quite legally, and large landless populations are pushed either into hamlets on barren soil or into the jungles of the big-city slums, especially in the Third World. Indigenous peoples on desirable lands are simply killed off or removed from their ancestral homelands, in a succession of small-scale holocausts that upset only a few academics and church-people in our own "civilized" parts of the world.

"Why don't they eat cake?" Why don't the world's poor revolt and build movements and societies that establish a measure of justice? It is not because they believe in non-violence, for in their own lives they know mainly of violence. It is in part because they lack the means of organization, and of counter-violence, but also in part because their established leaders, in much of the Third World, make common cause with one or more of the superpowers—chiefly the United States and Britain and France—that so diligently protect our world order against social and economic change.

Only rarely, as in Cuba and Vietnam and Nicaragua, or in Mocambique and Angola and Zimbabwe, has it been possible for movements of and for the poor (initially, at least), to revolt successfully against their former masters, at enormous costs of bloodshed and suffering. In the "Free World," under the banner of anticommunism, most authentic freedom fighters and movements of and for the poor have been butchered well before reaching the point of actually threatening the public order. Against Washington's inexhaustible arsenals, so freely dispensed to repressive regimes expecting trouble, one can only marvel at the courage and persistence of past freedom fighters in Nicaragua or Mocambique, and of those who fight in El Salvador and Guatemala today.

In April, 1982, when visiting Barbados for a meeting with cooperative Carribean leaders, President Reagan spoke of the "virus of Marxism" which must be kept out of the Western hemisphere.[2] That is the imagery that justifies the American overlordship over so many countries, in both hemispheres, countries that receive small amounts of economic and/or military aid and coincidentally guarantee the "economic freedom" that enables foreign firms to displace or employ local inhabitants and exploit natural resources at high profits; it is good business all around, except for those who are displaced or exploited and deprived of political opportunities to build less unjust societies.

If the reader will grant that our world order is authoritarian and brutal, perhaps he or she will still insist that the United States is a democratic and only moderately violent country. There are, to be sure, many countries that are more authoritarian and also more violent. But if we want to understand the violence of the world order, and to entertain some hope of learning how to change it, we must face the fact that behind the facade of electoral democracy and free speech in the world's most powerful nation are the realities of a corporate elite that determines which issues are to be left open to electoral and legislative influence and which are not.[3] Most of the time, American public opinion is successfully programmed to reject any and all ideas that can be associated with un-American ideologies like Marxism. Any and every effective idea of reducing or weakening corporate property rights, or of making private corporations subservient to agencies representing the public interest, is rejected or ignored. Even the mild proposal of "open books" for major corporations, for easy public scrutiny of what is being done with the nation's natural resources, has so far been left as politically dead; "there is already too much public interference with private enterprise," to cite a frequently heard refrain, from the political Center as well as the Right.[4]

The most damaging aspect of the *de facto* authoritarianism within the world's leading superpower at the present time is neither the extent of the violence in the cities, nor the ideological domination of electorates that are barred from seeing the alternative possibility of a non-violent world and from choosing to build a democratic, non-violent social order. The most damaging aspect is the paranoia that the system has built against the "virus" of communism. This has led to mounting military preparations for risking, and preparedness to risk, the very future of humankind, and has barred a rational awareness of the most urgent of all defense and security needs today: serious negotiations that recognize the universally shared interest in achieving progress toward multilateral nuclear disarmament over the short range, and in struggling for near-total conventional disarmament as well, within the next decades.

The U.S. electorate has been left powerless to resist the American leadership in the postwar arms race, which goes a long way toward accounting for the mounting militarism in the U.S.S.R. as well. The increasing danger for both sides that the arms race entails was inaugurated, in my view, by the use of atom bombs against the Japanese in 1945, and was further stimulated by the attempted uses of nuclear blackmail against minor "enemy" states (and indirectly against the U.S.S.R.) on several subsequent occasions.[5] In the 1950s there were false U.S. allegations about a "bomber gap" and in the 1960s about a "missile gap," which in both cases led to accelerated arms buildups on both sides.[6] Little has been learned from these costly "mistakes" and their grim consequences. During its first year and a half in office, the current Reagan administration has been getting away with repeating equally unfounded allegations about present military inferiority in the West, as pretext for yet another massive escalation of the arms race. While there is at present a Soviet superiority in landbased missiles in the European "theatre," there is no way of challenging the fact that the NATO powers have a considerable global superiority in missile power and in military technology. It may still be argued that there is a *rough* over-all parity between the two power blocs, and I take this to be fortunate for both sides. If one side is in the lead, it is not the Warsaw bloc; and it is Moscow, not Washington, that consistently has pleaded for a mutual recognition of the principle of parity between the two blocs as a prelude to staged reductions in armaments on both sides.[7]

In the last few years significant proportions of the West European publics have broken loose from authoritarian nationalist molds by way of building rather massive anti-nuclear peace movements. Only in the last few weeks, as this is written (April, 1982), are there indications that large numbers of North Americans, too, are beginning to assert critical, even protesting and perhaps ultimately resisting attitudes against Washington's and NATO's ill-conceived military defense policies. How can those of us who work in the universities try to help build this movement, and defend it, to make sure it will not fade out? What role can academics in general, and political scientists in particular, try to perform in the present, most dangerous phase of humankind's long struggle toward a less violent world?

II

Ronald Inglehart's work has demonstrated that the liberation movements within our major universities in the 1960s reflected something new in the world: an onset of *postmaterialist values* in many young people who had grown up with a sense of security, relatively speaking, about their own private prospects in American society.[8] Also, they belonged to the "Spock generation:" many had from their earliest years been given the advantage of much security and freedom to develop a sense of personal power and responsibility over their own lives.

Inglehart's most recent paper indicates that postmaterialists who were students two decades ago now make up considerable proportions of influential categories of people, like members of free professions, civil servants, and management personnel.[9] They need no longer march in demonstrations, although some of them do, on occasion. They serve to strengthen the substantial anti-nuclear-energy movement in this country, as well as feminist and other progressive movements. At this time they may be about to extend their support to the growing peace and disarmament movements as well.

The same data, which are based on large European and Japanese as well as American population samples, indicate that postmaterialism, which enables people to become conscious of their own direct stake in the public good, and become *public citizens* instead of merely private, occasional citizens, is a next stage in moral development, beyond a mere obedience to laws and customs: it is a wider consciousness that, once gained, stays with us.

The development of postmaterialist values appears to require a sense of personal security and freedom during one's formative years, first of all. Secondly, we may assume that a liberal education (in the broad sense of a humanist education) can be of help. But the latter is not enough by itself. Inglehart's more recent data show a modest *decline* in rates of postmaterialism in the post-1960s student generation. In the early 1970s word got around that there might be massive unemployment ahead. To many an embattled Dean or Provost this may at the time have seemed a godsend: fewer students now felt they could afford a strong political conscience as a guide to their own practical decisions. Once again there was a trend for most students to settle for subservience on the campus and for lowering their ambitions and taking "practical" courses with "safe" career options in mind. Many in effect opted for training in skills rather than intellectual education.

As academics we may regret that we have little influence over the larger economic system with its problems of recessions and inflation as well as of deepening structural unemployment. It is too bad that improved educational systems are not sufficient to educate most young people toward becoming public citizens. But good educational systems are necessary, even if insufficient. Some youngsters will always survive, with their own moral bearings and intellectual capacities intact, the anxieties involved in growing up in an economically oppressive, unfair, and unpredictable system; they will be fit for education, as distinct from mere training and grooming for jobs within some hierarchy or other. Young people who are secure and free enough to be educated are the best hope for a future for our society, and our universities must be ready to engage them in the best possible educative situations and encounters.

I shall in these reflections leave aside the topics of child-raising and primary and secondary education, although these are issues with an even weightier bearing on the prospect for democratic citizenship. Let me make only one assertion here, because this point is so often overlooked, though difficult to contest: possibly the greatest asset of the growing feminist self-assertion for our society's future hopes is that so many more youngsters in their homes now are exposed to *joint* decision-making within the family or between parents, based on reasoning things out, rather than to decisions based on male (or female) dictatorship, with orders issued and not much questioning tolerated. The strength of this trend may be contested, but hardly its relevance to the development of psychological capacities for the children to become democratic, public citizens.

The degree of a university's relevance to politics is best indicated, in my view, by the amount and quality of political education that goes on, in and out of the classrooms, involving students and teachers as political equals. Not as equals in all respects, to be sure, but as equals in the sense that we must be equally open to learn from each other, across the generations, and above all on issues of the *relevance* of our academic work to political aims and values and standards. Social and political hierarchies always reduce the ability or the incentive to really listen and learn, on both sides of every step of the ladder.

I find it absurd to teach politics and not treat students as politically equal citizens, inside as well as outside the university. If we want to attain optimal use of our critical capacities, among teachers *and* students, we need to develop academic communities based on mutuality and trust; for political education is *dialectical* or it isn't political education.

All our universities cultivate positivist knowledge and neglect dialectical inquiry. They are dedicated to truth in the abstract, and to endless collecting of data; not to justice or universal human rights, or even to life over death, except in our medical faculties. Witness how many academics go to work for the war industries, without ever being ostracized by their colleagues; in my own field witness a Jeane Kirkpatrick going to work for the Reagan Administration, perhaps being selected for the Ambassadorship to the United Nations on account of her well-known distinction between human rights violations in authoritarian states, which she sees as a lesser evil, and totalitarian violations.[10]

How can we aim at reforming the structure and functions of our universities, so that faculty and administrators become more accountable to their society, including the future generations, while at the same time becoming less accountable to governments, and to private industries, corporations, and foundations? Only a few suggestions can be attempted here:

(1) Academia's independence of governments in our part of the world appears reasonably well protected at least for the leading and financially relatively secure universities, but that may well be true only as long as positivism and the spirit of service to regime interests and to established ideologies continue to prevail. Our academic freedom should be tested and extended by more frequent and searching teach-outs on the major and most contentious issues in our society, with attempts to enlist the most articulate and knowledgeable representatives of all views. Also, universities should push for more direct access to the major media, with free political discussions of the major issues, to safeguard the public's right to hear and to see, and to stimulate a wider political consciousness.

(2) Academics should take more interest in pushing for continuing systematic scrutiny of the scientific value and the political relevancy and implications of foundation-sponsored research activities, especially those that are given large grants. Foundations, too, should be publicly accountable, over time, for their investments; the public interest surely is best served by open books and by continuing, well-informed, critical examinations and debates about their policy priorities, also outside their own boardrooms.

(3) Universities should in principle be governed by Boards of Trustees that are elected by two, approximately equally weighted, constituencies only: faculty and students. Administrators as other service personnel should be responsible to these elected Trustees and should be replaceable within the higher echelons. Annual or biennial elections to the Boards of Trustees, or rather to the Assemblies from which these Boards should derive their members and their powers, should be preceded by public campaigns that raise issues of academic standards as well as of moral and political good for society as a whole. Thus we should all aim at matching the privileges of academic life with actual responsibility for serving the good of all.[11]

(4) There is no way to establish direct representation for the future generations, whose interests should be a major concern for responsible universities. The best we can do, apart from organizing many continuing workshops on alternative futures, and supporting large research projects on the environment and on ways to protect it, is to make sure that the younger generations (the students) within Academia are given approximately as much political power as the older generations (the faculty), and that the dialectics of continuing *public* discussions of priorities in future studies take place, along

with discussions of how to build peace, how to prevent war and famines and exploitation and other human and environmental destruction. It should be the responsibility of universities to make sure that all these urgent issues are kept alive and salient, and that all important information and all relevant views are made readily available to all who are capable of caring about them, inside and outside the universities and school systems.

III

What can and should politically responsible political theorists be doing these days? Many seem to forget that humankind now is an acutely endangered species. In Christopher Isherwood's metaphor, I believe, they keep on lecturing on navigation even while our ship appears to be sinking. Indeed, some colleagues who were influenced by the late Leo Strauss keep on lecturing mainly on *ancient* navigation and appear to take little interest in keeping our ship afloat. While I value their kind of scholarship, I do so in the same way that I value good music: as inherently enjoyable and probably good for the soul but not as political theory of relevance to our own world's urgent problems.

I am equally critical of other colleagues who insist that they are *empirical* theorists and researchers only: the positivists, the straight behavioralists. They forget that knowledge, as distinct from mere data, is dialectical as well as factual, normative as well as empirical. Many of these colleagues even insist on reserving the terms "research" and "scientific method" for purely empirical work. As C. Wright Mills has demonstrated so well, this has been a very effective way of avoiding contentious political issues.[12] Pseudopolitics is promoted instead; political behavior is reduced to consumer behavior, and political action for just ends to "deviant" behavior.[13]

Do not misunderstand me: I do not denigrate behavioral research, including opinion surveys and voting research. We need all kinds of data, even though we must avoid the fallacy of thinking that conventional behavior research in the context of empirical theorizing is all there is to political inquiry. It is only half of it.

The other half is our concern with justice, freedom, human rights, and individual and collective security. These aspects of politics cannot be left out, if empirical research is to have any value. Normative aspects of politics require systematic scientific inquiry no less than empirical aspects. They belong together, in individual study and consciousness as well as in joint dialectical testing of the truth-value and the political significance of our work, on a continuing basis. This is what, in particular, university workshops on the future must be about, in politically relevant academic communities.

Politics, most generally speaking, is the difference between what is and what ought to be. Practically speaking, politics is the difference between what is likely to happen unless we think and act, and what can, at best, be achieved by carefully planned joint action. Politics is a dialectical concept: the tension between (in principle practical) ideals of justice and freedom, and realities of lopsided power and oppression.

In general terms I take it that there are three most politics-relevant tasks of political theory. The first task is critical: to analyze and expose ideology in the service of domination and oppression; even in the service of death, in much of the Third World today, for "superfluous" unemployable populations.

The second task of political theory is to work out improved strategies of political education and political resistance against the powers that be. We must work to identify what is viable and life-serving in the liberal-democratic ideology (as C.B. Macpherson has been doing, for example)[14], while forcefully discarding the liberal legitimation (in even as advanced a liberal theorist as John Rawls)[15] of the jungle conditions that prevail in today's world.

The third task of relevant political theory is constructive: aims and values and limitations on means must be formulated, critically analyzed, and dialectically argued out, among politically concerned academics and others. For example, beyond the task of resisting or delimiting the powers of the state and the multinational corporation we must seek to achieve clarity about what powers we wish to enlarge when state and corporate powers shrink. I happen to be a human survivalist first and then a democrat but not a liberal; I am a human rights-ist and a community-ist (not exactly the same as a communist): the ultimate aim that I see, as well as the road toward that aim, is in the direction of basic human rights for all, everywhere (those related to the most basic human needs taking precedence over those related to less basic needs), and, therefore, in the direction of limitations on the extent of property rights and, more so, on corporate rights of many kinds. Secondly, the way that I see involves work to strengthen and democratize and politically activate local communities, and to encourage and support cooperative enterprises and democratic planning.

IV

Mulford Sibley's terminology differs in various respects from mine, but I like to think of our conceptions of political value priorities as being closely related. Certainly I feel indebted to his inspiration and example, as a human being as well as a scholar. He would, I think, consider me a rather utopian theorist, but in his book that is no term of opprobrium:

> The vision of a utopia can maintain the tension which ought always to exist between patterns of life in existence, on the one hand, and the ideal, on the other....
> Utopia building is eminently practical. It helps save us from the illusions which both revolutionary leaders and defenders of the status quo constantly tend to propogate. By keeping before us a relatively remote goal, it prevents us from uncritically embracing any short-run panaceas. It helps us see civilization in perspective and to realize dramatically the enormous distance between what is and what ought to be.[16]

II
Images of Utopia

Eight

Utopia and the Family:
A Note on the Family
in Political Thought

Lyman Tower Sargent

Utopian fiction has traditionally been studied through analyses of a few of the "greats" or by tacking together a series of plot synopses from a specific time period. Neither approach is particularly useful to the student of political thought even when the work is done with skill and imagination. The first approach, through the "greats," ignores the complexity of the utopian tradition even when it provides interesting insights into the authors involved. The second approach usually leads to extreme oversimplification since no individual work is given adequate consideration and themes or patterns go unnoticed.

Some justification for choosing one of these approaches is found in the sad state of scholarship on utopianism. Until recently, there was little or no serious attention given to the two central problems faced in dealing with any literary genre—definition and bibliography. Fortunately both problems have been addressed by various scholars in recent years and the situation is much improved.

Given the state of scholarship, there is another approach that makes it possible to move beyond analyses of individual texts— focusing on sub-themes within utopianism. While this does not allow presentation of whole societies (one of the major virtues of the utopia as political thought), it does allow for the examination of one aspect of a large number of utopias. Since there are hundreds of utopias from many times and places, examining a sub-theme can help illuminate differing treatments that reflect those times and places. While such an approach is suggestive rather than definitive, it is possible. A definitive study will not be possible until there has been more work on the history of utopianism.

I have chosen to focus on the family because such an example illustrates the value of the utopian tradition in the history of political thought. Utopianism is the only tradition in political thought normally including a discussion of such supposedly non-political institutions as the family. Today most scholarship on the history of political thought recognizes that an understanding of the family and other social institutions falling outside the political narrowly defined is essential in our attempts to comprehend the full range of political thought at any time and place. Many writers of utopias recognized this, and, therefore, provide a series of commentaries on the roles of "non-political" institutions in developed political theories. In this essay I look at images of the family, primarily in the eutopia or positive utopia, to see what changes are proposed in the family (designed to strengthen society) and in society (designed to strengthen the family).

It is most appropriate that an essay on two such unconventional topics for political theorists as utopias and the family should appear in a *festschrift* for Mulford Sibley. After all, he was the pioneer of utopian studies in political science,[1] and he constantly reminded us to be aware of defining the political too narrowly. He taught us by word and deed that what the world saw as unconventional was very likely just the place to look for truth.

A utopia is a species of prose fiction which describes a non-existent society in some detail and is located in time and space. The works identified by this definition may be subdivided into the eutopia or positive utopia, the dystopia or negative utopia, and the satirical utopia. I shall discuss the first two subcategories but emphasize the former. While almost all utopias have some satirical elements,[2] the satirical utopia *per se* (typified by Samuel Butler's *Erewhon)* does not lend itself readily to analysis for social and political thought. I shall use a chronological approach because it allows me to check for patterns of development, and I shall mention only those works and those parts of the works which are directly relevant to the theme. The utopia is predominantly an Anglo-American and Western European phenomenon, at least until the latter half of the twentieth century, and I shall concentrate on the Anglo-American tradition. Apparently more utopias have been published in the U.S. and the U.K. than in all the rest of the world put together.[3] I will make a few cross-cultural comparisons where the literature allows.

Since utopias often propose novel institutions to replace the institutions with which we are familiar, there is some problem with how one defines "family" so that none of the richness of the utopian proposals is lost but without being so vague as to include all of society. For the present purpose, I shall define the family as that institution which is the focus of socially approved sexual relations and child-rearing. Since it is possible to have socially approved sexual relations and child-rearing without having anything like what we call the family, part of this paper will be concerned with suggestions which include the disappearance of any institution resembling what we now call the family.

There still remains many areas in which the discussion of the family will shade off into consideration of the status of women, sexual relations, and education. This can't be helped. For some authors the role of the family is so central that all these areas are rooted in the family. Other authors consider one or more of these points more important than the family and remove them from the family.[4]

Utopias Before More. Whether or not one considers Plato's *Republic* an eutopia (and there is a case for either position), it is traditional to start with it. For Plato family life got in the way of more important things, at least for those parts of the population he treats in detail. For the average worker the family was acceptable, perhaps even desirable. For the rest of the population it was an intrusion because, first, it could take one's thought away from the Good; and second, it could (and ultimately would) interfere with the Philosopher King's reasoned stewardship of the *polis*. As a result the family must be abolished.

Although there is considerable controversy over the intent of Plato's treatment of women,[5] he did present a society where women could achieve something approaching equality, in large part because the family was abolished. Education (the central concern of the state) must not be influenced by family concerns. Sexual relations limited to the family would not produce the best children. The good state must abolish the family to achieve the good life.

Another early utopia, "Heliopolis" by Iambulus as reported by Diodorus Siculus, abolished the family for similar reasons. The people lived in kinship groups of no more than four hundred, each ruled by the eldest male. Individuals live one hundred and fifty years. "They did not marry wives, but had their women in common: the children so born were brought up in common and treated with equal affection by all. While they were infants the women who suckled them often exchanged their charges, so that even the mothers could not recognize their own children; consequently there was no jealousy among them, and they always lived without any quarrels, counting concord the chief of all blessings."[6] Here, then, the family, particularly the ties between parents (mothers specifically) and children, is seen as a, if not the major source of conflict in society. Rid society of the family and life will be much more pleasant for all.

A "community of wives" was often suggested and widely discussed in ancient Greece as a replacement for the traditional family. In addition to Plato and Iambulus, Zeno advocates it in his *Republic*.[7] Aristotle rejects it in the *Politics*. Aristophanes uses the institution satirically a number of times.[8] Thus, the position of women in society, their relationships with men and, to a lesser extent, with other women, and the place of the family in society were common issues in Greek thought. Utopias were only one of many expressions of the debate.

For many ancient Greek and Roman writers, the family symbolized the intrusion of the private on the public. Public life was more important and private life should be kept hidden. This was true in Athens. Sparta virtually abolished private life altogether. "Community of wives" was one way of further diminishing the role of the private and emphasizing the public.[9]

The emphasis on public rather than private continues throughout medieval utopianism which was primarily expressed through monasticism and images of the earthly paradise, the noble savage and Cockaigne (Cokaygne). Thus, the tradition up to 1516 when More wrote *Utopia* was one that stressed public life and deemphasized the private and, particularly, the family.

More And Sixteenth-Century Utopianism. With *Utopia* the scene changes. While he still stresses public life, the family is one of the central foci of his society, and it remained such in most utopias (with a few French exceptions) until the nineteenth century.

The family of More's society is authoritarian and patriarchal. The father is the ruler and the wife is subordinate, if not actually inferior. As More describes his hierarchical system, "The oldest...rules the household. Wives wait on their husbands, children on their parents, and generally the younger on their elders."[10] Elsewhere he says, "On the Final-Feasts before they go to the temple, wives fell down at the feet of their husbands, children at the feet of their parents. They confess that they have erred, either by committing some fault or by performing some duty carelessly, and beg pardon for their offense."[11]

This is not the nuclear family; it is closer to an extended family. "Girls, upon reaching womanhood and upon being settled in marriage, go to their husbands' domicile...male children and then grandchildren remain in the family and are subject to the oldest parent, unless he has become a dotard with old age. In the latter case the next oldest is put in his place."[12]

The family is not more important than the health of the city. Each family is composed of from no less than ten to no more than sixteen adults, and there are six thousand families in each city. If a family is above or below these figures, the balance is restored "by transferring those who exceed the number in larger families into those that are under the prescribed number."[13] The same thing applies among cities and between colonies and the mother country.[14]

Politically, the family is significant because the family rather than the individual is the basic electoral unit—thirty families comprising the primary district.[15] The family of ten to sixteen adults and each nuclear family within that group is the locus of social control since "husbands correct their wives, and parents their children, unless the offense is so serious that it is to the advantage of public morality to have it punished openly."[16] The parents of children who commit a serious offense (such as premarital intercourse) "incur great disgrace at having been neglectful in doing their duties."[17]

Thus, although the community takes precedence, the family is the next most fundamental social and political unit. This attitude, changed to a basis on the nuclear family, dominates utopias for the next three centuries.

There were few other sixteenth-century utopias, and on the whole they are little known. Except for the "Abbaye de Thélème" episode in Rabelais's *Gargantua* (1534), which says nothing directly on the subject, the famous description "Des Cannibales" by Montaigne (1580), which indicates that there is a polygamous system with no jealousy, and Antonio Francesco Doni's *Mondi cekestu terrestu e ubferbu* (1552-62), which follows Plato in abolishing the family, the families are patriarchal and authoritarian.[18]

For example, Thomas Lupton in his *Siuqila,* says approvingly that "There are no wives on earth more obedient to their husbands than ours be."[19] He goes on to discuss specific family arrangements in great detail addressing what he sees as a serious contemporary problem, disobedient children. If a government official has an unruly child, he loses his position on the principle that one who cannot rule his family should not rule in the state.[20]

Children are taught the Lord's Prayer and the Christian profession as soon as they can speak. If they do not learn them by age five, the father loses any office he holds and the child is taken away from the family.[21] Between twelve and twenty, disobedience results in being bonded as an apprentice until age thirty. After twenty they are whipped and lose all or part of their inheritance and possessions.[22]

The few English utopias in the sixteenth century are patriarchal and authoritarian. This contrast continues, with some exceptions, until the nineteenth century.

The Seventeenth Century. Among the utopias of the seventeenth century which treat the family in any detail, the first of significance is Johnn Valentin Andreae's *Republicae Christianopolitanae Descriptio,* known as *Christianopolis* (1619). The family described is a strong nuclear family. Marriage must have "the consent of the parents, consultation of the relatives, approbation of the laws, and benediction of God."[23] The important reforms which influence the marriage relationships are external to it. There is no dowry; furniture and housing are publicly provided; and, living in a well-ordered state, there will never be any economic uncertainty.[24] All children are raised by the state after age six, although parents can visit their children regularly. Andreae stresses the economic as well as the educational advantages of the arrangement. Children will never be a burden to their parents.[25]

Tommaso Campanella's *Civitas Solis, idea reipublicae Platonicae* (1623), known as *The City of the Sun,* follows Plato in completely abolishing the family. It also follows Plato in practicing eugenics. Francis Bacon, in *New Atlantis* (c1626), has the family as one of the foundations of the society.

The central issue in this period is illustrated by Andreae. In many of the utopias, children are taken out of the family and educated communally.[26] Although people want children, this being prior to Malthus, children appear to detract from whatever the focus of life for the parents (or at least the fathers) should be. This life focus is usually a combination of work and religion. The cares of family life, even mitigated by not having the goad of possible poverty, are too great.

This may explain some of the ambivalent attitudes toward women found in so many utopias. Some writers, such as Andreae, provide education for women, but the greatest honor for women in his society is still found in bearing children.[27] Most of the utopias provide traditional roles for women. The burden of family life is so onerous that it must be alleviated as much as possible, and where it can't be, the burden should fall on the shoulders of women so at least men can be free of it.

Although this may be overstating the case slightly, and both Bacon and Samuel Gott (*Nova Solyma*—1648) discuss the joys of family life, there is a clear ambivalence. For example, an interesting satire by Edward Howard entitled *The Six Days Adventure, or the New Utopia* (1671) establishes a short-lived government of women comparable to Aristophanes' *Ecclesiazusae* in which one of the women says that matrimony establishes rather "The tyranny of men, than the law of nature."[28]

The Eighteenth Century. The most important utopian works of the eighteenth century were not, strictly speaking, eutopias. Jonathan Swift's *Gulliver's Travels* (1726), which includes a utopia, and Daniel Defoe's *Robinson Crusoe* (1719-1720), which does not, produced innumerable imitators which dominate eighteenth-century utopianism. Regarding the issues discussed here, the eighteenth century is most noteworthy for the stress on the desirability of subordinating women.

Regarding the family as an institution, the eighteenth century in England was a time of proposed reform. Few major structural changes were suggested. Some of the specific reforms were easier divorce[29] and modifications in inheritance laws.[30] Otherwise the patriarchal family is the central social institution.[31] James Burgh is fairly typical of the English approach. In his utopia the head of the family is answerable for the conduct of all its members,[32] and each married man was given a parcel of land in order to make the family the foundation of the society economically as well as legally.[33]

Although similar reforms were suggested in some French utopias,[34] more radical changes were also proposed. The major writers were Denis Diderot, the Abbé Morelly, and Nicolas Esme Rétif de la Bretonne.[35] In each case they reject certain aspects of the nuclear family and propose significant alterations. In each case, it is the perceived failure of the family as the focus of sexual relations which most bothered the authors. They all proposed polygamy or what was later called "free love." At the same time, all three exhibit an ambivalence toward their own proposals. They all wrote other works describing stricter systems.

Morelly provides one of the neatest contrasts in that he presents, in the *Basiliade* (1753), a very free and open system where even incest was perfectly proper, and then in *Code de la nature* (1755), a list of marriage laws to carefully regulate the marital system. Rétif de la Bretonne does the same thing. First, he discusses the freedom of sexual relations and the temporary nature of marriage; then he establishes his so-called moral register which effectively determines the choice of marriage partner.

The central tension of family life for these French utopians is in its complex role both as primary or sole sexual focus with all of the sensuality, passion, etc., entailed and the child-rearing institution designed to teach reason, self-control, and temperance. Since the difficulty of maintaining the relationship as a sole, or even primary, sexual focus is manifest, some utopians have chosen to allow, even encourage, freedom there in order to maintain balance elsewhere. Others suggest restrictions on sexuality. The choice depends in large part on the author's attitude toward sex. Sex, free or controlled, becomes a central issue in the twentieth-century dystopia.

The Nineteenth Century. Many more utopias were written in the nineteenth century than in all previous centuries together. The single most important author was Francois Marie Charles Fourier, but his works were not typical of the century.

One of the most interesting utopias to contribute to the family debate was *The Swiss Family Robinson* (1812-1813).[36] It is part Robinsonade and part eutopia and can be seen as presenting the nuclear family as eutopia as long as two conditions are fulfilled: absolute isolation from the rest of the world and the provision of partners as the children reach maturity. Of course, without incest, neither is possible without the other being impossible. Even though the strains of isolation are clearly depicted, the life presented is a significant improvement over life in civilization. But even in presenting the nuclear family as eutopia, some fundamental problems are highlighted. Incest is not acceptable and isolation is too much of a burden. Some versions stress the point even more strongly by having the family emigrate in order to escape the impact which highly civilized life was having on the older children.

Jean-Baptiste Say in *Olbie* (1800) and Etienne Cabet in *Voyage en Icarie* (original title *Voyage et aventures de Lord Villiam Carisdell en Icarie*—1840) provide utopias with a solid family life. They, like many other utopians of the time, assume first that the family was the rock on which society was based and second, slightly in contradiction, if there is anything wrong with the family, it could be corrected by changes in other social institutions, such as the distribution of economic goods. The majority of writers of utopias in the nineteenth century believed that little or no change in the family was needed in the move to eutopia. For others it should be strengthened significantly.[37]

Some writers proposed reforms. They fall into two categories: those who suggest relatively minor changes in the courtship and marriage system,[38] and those who see the need for providing increased freedom, personally and/or economically for family members. For example, in Thomas Low Nichol's *Esperanza* (1860): "Every person here, who has arrived at the age of twelve years, has his or her own independent suite or rooms, with the simple necessities of furniture, at first, to be added to afterward, according to taste and ability. Each apartment is sacred to its owner, and free from all intrusion. Parent or friend cannot come without knocking, and no one asserts claim or authority. Privacy and entire individuality are thus secured."[39]

Of course, it can be argued that this destroys a central part of the family and goes much further than reform, but the author saw this as essential to both the individual and the family. Another popular reform was to ensure the economic health of the family by enabling each family sufficient land to always have a means of providing for itself.[40]

There were a number of writers who attacked the entire concept of the family as an institution. Best known of these were, of course, Fourier and some of the Saint-Simonians, but there were a number of others also. With a few exceptions these works all proposed what could be called a family of love (not to be confused with the English sect of that name). This was not merely a euphemism for the freedom of sexual access which was generally proposed, but an apt phrase for expressing what most of the authors had in mind. In all cases the authors saw the family, exclusive sexual access, and the system of morality developed on these as *a*, if not *the*, major impediment to achieving a good society.[41]

Fourier and the unknown American Calvin Blanchard took the most extreme positions. In both cases, young virgins of both sexes were initiated by the most experienced of the opposite sex. Together with James Lawrence earlier in the century, they proposed that sexual partners be chosen each evening. The whole notion of the family is rejected, in large part due to the bad results of exclusive sexual relations.

After Edward Bellamy there is one significant addition to, or revival in, the reforms proposed. There is a tremendous growth in the emphasis on removing certain activities, ranging from child-rearing to cooking and cleaning, from the purview of the family even when, in some cases, the family is a central concern. In most cases, the changes are justified as improving the lot of the children and/or the mothers. In some cases the justification is based solely on the perceived inefficiency of certain activities being repeated in so many different places.[42]

The nineteenth century saw the use of the utopian form to depict a wide variety of reforms, and a few radical changes, of both the family and society. But most utopias still assumed no significant change would need to be made in the family. The twentieth century, particularly its third quarter, changes that.

The Twentieth Century. In many ways the Twentieth Century is the most interesting. First, due in large part to the growth in publishing, more utopias and dystopias have been published than ever in the past. Second, authors have felt freer to directly criticize social institutions such as the family that have been more or less sacrosanct in the past. Third, more imaginative alternatives to the family have been proposed. At the same time, the nuclear family remains the major form in utopias for sexual relations and child-rearing. As a result, utopias reflect the social tensions of our times and imaginatively illustrate these tensions in ways that help illuminate them and might help alleviate, if not solve, them.

Five points can be made about the twentieth-century utopian attitude toward the family. First, all family forms and reforms are presented in the dystopia as well as in the eutopia. Second, the sexual freedom controversy and the role of sex as a potential freeing or controlling agent takes a central place in both eutopias and dystopias. Third, the family gradually loses its position as a central focus of society. Fourth, most recently the extended family, related and unrelated, has become a major theme. Fifth, the single sex (women) family becomes an important theme.

Since more utopian works have been published so far in this century than in the past four centuries put together, it is almost meaningless to cite specific works. But an analysis of most utopias published in English and a substantial number of those published in other Western languages does make a few generalizations possible.

Although the dystopia has been the dominant form in the twentieth century, eutopias have been published regularly and have had a mild resurgence in recent years. The fact that all family forms appear in dystopias as well as eutopias makes the point that changes in the family are insufficient to bring about sufficient change to transform society as a whole. The ambivalence toward sexual freedom illustrated by Evgenii Zamiatin's *We* (1920), Aldous Huxley's *Brave New World* (1932) and George Orwell's *1984* (1949), suggests that all social change can be used for both freeing and controlling. Perhaps this is why, for most of the century, the family is simply not as important in the literature as previously. If any form of human relationship can be both freeing and limiting, the focus of analysis is not likely to be clear. In fact, the major concerns of both eutopias and dystopias have tended more and more toward greater social variety and personal freedom.

In this light it is interesting that new versions of the extended family are beginning to be presented as a free family. A family with no clear internal authority structure, inclusive sexual relations, no defined sex roles, and communal child-rearing replaces all previous forms of the family, all of which are seen as essentially coercive.[43] But then why bother; what function has the family filled which requires its continuation in any form? If it is not child-rearing, sexual access, or role model, where is the family?

A totally new approach, the single sex family, has begun to appear in the past few years. Joanna Russ's short story "When It

Changed" (1972) followed by her *Female Man* (1975), Suzy McKee
Charnas's *Motherlines* (1978), Sally Gearhart's *The Wanderground*
(1979), and Donna J. Young's *Retreat: As It Was!* (1979), all show
ideal societies without men. The families are usually extended multi-
generational families.

Recent utopias that are usually labelled feminist (including the
single sex utopias) tend to propose the same changes in the family,
except that something like familial child-rearing is usually
maintained. But, of course, the family is now a multi-generational
related and unrelated group. In Marge Piercy's *Woman on the Edge
of Time* (1976) each child has three "mothers" (men are included and
modified so that they can breast feed) in order to break the usual
dependence on one or two individuals and give the child a variety of
early experiences. Ursula K. Le Guin, in her *The Dispossessed*
(1974), aims for a similar result through less drastic tactics. Her
society is organized so that the child will be exposed to many adults
in addition to the biological parents. They are also raised
communally from a fairly early age and spend a great amount of
their time with peers.

The answer to the problem of the family given by twentieth-
century utopias is unclear, but most argue that the family has failed.
Perhaps a radically new form, one which provides a non-coercive
setting for socialization with love in a society which increases
economic security together with an improved educational system
and radical decentralization of authority, could produce a
significantly better life.[44] This is the positive message of the
twentieth-century eutopias.

Conclusion. The utopia is a critical genre with its criticism taking
the form of alternatives that are better than the present. Looked at
quantitatively, utopias have opted for the family. Most have simply
assumed its continuation. The move to a better society, for most
authors, will not entail any change in the family. On the other hand,
there have been many alternatives suggested.

To some utopian critics everything about the family is wrong!
(1.) It is foolish to think that men (and later women) will be satisfied
with one or only one major sexual outlet. (2.) It is a terrible way to
breed. (3.) It is a worse way to raise children. (4.) It binds women to
specified and limiting roles. (5.) There is too much tension between
the sensuality and passion of sexual relations and the reason and
order needed in child-rearing. (6.) The patriarchal family is
dystopian and must be replaced.

Other utopian critics have taken different positions. (1.) Men
and women must limit their sexual activity. (2.) It would be more

trouble to control breeding. (3.) Any alternative child-rearing technique will be worse. (4.) Women should be limited; they are better off limited than free. (5.) The patriarchal family is ideal.

The alternatives proposed are an extended family—related or non-related, free love or promiscuity, child-rearing outside the family, and external reforms—e.g. economic security.

What is the significance of this for political thought? Any political theory must address the problems raised by these alternatives. The central difficulty is that noted by Plato, the tendency of family responsibilities to weaken the public activity of the individual. Many deal with this, as does Plato, by simply getting rid of the problem. Others, such as those who favor public child-rearing (and it should be noted that the upper and middle-class Victorian family and its child-rearing system fit this model) simply get rid of the children as a great nuisance. The feeling is that you cannot have an active, involved citizenry and the family.

Current approaches stressing the extended and single sex family appear to aim in the same direction but differ in one important way. These families are designed to provide freedom needed for political activity, sexual variety and good child-rearing. They can also be an exclusive community where all public activity is internal and external activity is considered of secondary importance. Thus they bring back into focus the central political problem. They may solve the problems of the family as a unit, but they may be as strong or even a stronger force keeping the individual from public roles.

Nine

Technology in the Digger Utopia*

James Farr

During the bold and heady days which followed in the wake of the first English Revolution, Gerrard Winstanley the Digger wrote and published "the first socialist utopia formed in the hopes of becoming a party program."[1] *The Law of Freedom in a Platform* was Winstanley's last work and its design of utopian laws and institutions captured the spirit of Digger ideology—socialism, democracy, and pacifism. These were daring visions for the mid-seventeenth century, a time known for its daring visions. Amidst the great lights of his age—from Hobbes to Harrington, Bacon to Newton—Winstanley's "candle" /510/[2] burns bright still.

Winstanley and the Diggers were dead two and a half centuries before they received attention commensurate with their historical significance.[3] In this essay I shall investigate the problem of technology in Winstanley's utopian political thought. As did most of his contemporaries, Winstanley praised technological advance. Yet much more than they, he grasped the need to submit technology to constant democratic scrutiny in order that it remain responsible, humane, and part of the "common treasury for all."

The general story-line into which I am placing the Digger utopia is an important and familiar one, thanks to the work of Mulford Sibley.[4] In one of a number of fine analyses, Professor Sibley has suggested that utopias fall into one of three general patterns as regards technology: (1) whole-hearted acceptance; (2) radical rejection; and (3) selective implementation.[5] On balance, Winstanley's utopian platform falls into the third category.

....
*I would like to thank Terence Ball, Clayton Roberts, and Dan Sabia for their helpful comments on an earlier version of this paper. I would also like to thank Mulford Sibley—among many other things—for having made me appreciate the importance of history and utopian thinking for understanding political theory, contemporary politics, and even ourselves. Past platforms like Winstanley's carry visions of the future in them still.

However, the Digger utopia also displays certain features common to utopias of the first two types. It is as if in Winstanley we find the ambivalence on technology which has marked human history from the very beginning. In broad outline, then, I shall narrate in some detail one episode in the history of utopian political thought in terms of the problem of technology. I write this also with a conviction that we still require utopian thinking, and that any such thinking must come to grips with technology. I believe, moreover, that only a socialist utopia committed to egalitarian participation in all areas of life and to an educational system which promotes virtue, not merely skills, can begin to deal humanely and effectively with the pervasive problem of technology. Winstanley and the Diggers—among others—helped us to see that in seventeenth century revolutionary England; a select band of contemporary thinkers—Mulford Sibley foremost among them—help us to see that today.

Winstanley's Utopian Political Thought

Utopian speculation was one of the visionary products thrown up by the turmoil of the English Revolution. Creative energies previously censored and obstructed by despotic government were suddenly unleashed. These energies assumed many practical and literary forms—including utopias, constitutions, and communities. The Digger communities, of which there were several,[6] were but more radical versions of the Puritan design to establish a City on the Hill. Puritans and Diggers alike believed that congregations of saints (differently understood) could make the world anew by their very example. In print and pulpit model constitutions were also drafted and debated—a phenomenon all the more remarkable in a land never to know a written constitution. The most important was the Leveller's *Agreement of the People*. Many English writers chose the format of utopian literature which Sir Thomas More had rescued from antiquity and given new life a century earlier. More's *Utopia* became a model for Francis Bacon in *New Atlantis*, as for Campanella in *City of the Sun*. The utopias of the 1640s and 1650s were as diverse and contradictory as the times which produced them. Their titles display that curious mixture of solemnity and Puritan sobriety on the one hand, with unbridled fancy and exotic imagination on the other. One hears the turmoil of those times in *The Christian Commonwealth* and *A Way Propounded*, and again in *Macaria, Oceana, Nova Solyma,* and *Olbia*.

In the midst of this ferment Winstanley wrote and published his own utopia "in a platform." Having remained silent during the chaos of the civil war, Winstanley finally spoke in 1648 by producing three sectarian and millenarian pamphlets.

Winstanley's thought took an even more radical turn in the *New Law of Righteousness*. Revealed to him "in a trance," the new law bade all men and women to "work together. Eat bread together; declare this all abroad" /190/. True to his revelation, Winstanley soon organized a community of Diggers—or "true Levellers," as they called themselves—at St. George's Hill in Surrey. The Diggers were mainly impoverished commoners forced off the land by inclosures and hard-pressed by a decade of bad harvests.[7] In the *True Leveller's Standard Advanced,* Winstanley next proclaimed the Diggers' intention to make the earth a "common treasury" for all. Not surprisingly, the Diggers soon attracted the hostility of the local landowners. Within a year the community was harassed out of existence, even after relocating to Cobham Heath. All the while Winstanley protested furiously. In a number of remarkable pamphlets documenting the Digger hopes and travails, Winstanley appealed to the principal agents of the Revolution: the House of Commons, the Army and Lord Fairfax, the City of London, the Clergy and Lawyers, indeed "all Englishmen." But alas, all were deaf. And so in 1650 Winstanley once again fell silent.

    The Law of Freedom in a Platform broke Winstanley's silence one final time. The work is without question among the most important theoretical contributions of the revolutionary period. As a work of political theory, the *Law of Freedom* falls somewhere between two genres: the fictional utopia and the model constitution. The platform is classically utopian in that it measures the immense distance between the possible and the actual. However, Winstanley foregoes the literary fiction standard to many other English utopias of his day. In the *Law of Freedom* we find no idealized account of Utopia, Oceana, Arcadia, Macaria, Bensalem, Olbia, or even the Land of Cokayne. Rather, Winstanley offered his platform as something of a rough blueprint or as the materials out of which a working commonwealth could be crafted: "Tho this Platform be like a peece of Timber rough hewd, yet the discreet workman may take it, and frame a handsome building out of it" /510/. But the vision of such a bold new political architecture makes it an implausible candidate for an actual constitution. Seventeenth century England was just not ready. The fact that certain laws and institutions could be implemented characterizes a draft plan like Winstanley's; but so does it characterize a fictional utopia. The agrarian law described in *Oceana* was Harrington's hope for England's reformation; and the Royal Society of 1662 modelled itself on Bacon's Saloman's House. So the dividing line between a fictional utopia and a model constitution is very fine indeed. What must be recognized is that the connection between utopian speculation and political theory aimed at institutional change is very close—a connection which is likely to be missed if one overemphasizes the idealism of utopia, as expressed in its being a "good place" located literally "nowhere," or if one contrasts "utopian" with "real" or "scientific."

Utopias like Winstanley's platform for true commonwealth deal essentially with institutions and, as such, are "eminently practical," as Mulford Sibley reminds us.[8] But utopian institutions also reflect political theories of the more systematic and critical kind. Utopias, in short, perform theoretical, critical and practical functions. In performing these functions utopias reflect their times, and idealize a world lost or one anticipated. Winstanley's utopia is no exception and his institutions reflect the socialist, pacifist, and democratic character of Digger philosophy.

The *Law of Freedom* continues and develops Digger ideology. But two related changes of emphasis take place. First, the earlier emphasis on individual moral regeneration as the key to a real reformation is more or less replaced by an emphasis on social and institutional change. Social and institutional relations are now taken to be causes of individual moral change.

I speak now in relation between Oppressor and oppressed; the inward bondages I meddle not with in this place, though I am assured that if it be rightly searched into, the inward bondages of the mind, as covetousness, pride, hypocrisy, envy, sorrows, fears, desperation, and madness, are all occasioned by the outward bondage, that one sort of people lay upon another /520/.

Winstanley, we might say, exteriorizes the problem of utopia and freedom. A second change accompanies the first. More than any previous Digger pamphlet, the *Law of Freedom* concerns itself with laws and the external regulation of behavior. There must now be "suitable laws for every occasion and almost for every action that men do" /582/. The *Law of Freedom* is, we might say, Winstanley's most "Puritan" work. Law—not just love—must make true commonwealth.

These changes notwithstanding, the *Law of Freedom* is a decidedly Digger platform. Land, labor, and goods are shared as part of the "common treasury for all." There are laws to prevent idleness—aimed no doubt at the idle rich, as much as at beggars. "Every one shall be brought up in Trades and Labors," and consequently "all Trades shall be maintained with more improvement, to the enriching of the commonwealth" /526/. Storehouses for common collection and distribution are established for food, raw materials, and finished products. After all, what is freedom but the "free enjoyment of the earth" /520/, and the earth itself but a "common storehouse" /252/? "As every one works to advance the Common Stock, so everyone shall have a free use of any commodity in the Storehouse...without buying and selling" /583/. Indeed buying and selling would be outlawed, as would money. Reversing Midas, gold and silver would be transformed into ordinary "dishes and other necessities" /595/. On the basis of this economic transformation, all institutions of English society would be changed. "There shall be no Tyrant Kings, Lords of Manor, Tything Priests, Oppressing Lawyers, exacting Landlords, nor any such pricking bryar" /535/.

Winstanley's socialism is Janus-faced. It looks back to the peasant communalism of the middle ages and foward to the proletarian movements of the next three centuries. True commonwealth is populated, as it were, by Joachimites and Anabaptists, Chartists and Wobblies. The simplicity of life and needs is surely pre-modern, as is Winstanley's view of small-scale science and technology. But Winstanley's overall vision is in many ways historically precocious, not medieval at all. Many medieval utopists had made utopia heaven, and heaven utopia. Winstanley, on the contrary, is forthright in his this-worldliness. Why, he asks, must "the poor people...be content with their poverty" with a "promise of a Heaven hereafter?... But why may we not have our Heaven here (that is, a comfortable livelihood in the earth)?" /409/. More importantly, he stresses the primacy of labor and production over distribution. This allows him to grasp a crucial point about exploitation. In history as a whole Winstanley discovers that "the difference between Lords of Manors and the poor, about the commons land, is the greatest controversie that hath rise up these 600 years past" /420/. But it wasn't just land, but labor which was at the heart of this exploitation.

The Inferior Tenants and Laborers bears all the burdens in laboring the Earth...: and yet the Gentry, who oppress them, and that live idle upon their labors, carry away all the comfortable livelihood of the earth /507/.

All rich men live at ease, feeding and clothing themselves by the labors of other men, not by their own.... Rich men receive all they have from the labourers hand, and what they give, they give away other men's labours, not their own /512f/.

The materialist interpretation of history and the theory of surplus value may well be a long time coming, but Winstanley has here already grasped the root of the matter.

Winstanley designed his utopia, then, to rectify class exploitation. But he was well aware that his vision was wholly out of step with the England of 1652. He must have sensed that his readers would have thought his ideas to be extravagantly anachronistic at best; and at worst only institutionalizable by armed force. So Winstanley came up with an ingenious suggestion. He claimed only to want the "ancient commons and waste lands" /513/ and such property as was donated by willing owners. "And for others, who are not willing, let them stay in the way of buying and selling, which is the Law of the Conqueror, till they be willing" /513/. In short, Winstanley offered an interim program for a dual commonwealth. A true commonwealth could coexist alongside the property-sanctifying one already in existence.[9] In this way the commoners could have the commons land, and the landlords their enclosures.

In sketching this visionary program, Winstanley thereby bolstered his pacifism: "I do not say, nor desire, that every one shall be compelled to practise this Commonwealth's Government" /513/. Rather, as Gandhi and the utopian socialists would later, Winstanley hoped that good example would ultimately persuade gentry and freeholders to surrender private property and gain a community. Here Winstanley echoes the pacifism which consistently and nobly marked the Diggers' conduct even amidst much harm and physical abuse. To soldiers and bullies he proclaimed: "We abhor fighting for Freedom. . . : and do thou uphold it by the sword we will not; we will conquer by Love and Patience, or else we count it no Freedom" /378/.

It merits observing, however, that in the *Law of Freedom* Winstanley appears to compromise his pacifism to some degree by legislating capital punishment for extreme crimes. Puzzling at the possible inconsistency here, Mulford Sibley suggests Winstanley's possible motive: "Perhaps his harsh discipline is in part a reaction to what Winstanley regards as the centuries of exploitation to which the people of England have been subjected: he expects the exploiters to resist."[10] This may also account for Winstanley's justification of popular defence by "force of arms. . . against, any Invasion, Rebellion, or Resistance" /539/. Even with these surprising twists in mind, however, Winstanley still trusts that his platform alone "will turn swords into ploughshares, and settle such a peace in the Earth, as Nations shall learn War no more" /513/.

The *Law of Freedom* also expresses a democratic creed. The fact that Winstanley's utopian political theory is both socialist *and* democratic is especially noteworthy because other socialist utopias, like Plato's or Campanella's or debatably More's, are exceedingly non-democratic. Winstanley's plan for universal manhood suffrage was far ahead of the limited franchise proposed by the Levellers—the only other remote contenders for the title of democrats during the English Revolution. Winstanley retained Parliament as the supreme and sole "Head of Power" /562/ and demanded that Members of Parliament be elected yearly for single terms to ensure democratic accountability. All other public officials would also be elected annually, including ministers, bureaucrats, postmasters, justices, and military officers. More generally, a democratic and participatory way of life (and not just democratic political institutions) invigorate the Digger utopia. There would be no lawyers; judges would pronounce "the bare letter of the law" /554/; and the law would be in English, not French, Latin, or legalese (as it remains today). In this way, all commonwealthmen would know the law and be able to speak for themselves in court. Even Sunday meetings were democratic. During gatherings any individual could speak, not just ministers. All of God's children had the light within. God was no doubt a democrat; Christ was the "Head Leveller" /390/.

Finally, the single most important democratic mechanism of the *Law of Freedom* was the continuous referendum on all acts of Parliament. This alone would insure that all "new laws must be by the Peoples' consent and knowledge" /559/. Whenever Parliament proposes a law it must "make a public Declaration thereof to the people of the Land...; and if no Objections come in from the people within one month, they may then take the people's silence as a consent thereto" /559/. Winstanley did not elaborate on the details, nor did he suggest how deadlocked Parliaments might move ahead in the face of public dissent. He clearly envisioned a more enlightened and informed electorate whose sense of democracy would come increasingly with the practice of it. So too their concern for the public good. The Quaker principle of consensus seems to guide Winstanley here—as indeed do many other Quaker principles, like pacifism, the seeking after truth, and the belief that religious experience is an "inward light and power of life within" /234/. Consensus on public issues should result as long as "common interest" and not "particular interest" informs the peoples' choices /559/.

Science and Technology in the Digger Utopia

Winstanley's utopian political theory, to say the least, was an amazing achievement, especially given its origins. Three years after the conclusion of a nasty, brutish, and protracted civil war, whose true victors were the rural gentry and the urban bourgeoisie, Winstanley crafts a platform for a socialist, democratic, and peaceful commonwealth. Surely he dissembled not when he claimed never to have learned his first principles in books. But if one listens closely, one can hear the tumult of voices which characterized the excitement, novelty, and fecundity of seventeenth-century political debate.

Winstanley engaged his age and had new things to say about the role of science and technology in utopia, as well. Seventeenth century utopians, particularly Bacon, Campanella, and Hartlib, were almost possessed by the new experimental science. Indeed the connection between utopia and science was particularly strong. For example, the Royal Society founded in 1662—which Sibley rightly marks as "the symbolic initiation of the new age" of science and technology—was inspired and even patterned after Saloman's House in *New Atlantis*.[11] The utopians, and the educational reformers generally, believed that science served two masters: it glorified God, whose works it discovered and marvelled at; and it benefitted Man by useful technological invention. God, science, and human technology formed a new trinity in the saintly but practical minds of the seventeenth century.

Our Digger philosopher shared this general enthusiasm for science. Although Winstanley was never in the front ranks of scientific speculation, nor became Lord Chancellor as did Bacon, nor founder of a scientific college as did Hartlib, the *Law of Freedom* is of premier importance precisely because it tells us so much about the popularization of science at a time when popular scientific education was virtually nonexistent, and when science was still hedged around by astrology, magic, and traditional religion.

Despite his enthusiasm, however, Winstanley never glorified science and technology. Indeed he limited them in true commonwealth to preserve democratic and socialist institutions. It is for this reason that, on balance, I would place the Digger utopia in the third of Sibley's three types of utopian appropriation of technology:

(1) whole-hearted acceptance of complex technology, without limits, as a key to the good life; (2) radical distrust of technological development; and (3) the adoption of some forms of technology and the rejection of others.[12]

The third—"selective implementation"—type best captures Winstanley's intentions. But the fit is perhaps not perfect, and indeed we find hints of the first two types as well. The *Law of Freedom* is something of a complicated document which records man's historic ambivalence on technology.

True commonwealthmen breathe the new air of science. This was not to spite God, as moderns might suppose, but to praise Him: "To know the secrets of Nature, is to know the works of God; and to know the works of God within the Creation, is to know God Himself, for God dwels in every visible work or body" /565/. The pantheism and plebeian materialism which pervades such a view makes for a curious union of mysticism and rationalism. From mystical trances Winstanley uttered revelations of "the great Creator Reason" /251/. Indeed in praising God and coming to know Him, we can only approach Him rationally and experimentally through His works in nature, through "motion or growth...the stars and planets...grass, plants, fishes, beasts, birds, and mankind.... To reach God beyond the Creation is a knowledge beyond the line or capacity of man to attain" /565/. So it is that like the Quakers, of whom he might be numbered,[13] Winstanley praised "experimental religion" /40ff/. Such views made for a certain skepticism, as well. It was not just doubting but "wise-hearted Thomas to believe nothing but what /there is/ reason for" /523/. Puritan divines, naturally enough, found these views heretical, even atheistic. But Winstanley was not unnerved by such charges. Indeed he returned the slander.

The subtle clergy can but charm the people.... Their divining Spiritual Doctrine is a cheat; for while men are gazing up to Heaven, imagining after a Happiness, or fearing a Hell, after they are dead, their eyes are put out, that they see not what is their birthrights, and what is to be done by them here on earth while they are living /569/.

Even Hobbes' sneers at the "kingdom of Darkness" in *Leviathan* were more generous.

Digger eyes are cast upon God then when they seek "experimental knowledge in the things which are" /564/. It is "in every Trade, Art, and Science," therefore, that men "finde out the Secrets of the Creation" /577/. In short, the technological inventions appropriate to humanly-scaled Trades and Arts are "knowledge in the practice, and it is good" /579/. Technological innovation is positively encouraged in the Digger utopia and the democratic spirit pervades the encouragement:

In the managing of any trade, let no young wit be crushed in his invention, for if any man desire to make a new tryall of his skill in any Trade or Science, the overseers shall not hinder him, but incourage him therein; that so the spirit of knowledge may have his full growth in man, to find out the secret in every Art /579f/.

Such activity is not only to be encouraged, but rewarded. "Let every one who finds out a new invention have a deserved honor given him" /580/.

Winstanley cleverly redesigned two traditional offices—the ministry and the postoffice—to ensure the success of a scientific and democratic polity. There was no love lost between our Digger philosopher and Anglican and Puritan divines, for reasons we have partly seen. But Winstanley would keep a new model ministry in true commonwealth, not, it should be emphasized, to enforce any particular religious doctrine nor even to have a civil religion. Rather, a Sabbath day organizer was crucial for the solidarity so essential to a communitarian society. The people must "meet together to see one anothers faces, and beget or preserve fellowship in friendly love" /562/. The minister's role was minimal. He or she read both the "law of the Commonwealth" and "the affairs of the whole land as it is brought in by the Post-master" /562/. But since wits need exercising the minister may also give speeches or sermons on a delimited range of topics, sometimes on history and government, "sometimes on the nature of Mankind" /563/. But most importantly, "speeches may be made, of all Arts and Science, some one day, some another; As in Physick, Chryrurgery, Astrology, Astronomy, Navigation, Husbandry, and such like" /563/. Speechmakers, much less sermonizers, as we all know from experience, are infamous for holding forth. So Winstanley, the unabashed true Leveller, would have the minister stand down on demand.

He who is the chosen Minister for that year to read, shall not be the only man to make sermons or speeches: but every one who hath any experience, and is able to speak of any art or language, or of the Nature of the Heavens above, or of the Earth below, shall have free liberty to speak when they offer themselves /564/.

The only criterion which Winstanley demands is a simple, but scientific one:

And every one who speaks of any Herb, Plant, Art, or Nature of Mankind is required to speak nothing by imagination, but what he hath found out by his own industry and observation in tryal /564/.

In this way, ordinary scientific and technical knowledge speaks from the hearts and minds of ordinary men and women; and the old ministers—who are but "Witches and Cheats" /597/—can no longer fool the plain-hearted people with their mysteries and incantations.

The postmasters also serve the cause of Digger science and technology. Besides the likely task of providing "speedy knowledge," the postmasters were to perform a somewhat unlikely task. "If any through industry of understanding have found out any Secret in Nature, or new invention in any Art or Trade, or in the Tillage of the Earth" /571/ then the postmasters were to spread this news, too. Casting patents to the wind, the postmasters were to help fertilize the land with knowledge. "When other parts of the land hear of it, many thereby will be encouraged to employ their Reason and industry to do the like, that so in time there will not be any Secret in Nature, which now lies hid" /571/. The obvious point is that Winstanley was using and reforming the postal service to secure both democratic and scientific results. Indeed it has even been argued that "Winstanley was slightly ahead of actual developments in the postal service of England.... It was not until Oliver Cromwell's Post Office Act of 1657 that a comprehensive system with a postmaster general was established."[14] Although it is doubtful that it was Cromwell's inspiration, it would be ironic, nay tragic, if the candle Winstanley set forth before the Lord Protector's door illuminated the way not to true commonwealth, but to a postal system.

Surely it is no exaggeration, then, to say that in the *Law of Freedom* we find "one of the most magnificent panegyrics of rational science, with its feet on the earth, to be found in the whole of seventeenth century English literature."[15] Neither Bacon nor Hartlib, nor Hobbes nor Boyle, outdo Winstanley on this score. Our Digger philosopher made science and technology part of everyday life—in the trades, in the pulpit, in the mailbox. It would be wrong, however, to conclude from Winstanley's panegyric that his utopia whole-heartedly embraces complex technology. Despite some shared elements with Bacon and Hartlib, the Digger utopia is not a full-fledged instance of Sibley's first category. There is the obvious point that Winstanley set his sights on a relatively simple and small-scale technology. But much more importantly, utopians who whole-heartedly accept technology characteristically commit themselves to one or all of four further points.

First, their commitment to technology entails specialized education for, and sometimes rule by, a narrow elite. This, for example, was Bacon's view, whose fellows of Saloman's House were uniquely well-educated in New Atlantis and were consequently self-perpetuating scientist guardians of both technology and polity. Secondly, most utopias of whole-hearted acceptance develop a domineering, even imperialistic, attitude towards nature. Again Bacon is paradigmatic. He argued that by technology we "control" nature and make her "submit to our experiments," thus "enlarging the bounds of human empire to the effecting of all things possible."[16] Thirdly, in Sibley's words, technology is understood to be "the key to the good life." That is, causally, and perhaps ethically, technological innovation makes for the good life. The more technology, the better our lives. Finally, utopians of this kind never provide mechanisms of popular oversight. Technology is granted a life of its own. When introduced it is developed without consideration to consequences. And if unwanted consequences develop, it is simply assumed that still newer technology will arrive to relieve us. More technology means more technology.

Winstanley will have none of these. First, his view of education was democratic and anti-elitist. As such, Winstanley's views were "strikingly modern in comparison with the traditional concepts of his day."[17] Education in true commonwealth would be universal and life-long. Winstanley would have shared the belief of Mulford Sibley's own latter-day utopians that "true rule implies education in its broadest sense."[18] Winstanley conceived of education as both practical and humanistic, and he refused to allow a class of scholars to remain idle while others worked. That was the principal failure of the educational system under "kingly government" where scholarly idleness in the universities was like "the standing ponds of stinking waters" /238/. Winstanley's vision is the antithesis of the elitism and narrow intellectualism which pervades Bacon's Saloman's House, or even John Milton's proposals for education. "Let no young wit be crushed" was the motto of Digger pedagogy.

Secondly, Winstanley would have winced at Bacon's boasts of "human empire" over nature. By contrast, Winstanley spoke of scientific knowledge enhancing the "beauty of our Commonwealth" and providing "nourishment and preservation" and "enjoyment of the earth" /519f, 571/. Moreover, he implies that only those forms of technology which preserve the beauty and enjoyment of the earth should be engaged in, since he limits trades to those "which mankind should be brought up in" /577/. That is, Winstanley proposes an ethic about our relationship with nature which should not be violated by technological progress. In this regard he shares some of the views of later utopians who were decidedly anti-technological. In William Morris' *News From Nowhere,* for example, just as in the *Law of Freedom,* money is not used, goods and services are exchanged solely on the basis of human need, and the spiritual union with nature is valued as part of life itself.[19] In this somewhat ambivalent way, the Digger utopia is built upon some of the very premises which later utopians would use to radically reject complex technology.

Thirdly, Winstanley actually reverses the relationship between technology and the good life which characterizes those utopians who accept technology whole-heartedly. The latter regard technology as the causal and ethical key to the good life. But this puts the matter on its head, Winstanley would say. In his platform he sets the matter aright:

When men are sure of food and raiment, their reason will be ripe, and ready to dive into the secrets of the Creation, that they may learn to see and know God...in all his works; for fear of want, and care to pay Rent to Taskmakers, hath hindered many rare inventions /580/.

Only a just society can provide the good life, and the freedom which is that life. Science and technology are not its producers, but one of its products.

Finally and most importantly, Winstanley's parliamentary referendum subjects technological implementation to popular discussion and democratic decision-making. The referendum was designed to ensure democracy in this as in all other matters. Since there must be "laws for every occasion" /528/, Parliament (by implication) must legislate on matters of technological implementation which affect the "common treasury." As with the medievals, so with Winstanley: "Whatever touches all, must be judged by all." In the month between Parliament's proposing a law and its final passage, the people must be informed and their support solicited. The burden of proof would lie with those MPs who favored the law supporting technological change. After all, the people need not provide alternatives when they use their veto. During this month, the public, counselled by partisans of change as well as by partisans of preservation, would register their final say. Obviously for the referendum to achieve its democratic goals a minimal scientific education would be required of all. This, as we have seen, Winstanley sought to institute. Moreover, extra-technological concerns could surely guide new legislation. Winstanley's abiding concern for the "poor oppressed people" made him favor technological innovation which reduced unnecessary toil, but not when it displaced people from their work, or when it made them dependent on the changing technical composition of work. Neither Luddites nor romantics, the Diggers nonetheless would not have technological growth at any cost.

Surely, modifications in the Digger plan would be required for the complexities introduced by larger populations, more complex technology, and the like. But the important point is that in the Digger utopia the spirit exists, and with modification so too the mechanism, to keep technology under democratic rein and to ensure its service for human needs. It is this spirit which makes the Digger utopia a unique seventeenth century utopia of selective technology.

Winstanley was, if nothing else, a visionary. Sadly, not all his visions were uplifting. Despite his efforts to stem the tide, he knew that science, technology, and knowledge itself, when not harnessed to a vision of justice, equity, and true freedom, bring about their opposites. This Winstanley felt deeply, and perhaps with a sense of resignation. *The Law of Freedom* begins with a hopeful buoyancy that knowledge in the form of his platform might, like a candle, light the way to the good life. But alas, not all knowledge is of this kind. What begins with hopeful buoyancy ends in a lament: "Knowledge, why didst thou come, to wound, and not to cure?" Winstanley's parting poem could be hung over our age, as well as his:

Here is the righteous Law, Man, wilt thou it maintain?
It may be, is, as hath still, in the world been slain.
Truth appears in Light, Falsehood rules in Power;
To see these things to be, is cause of grief each hour.
Knowledge, why didst thou come, to wound, and not to cure?
I sent not for thee, thou didst me inlure.
Where knowledge does increase, there sorrows multiply.
To see the great deceit which in the World doth lie.
Man saying one thing now, unsaying it anon,
Breaking all's Engagements, when deeds for him are done.
O power where are thou, that must mend things amiss?
Come change the heart of Man, and make him truth to Kiss:
O death where art thou? wilt thou not tidings send?
I fear thee not, thou art my loving friend.
Come take this body, and scatter it in the Four,
That I may dwell in One, and rest in peace once more.

Ten

Computers, Cables, and Citizenship: On the Desirability of Instant Direct Democracy*

Richard Dagger

Mulford Sibley is not the sort of scholar who makes a career of elaborating variations on a theme. There are recurring themes in his work, however, and I want to sound two of them, participatory democracy and technology, in this essay.[1] These themes may be joined in a number of ways, but here I shall take up only one—the possibility that advances in communications technology may actually promote democracy by extending and enhancing opportunities for political participation.

This possibility has been raised by several writers who have noticed that computers and coaxial cables now enable us to establish an instant direct democracy.[2] With the aid of computers and cables, it seems, we could install electronic voting devices in the homes of all citizens, disband our legislative bodies, and proceed to set policy by the direct vote of the electorate. What had hitherto seemed suitable only for the Greek *polis,* the Swiss canton, and the New England town now seems conceivable, at least, in the modern nation-state.

To say that something is conceivable is not to say it is desirable, of course, and the latter point is my concern here. Is instant direct democracy a desirable form of government? I think not. It is an attractive prospect in some ways, to be sure, and I shall note some of

....

*An earlier version of this paper was prepared for the American Political Science Association Ethical Issues Seminar on "The Status of Citizenship," Washington, D.C., August 1980. I am indebted to James Dick and Daniel Sabia for their comments on that paper, and I am especially grateful to Nannerl O. Keohane, the seminar leader, for her criticism and encouragement.

these in this paper. But it also has its drawbacks, notably its tendency to render political action less meaningful, rather than more, than it is at present. To put the point in terms I shall define later, instant direct democracy threatens to discourage people from acting as ethical citizens. I must emphasize at the outset, though, that my criticism is aimed only at this particular form of direct democracy. For that reason, it seems best to begin with a sketch of instant direct democracy.

As a preface to this sketch, I should like to enter the following qualifications. First, in order to avoid the charge that I have merely set up a straw man, I try to portray instant direct democracy in the most favorable light. Some readers may suspect that I overstate the case in its behalf. Second, some of the features of this sketch, such as the terms of office for president and judges, are somewhat arbitrary. Those who do not think that the president in such a system should serve a term of one year may trim or extend the term as they see fit, making similar adjustments to similar features of the scheme. Third, because I try to outline an instant direct democracy which is as direct and as democratic as possible, I do not consider the possibility of using computers and cables to create a mixture of representative and direct government. Some of the arguments against the pure case of instant direct democracy may tell against these mixed forms, others may not. Finally, I simply suppose in the following sketch that instant direct democracy is in operation. This may seem unfair, for I neglect the possibility that a gradual transformation might be necessary to prepare citizens to meet the demands of the new institutions and procedures.[3] But my purpose is to consider the claim, advanced by at least one proponent, that instant direct democracy will itself lead to a change in the habits and attitudes of the citizenry.[4] Given this concern, it seems fair to proceed in an admittedly ahistorical manner.

I

Let us suppose that the government of the United States has somehow been converted into an instant direct democracy. As with all forms of direct democracy, the basic premise of this regime is that the people, not their intermediaries, should themselves determine the policies which govern their lives. To make this possible, a computer console has been installed in the home of every member of the electorate. These consoles, connected by two-way cable television to a computer in the capital, allow the citizen to cast a vote on an issue by touching one or more buttons.[5] For some issues the voters may be asked to rank their preferences among a number of alternatives; for others they may be able to select from Approve

Strongly, Approve, Don't Care, Disapprove, and Disapprove Strongly. This allows voters to register intensity as well as support for or opposition to a proposal, although the range of intensity is quite limited. The voter may cast no more than two votes for or against a proposal, that is, so that someone who votes Disapprove Strongly (or Approve Strongly) will have cast the maximum number of votes on an issue. In every case, a proposal is adopted if it receives more positive than negative votes.

In this instant direct democracy the citizens themselves are the legislators, and each week they vote on one or more issues. This referendum is conducted via cable television, where the proposals of the week are announced, then debated by their proponents and opponents. These debates are rebroadcast at various times throughout the week so that everyone may see them, and at the end of the week the referendum is held. The polls are open, so to speak, at three different times during the day to give everyone a chance to participate. Those who cannot be home at any of these times can arrange to vote at a post office, library, city hall, or public office of some sort.

The executive and judicial branches of government play important, but diminished, roles in this scheme. The executive branch is responsible not only for carrying out policies approved by the electorate, but also for providing regular televised briefings on matters of public concern. The president is elected by direct popular vote to serve a term of one year in office. A president may be re-elected, but not to consecutive terms, and the man or woman who holds this office may be removed at any time by the vote of the majority of the electorate. Although the president exercises certain emergency powers, they do not include the authority to introduce or veto legislation.

The president appoints the members of the national judiciary, but nominees must be approved by a majority of those voting in special referenda, with the pool of eligible voters comprising the citizens who live in the jurisdiction in question. Every citizen may vote for or against a nominee to the Supreme Court, that is, but only those who reside in the relevant jurisdiction may vote for or against a nominee to a Court of Appeals or a District Court. Once admitted to the bench, judges remain subject to recall throughout their tenure. They apply and interpret the law, but they are not allowed to declare a policy approved by the citizens to be *ultra vires*.

These are the basic features of an instant direct democracy. I shall now add a bit more detail to the sketch by anticipating some practical objections which may be brought against a scheme of this sort.

The first objection is that it will prove too expensive. This claim cannot be refuted, strictly speaking, because no one (to my knowledge) has calculated the costs involved. We do have some idea, though, of how much it costs to maintain Congress—about $519,000,000 in personnel costs alone in 1974, for instance[6]—and in light of this one may wonder whether instant direct democracy might not prove less expensive than our current form of government. One may also ask, what makes something *too* expensive? According to one advocate, the argument that instant direct democracy is "prohibitively expensive" is a "highly disreputable argument. If we have any serious regard for the value of democracy, then we ought to be prepared to expend resources on it. A society which prefers to allocate resources to the pomp of Government, and to royalty, presidency or members of the inner caucus of the Party, has failed to take democracy seriously enough."[7]

Another objection is that instant direct democracy invites fraud. A number of safeguards can be employed, however, including steps to insure that only the person to whom it is assigned can operate a console. This could be accomplished by using cards and codes, as automatic cash machines at banks do; or the consoles could be designed to require the thumbprint of the assigned person before registering a vote.[8] The same measures could prevent voters from voting more than one time on any issue. Other precautions, such as security screening and "failsafe" procedures, could protect against the possibility of tampering with the computer.

This leaves the most serious of the practical objections: the charge that the electorate will be at the mercy of those who set the agenda. How issues are formulated, what proposals are put before the public, even the order in which alternatives are submitted to the vote—all these are important problems which cannot be settled by the people's vote, for they must be settled before the people vote. This is to say that at least one set of intermediaries is necessary even in an instant direct democracy. The problem is to see to it that the intermediaries are under the control of the people, not the other way around.

To meet this problem we may suppose that once a year the citizens elect an Agenda Committee. This committee formulates proposals which its members present on television at the end of each week's referendum, and any proposal which draws at least a third of the votes cast is selected. When this is done, the Agenda Committee chooses speakers from its ranks to take part in the televised debate on the merits of the proposal(s) in question, then sets to work to formulate the proposals for the following week. Like the president and judges, members of this committee are subject to recall at any time. In this way the Agenda Committee, the sole indirect element in this instant democracy, remains subject to the control of the citizenry.

This is only a sketch of instant direct democracy, of course, not a full portrait. Nevertheless, it should serve to indicate that a direct democracy of this sort is neither hopelessly far-fetched nor absolutely inconceivable. With this in mind, let us now consider its attractions.

II

Instant direct democracy promises to be an attractive way to conduct a nation's affairs in several respects. There is no legislature, to begin with, so the problems associated with representative government are problems no longer. There is no need to worry about whether representatives should act as delegates or trustees, for instance, or in what proportion they should mix these roles. Moreover, direct democracy guarantees that no one will be either under—or over-represented. As matters now stand in the United States, the Senate in one way and the House in another give more weight to some person's preferences than to others'. In the Senate, the citizens of the less populous states enjoy an advantage because every state elects two Senators. In the House, with its single-member districts, those who do not vote for the successful candidate—and this may be a majority of voters when there are more than two candidates—can be said, in a sense, to have no representative at all. Problems such as these vanish in a direct democracy, where everyone has an equal part in setting policy.

Equality figures also in the second attractive feature of instant direct democracy: the reduction of the influence of interest groups. In a representative government, the representatives of interest groups typically gather in the capital to try to influence the representatives of the people. In many cases interest groups even do what they can to determine who is elected to the legislature. The abolition of the legislature might not bring a halt to the lobbying efforts of these groups, but it would certainly hinder them. Insofar as the Agenda Committee in the preceding sketch assumes some of the functions of a legislative body, it will also afford some opportunities for lobbying. But insofar as these functions will be limited, we may expect that the opportunities for lobbying will be limited as well.

Direct democracy also promises to end or minimize some of the legislative maneuvers which characterize representative government. There would be no filibuster in an instant direct democracy, for example, nor would there be committee chairmen from "safe" districts to delay the passage of laws favored by a clear majority of the people. For better or worse, log-rolling and pork-barrel politics in general will be nearly impossible in such a system. This is not a necessary consequence of direct democracy, to be sure, for direct democracy does not itself eliminate strategic voting. It is a consequence of *instant* direct democracy, however, because the large number of voters and their isolation from one another will prevent them from sending signals, "thus reducing the scope for strategic behavior to its bare minimum...."[9]

We may note, too, that instant direct democracy will probably not suffer from what many consider to be a major defect of contemporary American government—its emphasis on personalities rather than issues. This tendency may be more pronounced in the United States than elsewhere, but it is likely to appear in all representative governments. When we have to choose a representative, after all, we usually want to know something about his or her character. In a large polity where access to the mass communications media is widespread, this concern for character seems to degenerate into a concern for personality, image, or "charisma." This is in marked contrast to instant direct democracy, where the issues themselves are likely to be at the center of attention.

Some may also find instant direct democracy attractive, finally, because it is free from the intolerance and pressure to conform which, in the eyes of critics, characterize other forms of direct democracy. On this view, direct democracy of the sort found in face-to-face societies purchases community and equality at the expense of more precious values, liberty and privacy. As one critic puts it, "direct democracy effaces boundaries and separations, while subjecting everything to the publicly political imperative. This imperative repels the exploration of possibilities in nonpublic life that the spirit of representative democracy fosters."[10] Not everyone accepts this criticism of the traditional forms of direct democracy; yet those who do should recognize that an instant direct democracy will differ from the traditional forms, largely because it is not confined to face-to-face societies. Given the size of the body politic and the isolation of citizens voting in the privacy of their homes, instant direct democracy seems to preserve the desirable features of other forms of direct democracy while minimizing the prospect of smug or brutish intolerance.[11]

In all these respects instant direct democracy appears to be an appealing system of government. These are not the only respects which matter, though, and in the remainder of this paper I shall

argue that more important considerations count against
government by electronic referenda. We may also expect that some
people will not agree that all the features mentioned above are to be
counted in favor of instant direct democracy; indeed, I turn the last
feature against it later in this essay. The purpose of this section,
however, is not to provide a conclusive argument, but to suggest that
this novel form of direct democracy should not be rejected without
consideration—for there is something to be said in its behalf.

III

Any advocate of instant direct democracy must expect that he
or she will soon face the challenge, "Are the people of this (or any)
country willing and able to govern themselves in this way?" There is
abundant evidence to suggest that they are not. Sidney Verba and
Norman Nie report, for example, that 22% of the electorate of the
United States take no part in politics; another 67% participate only
occasionally.[12] When researchers study levels of political awareness
and information, furthermore, the surveys almost always reveal
that most people are ill-informed, misinformed, or uninformed. In
these circumstances it is easy to understand how some might fear
that the policies adopted by an instant direct democracy will prove
to be short-sighted, ill-conceived, and ultimately disastrous.

This is the kind of argument we associate with elitists,
democratic and otherwise. Because the people lack the capacity to
deal with the difficult issues in politics, the argument holds, they
ought to entrust their governance to those who are wiser, more
prudent, and more public-spirited. Yet even an advocate of
participatory democracy may conclude that instant direct
democracy goes too far. Thus C.B. Macpherson says that the most
democratic government we can hope for at the level of the nation-
state, even with the aid of computers and cables, must still be a
mixture of direct and indirect government. Some form of
representation is necessary, as he sees it, if questions are to be
formulated properly and if inconsistent demands are to be
reconciled. Otherwise, voters would

> very likely demand a reduction of unemployment at the same time as they are
> demanding a reduction of inflation, or an increase in government expenditures along
> with the decrease in taxes.... To avoid the need for a body to adjust such
> incompatible demands...the questions would have to be framed in a way that would
> require of each voter a degree of sophistication impossible to expect.[13]

Participatory democrats and elitists may agree, then, that
instant direct democracy requires too much of the average person.
But there is at least one political philosopher who is not persuaded

by this argument. Robert Paul Wolff is, he says, "a good deal more than half in earnest" about the proposal for instant direct democracy he advances in his *In Defense of Anarchism*. There Wolff anticipates the criticism just set out and offers the following rebuttal:

The initial reponse to...instant direct democracy would be chaotic, to be sure. But very quickly, men would learn—what is now manifestly not true—that their votes made a difference in the world, an immediate, visible difference. There is nothing which brings on a sense of responsibility so fast as that awareness. America would see an immediate and invigorating rise in interest in politics. It would hardly be necessary to launch expensive and frustrating campaigns to get out the vote. Politics would be on the lips of every man, woman, and child, day after day.[14]

Whose position is more plausible, Wolff's or the critics'? I must side with the critics. For we need not believe that the average man or woman is stupid, selfish, or irrational to believe that instant direct democracy is too taxing a method of government. What disqualifies most of us as policy makers may simply be the lack of time to become suitably informed about the complex problems we face as a nation. Because these issues are so complex and so entangled, one may have to be a full-time student of politics to acquire the necessary grasp of these matters. There may be much that instant direct democracy can do to increase our political sophistication, but it cannot itself give us the time to learn all we would need to know.

Time is not the only consideration here, of course. People seem to "find time" for matters which are important to them, and it is possible that the number of those who take an interest in political questions may increase dramatically with a shift to instant direct democracy. This is Wolff's position. In his view, the real source of the average person's apathy is the realization that his or her voice is too faint to be heard in our elite-dominated political system. If he sees that his vote actually makes a difference, then the average person may attach more significance to public matters and find the time to inform himself about them.

Wolff's account of the cause of political apathy may be true, if not the whole truth of the matter. If we grant this, however, it still does not follow that the creation of an instant direct democracy is the cure for this malady. For it is far from apparent that the citizens of an instant direct democracy will see that their votes make "an immediate, visible difference" in the world. *Their* votes will certainly make a difference in this system, for *their* votes determine the outcome. But the individual voter is not likely to find that *his* vote makes a difference. As one voter among millions, he may conclude that his vote is utterly insignificant; and this may lead to the further conclusion that time spent gathering political information is time wasted.

This conclusion is at least as likely as that which Wolff foresees. If the voters perceive that their individual votes are insignificant, we cannot expect them to develop the sense of responsibility that follows, according to Wolff, from the awareness that their votes matter. It seems, instead, that the sense of reponsibility is what now brings many people to the polls in a national election, for it is nearly certain that any individual's vote will have no affect on the outcome.[15] What an advocate of instant direct democracy must show is that some feature(s) of this system would instill a heightened sense of responsibility in the citizens, thus encouraging them to take an active part in public affairs. Wolff fails to do this.

So Wolff's claim is implausible. Yet we must be careful to note what this implies. Even if Wolff is wrong, it does not follow that the critics of instant direct democracy are right when they contend that the result of this system will be contradictory, imprudent, and disastrous policies. This *may* happen, just as it *may* happen that people will meet their responsibilities. But there is a third possibility—that most people, aware of the insignificance of their individual votes, will simply ignore the referenda and leave the resolution of policy to that small group who find politics enjoyable or compelling. If this should happen, we would have no cause to worry—no more than we already have, anyhow—about the soundness of policy in an instant direct democracy. But is the risk worth taking? It may be if govenment by electronic referenda has something else to offer us. For sound policy is not the only thing to be desired from political institutions and processes; we may also want institutions and procedures which enrich human life. This goal cannot be reached unless people are encouraged to act as citizens, however, and this instant direct democracy is unlikely to do.

IV

In this section I shall argue that instant direct democracy is undesirable as a form of national government because it threatens to discourage citizenship. If this claim seems odd, it is probably because we now use "citizen" in an attenuated sense of the word. All the more reason to begin this argument by distinguishing between two conceptions of citizenship.[16]

When we call someone a citizen nowadays, we ordinarily mean only that he or she is legally entitled to participate in public affairs. Whether one does what he is entitled to do—whether one actually participates—is seldom regarded as a test of one's citizenship. Our modern view of citizenship tends to be passive and legalistic, in other words, a matter of privileges and immunities rather than duties and responsibilities.

In contrast to this is the conception of citizenship bequeathed to us by the ancient *polis* and *civitas*. On this view citizenship is, or ought to be, a public vocation which requires us to take an active part in matters of public concern and to act with the interests of the community in mind. This conception, with its emphasis on the responsibilities of the citizen, no longer prevails, but neither has it vanished. We still attach "good," "ethical," or "responsible" to "citizen" when we want to distinguish a "true" citizen from those who are citizens merely in the legal sense of the word, for instance. When we do this, we invoke the ethical conception of citizenship.

We have, then, two different, if not entirely distinct, conceptions of citizenship. According to the first, citizenship is essentially a matter of legal status; according to the second, it is essentially ethical. The ethical conception presupposes the legal because it takes the right to participate in public affairs as a necessary condition of citizenship; but it also considers this right to be far from sufficient in itself. In this sense we still share the ancients' conviction that those who consistently fail to exercise their rights and meet their responsibilities as citizens are not really citizens at all. This is the sense I draw upon when I say that instant direct democracy is likely to discourage (ethical) citizenship.

Assuming for the moment that instant direct democracy will have this effect, why should we care? What is the value of (ethical) citizenship? Perhaps the best answer begins with Aristotle's definition: "as soon as a man becomes entitled to participate in authority, deliberative or judicial, we deem him to be a citizen...."[17] This suggests that citizenship both recognizes and cultivates the faculties of judgment and deliberation. To be accorded the status of citizen is to be recognized as one capable of leading a rational, self-governed life—and as one who has a right, following from this ability, to participate in the government of the community. Those who are denied this recognition, even if they are ranked as "second-class citizens," are demeaned as less than fully rational and as unworthy of equal respect and concern.

As the status of citizenship recognizes one's human faculties, so the life of the citizen cultivates them. A person becomes a citizen in the legal sense of the word when he or she (*pace* Aristotle) appears to be ready to participate in authority. Yet it is through this participation—through judging and deliberating—that one develops these capacities. This is to say that citizenship enriches lives by promoting both mental and moral growth. Certainly the problems the citizen faces *qua* citizen are often complex, whether they are primarily technical questions—what will the effects of a tax cut be?—or questions of strategy—how can we persuade others to vote with us on this issue? We need not fear, then, that anyone who takes the vocation of citizenship seriously will lack for mental exercise.

Nor need we fear that the moral muscles of the citizen will grow flabby from lack of use, for (ethical) citizenship calls these into play as well. It does this in at least two ways. First, (ethical) citizenship requires the individual to look beyond private interests to the interests of the community. In this fashion the public vocation of citizenship demands that the citizen's judgment and deliberation be employed in the service of the community. Second, citizenship promotes moral growth by leading the citizen to confront the fundamental question, how should we order our life as a community? For however technical, trivial, or prosaic political questions may seem to be, they refer ultimately to a way of life—an ethos—and are therefore ethical questions.

There is ample reason to believe, then, that the civic vocation promotes both moral and mental growth, thereby enriching not only the life of the individual, but the life of the community as well. This seems to warrant the conclusion that (ethical) citizenship is valuable indeed. Any method of government which encourages it is desirable, *ceteris paribus,* and any which discourages it is not. What remains is to show that instant direct democracy falls into the latter category.

When I say that instant direct democracy is likely to discourage (ethical) citizenship, I do not mean that it is unique in this respect. In many ways it will only extend certain conditions which already prevail in modern nation-states. One of these is the overwhelming size of the nation-state.[18] As I noted in the discussion of Wolff's argument, the knowledge that one's participation is virtually insignificant may well lead the individual to withdraw or abstain from political activity. There is also reason to believe that the individual's willingness to cooperate in public projects decreases as the size of the public increases. More than 200 years ago Montesquieu observed, "In a large republic, the common good is sacrificed to any number of other considerations; it is subject to exceptions; it comes to depend upon accidents. In a small republic, the public good is more keenly felt, better known, closer to every citizen; abuses are spread less widely, and consequently, are less tolerated."[19] More recently and more formally, others have demonstrated that members of large groups have little incentive to cooperate in a group venture when they can be free riders.[20] This implies, other things being equal, that the larger the body politic, the less the likelihood that people will cooperate freely to achieve public goods and the greater the likelihood that coercion will be required.

We cannot blame the size of the nation-state on direct democracy, instant or otherwise, of course. But unlike some forms of direct democracy, such as those that call for the decentralization of political authority, instant direct democracy offers nothing to reduce or counteract the effects of size. The ability to vote at home may make voting easier and thus more attractive for some. But when the individual casts a vote in a national referendum, he should soon become aware of the futility of this action. The immensity of the polity and the insignificance of the individual's vote will be brought home on cable television.

The size of the nation-state contributes also to another condition hostile to (ethical) citizenship—the lack of community. If an individual is to take the part of the citizen, he usually needs to feel a part of a community whose concerns are his concerns. We cannot expect many people to act with the public good in mind if that public holds no meaning for them. What we should expect in these circumstances is that many will fail to participate in politics, while many of those who do take part will simply regard their participation as the public pursuit of private ends.

This, again, is not the fault of instant direct democracy. It is, however, a problem which the electronic referendum is likely to aggravate. By enabling us to vote in the privacy of our homes, instant direct democracy may isolate us still further from public contact. In such a system we may lose even the slight contact now involved in going to the polls, standing in line, and casting one's ballot. Little as it is, this public effort should remind us that voting is a public act which carries with it public responsibility.[21] In an instant direct democracy this reminder may well disappear. Certainly it will be difficult to stir people to act on behalf of the public when the public is only a vague notion referring to something beyond one's walls.

Finally, we should note that instant direct democracy will probably accelerate the tendency for politics to become a spectator sport, or perhaps a television game show. This may occur as politics is reduced to little but voting. The elements of politics which contribute to the enrichment of life—debate, compromise, deliberation, for instance—are likely to vanish as the mechanical act of voting in the privacy of one's home, free from the frustration of confronting others with different views, becomes almost the only connection between most citizens (in the legal sense) and public life.

Judgment will not be sharpened by this process; deliberation will not be fostered; and the capacity of citizenship to enrich the life of the individual and the community will go unrealized.

Whether one takes these to be telling criticisms of instant direct democracy will depend, in the end, on the value one attaches to (ethical) citizenship and participatory democracy. If one believes that citizenship is merely a matter of legal status and that political participation is primarily a means of expressing personal preferences, then the prospect of wedding computers and cables to democratic government may prove quite attractive, for it promises an efficient and accurate way of registering the preferences of the populace. Democracy, on this view, is desirable because it affords everyone an equal opportunity to protect or promote his or her interests. This is the vision which seems to inspire many writers in the traditions of utilitarianism and welfare economics. Others, Mulford Sibley among them, find this vision narrow and cramped. And if one believes that political participation can and should be something more than a way of registering preferences—that it is valuable as a way of cultivating abilities and strengthening social bonds—then the prospect of instant direct democracy is disquieting indeed.

V

All this is to say that instant direct democracy threatens to devalue politics by converting an activity into a process, thereby discouraging (ethical) citizenship. Since the quality of the policy it will produce is also suspect, we have reason to conclude that we should not be striving to establish a government by electronic referenda. These criticisms apply only to *instant* direct democracy, however, not to other forms. There may be more to be said for more decentralized versions of direct democracy or even for more localized forms of instant direct democracy.[22] Attempts to combine elements of the instant referendum with representative government may also prove quite attractive.[23] The opportunities exist; it remains for political theorists to explore them.

What I wish to suggest is that we attend to two themes in Mulford Sibley's work as we explore these opportunities to remodel our political system. We should remember that political participation is a means of enriching life and that technological advances do not always bring corresponding advances in the political realm. When we examine the ways in which computers and cables may be used to reform our political arrangements, then, we should keep one question in mind: How will these changes affect the vocation of citizenship? There is little incentive to follow this vocation now; to discourage it further is to risk its complete loss.

Eleven

Authority and Freedom in Sibley's Utopia*

Daniel R. Sabia, Jr.

Mulford Sibley's sketch of a utopian world order in *Nature and Civilization* is accompanied by discussions "of the relation of authority to freedom."[1] In his view, authority and freedom ought to be reconciled; and under utopian conditions, he argues, such a reconciliation is possible. Because this Rousseauian contention is apt to be viewed with skepticism, I want in this paper to explicate and defend the theory of authority implicit in *Nature and Civilization,* and demonstrate how and under what conditions that theory reconciles authority and individual liberty. I begin, in the first half of the paper, by sketching both the theory and the proposed reconciliation. In the remainder of the paper, I consider various objections, hoping in the process not only to defend Sibley's position, but to deepen or broaden our understanding of these frequently contested concepts and of the relation between them. The central thesis I hope to sustain is that Sibley offers us a coherent, normative theory of authority that is equally sensitive to the demands of a just—and free—conscience and the need for social order and collective action.

The Background: Politics and Justice. Sibley's theory of political authority must be understood against some background conceptions of politics and justice. Defined as "the art of deliberately creating order and directing human collective affairs," politics is in Sibley's view a kind of natural necessity (256). The only

....

*This paper is in some respects continuous with earlier (unpublished) essays dealing with authority and freedom and supported by grants from the National Endowment for the Humanities to the American Political Science Association. I wish to thank these organizations for that support.

alternative to politics so conceived is to be ruled by chance and blind custom; and in contemporary civilization this is not a viable (nor is it a desirable) alternative. Consequently, "anarchist arguments" that deny the necessity of politics are mistaken, for "society will be 'ruled' in any event—either by standards fixed beforehand and then implemented or by ad hoc actions of various kinds, some of which (e.g., 'lynch law') might be very dangerous" (109n.).

Unfortunately, the "standards" by which political rule is guided in every community are always more or less unjust. This is the result, primarily, of human ignorance and corruption. The first of these deficiencies can be addressed by a political theory, and by an enlightened citizenry, which seeks to identify those "principles [or standards which] are to guide us in political direction and control;" and this "search for guidance..we call the quest for a definition of justice (or righteousness) and its implications" (62). Sibley holds that such a quest is not quixotic. Although "we do not live in a world where the norms of justice are completely known," he is convinced that these norms are knowable, that many are already known, and that many are instantiated to some degree in institutions and laws despite human ignorance and corruption (91).[2]

Substantial parts of *Nature and Civilization* are given over to the identification and explication of the norms of justice, and of their implications, as Sibley understands them. A number of basic norms and related propositions which serve as "starting points" for the "discussion of justice" are identified early in the work and are elaborated thereafter. Included are broad norms or principles to the effect that justice demands respecting both the uniqueness and the social nature of human beings; that justice requires the subordination of material to spiritual and intellectual goods; and that violence is unjust (66-67). Later we learn more specific norms: for instance, that religious and intellectual freedoms must be protected and promoted (92); that all persons are entitled to material goods (103); that distribution according to need is just (240); and that capital punishment is unjust (148).

Our knowledge of the fundamental norms of justice rests on our "intuitions." (Together with our knowledge of facts and probable consequences, these intuited norms provide the bases for just decisions and judgments regarding specific actions, rules and laws, institutions and practices.) It should not be supposed, however, that our "intuitions" are based on or are equivalent to our untutored "feelings." They are not. Nor are they mystical insights or innate ideas. And they are by no means infallible. As I understand Sibley's view, our intuitions are, at bottom, simply the ideas we have of the fundamental or basic norms of justice—ideas which "may, of course, be objectively mistaken" (66). Avoiding mistakes is made possible, though not certain, by substituting *considered* intuitions for our intuitions. Considered intuitions or ideas reflect the interplay of our reason with two kinds of virtually continuous experiences or "dialogues." In one, we "exchange experiences of primary values and value hierarchies with our fellow human beings" (66); in the other, we engage in "a kind of dialogue between the standards fixed by our society and our individual testing of those norms in our experience" (90).[3] Through both kinds of dialogue our intuitions are developed and shaped, amended and clarified, and, probably, brought closer to objective truth.

All of these arguments and conceptions inform in important ways Sibley's theory of political authority. The indispensability (and desirability) of politics requires that we reject anarchist options and that we seek instead to replace forms of rule based on might by forms of rule based on right. The conviction that many of the norms of justice are known, and that all are knowable, insures that this quest is practicable. And the argument that our knowledge of justice depends on continuous dialogue indicates how a form of rule based on right is itself to be ordered.

The Theory of Authority. Sibley's discussion of political authority begins with a definition and a question. "Broadly speaking," he says, "authority may be thought of as the *right* to act or not to act, and political authority, of course, implies the right to act in relation to collective affairs" (93). Given this definition, he continues, the central "question becomes: What authorizes, or what constitutes, the basis for authority?" (94). On what basis, in other words, is a right to rule established and justified?

Sibley's answer to this query proceeds from the essentially Weberian idea that the "basis" of authority is perceived legitimacy. Regimes and laws are authoritative, he suggests at first, if they embody "community standards which are regarded as authoritative" (94). The problem with such a Weberian theory is that the standards in question may not deserve their reputation. In particular, so-called community standards may actually reflect only the opinions, biases, or interests of rulers, or of some dominant segment of the community. In these cases, the allegedly "authoritative" standards embodied in the practices of a regime or in specific laws and decisions are not authoritative at all—or they are, more likely, "only partially 'authoritative,' the other part being corrupted by special interests and piratical elements" (94). Like justice, authority is usually a matter of degree.

Genuine or non-relative authority must rest, then, on a different basis. Regimes and laws are "truly" and "fully" authoritative, Sibley argues, if and only if they embody standards which reflect or "appeal to a common ordering of values and to reason.... And if the standards achieve this level, then they presumably coincide in considerable measure with what the community and its members think of as desirable."(94).

It is important to understand both what Sibley is, and is not, asserting here. He wants to reject any theory of authority that holds or implies that the mere widespread acceptance of a set of standards renders regimes or laws (fully) authoritative if those regimes or laws embody or conform to those standards. On the other hand, he is not (quite) claiming that the standards accepted by community members and embodied in regime practices and laws must be just standards. Rather he is claiming that such standards must "appeal to a *common* ordering of values and to reason"—they must, in other words, reflect a genuine consensus of community members about what is just or desirable. If they reflect such a genuine consensus, they are genuinely authoritative because they represent the considered judgment of the community that they are (or are derived from) just norms. The authoritativeness of the standards does not guarantee their being just (for the considered judgment of the community may be in error), but it makes their being just probable. For these reasons genuine authority, and the probable development and maintenance of just institutions and rules, can only exist in a truly democratic society of a kind Sibley will incorporate into his sketch of the utopian world order.

Before turning to this sketch, we need to ask how political authority, understood as the right to rule, is justified. Sibley provides two defenses of political authority, both of them dependent on or connected to his argument, earlier described, that political rule is unavoidable. The necessity for "creating order," he argues, includes taking into account the evil nature and contentious relations of men and women. Specifically, laws and rules, police and judges, are needed in order to "restrain" and to "correct" the "wickedness of men" so that stable and civil relations can be realized in human communities (94, 96). Additionally, political authority is needed in order to realize collective action and to articulate common ends. Here Sibley borrows from St. Thomas and uses St. Thomas to defeat the argument of anarchists and others that "if only men could cease to be wicked...authority could disappear." Against this argument Sibley counters that, were men angels, we "should still have to make decisions about the good common to all, which no one individual or group of individuals, acting in their individual capacities, and however virtuous as individuals, could determine" (95).[4]

Granted, then, that political rule is inescapable, the right to rule is justified on the ground that, in its absence, civil relations, collective action, and the articulation of common ends could not be achieved—or would be achieved through force or intimidation. Since the latter option is unjust, the search for a genuinely authoritative political order is a major task of political theory and political action. In the realm of theory, this quest translates into the request for the construction, in speech, of a utopian order. Such a construction—given Sibley's theory of political authority—would detail the political procedures, institutional structures, and socioeconomic conditions that would enable citizens to develop a genuine consensus on the standards which, in turn, would underlie or be reflected in all political decisions and actions. As we have already noticed, the development of such a consensus would not guarantee the justice of regime practices and laws (given humankind's propensities for error and wickedness), but it would be most likely to do so.

The central characteristic of such a political order would be its democratic procedures and features. Two interrelated arguments support this prescription. The first of these arguments is perhaps the more fundamental since it is entailed by Sibley's convictions: that our knowledge of justice reflects our considered intuitions the development and potential validity of which requires continuous dialogue and exchange of ideas with others; and, that genuine consensus is the basis for genuine authority. From this it follows that an authoritative and potentially just political order must be democratic and, ideally, must be a direct democracy. Only in a direct democracy are citizens guaranteed the right to initiate and participate in dialogues concerning the rules which shall govern the community, and to report on their experiences under prevailing rules. Thus a central goal of a utopian polity must be the transformation of the very essence of politics from a "struggle for power" to "the development of genuine authority through free debate and exchange of ethical and aesthetic experiences" (288).

Secondly, given the frequency with which laws in existing polities are "corrupted by special interests," it is imperative that we rectify this situation by, again, adopting the ideals of direct democracy. Only in a direct democracy is it possible to insure that laws and practices reflect a "common will" or "genuine consensus" that is both free from corruption and "represents the transcendence of individual policy positions and the attainment of a group view which is probably better than any individual view or combination of individual views" (268). This possibility can moreover be strengthened by adopting the rule of unanimity. Thus is such a rule—or more accurately a Quaker version of this rule—adopted in Sibley's utopia: "discussion continues until no one strongly objects to a given proposal" (267).[5] Decisions reflecting such a common will or based on such a genuine consensus would be fully authoritative. But can the practice of direct democracy guarantee these results?

Sibley recognizes that guaranteeing these results on a continuous basis is, even in utopia, virtually impossible. There are two reasons for this. First, these results are possible only when, in addition to the practice of direct democracy, certain other, *very* utopian conditions prevail: "relatively small size of basic decision-making units, absence of serious factional rifts . . ., strong emotional ties, repudiation of luxury, . . . elimination of significant class distinctions," and more (285).[6] Of course these conditions are, to some extent, realized in Sibley's utopia—which explains why the philosophers there "are fond of quoting Rousseau"! (285). But the problem for Sibley's utopia is that, given the necessity for a *world* order, decentralization of political (and hence authority) structures can only go so far. Consequently, it is only on the "neighborhood" level—the basic decision-making unit in his utopia—that consensus as a rule rules. As one moves up through decision-making units representing areas greater in size and peoples greater in number and diversity, the frequency with which consensus—and hence genuine authority and probable justice—emerges declines. The conditions making consensus possible simply "are not present, or [are] present only to a limited degree, at assemblies above the level of the neighborhood" (285).[7]

The second factor inhibiting consensus consists of two related constraints on decision-making which would by Sibley be termed "natural." It is for Sibley a fact of nature that people are *individuals;* and it is a demand of justice that this fact of nature be respected.[8] Accordingly, no utopian society can seek uniformity or conformity but must, instead, respect and tolerate diversity of opinion. As a result, achieving a common will, *even at the neighborhood level,* is usually "a time-consuming process" (267). But that other great natural constraint—the constraint of time—conspires with diversity of opinion to demand, on occasion, resort to majority rule. At best "only an unhappy expedient," the resort to majority rule must be permitted in even a utopian world given the necessity for decision-making in the face of persistent dissensus and under the constraint of time (268, 285).

Authority and Freedom. I have so far implied that Sibley's utopian call for a Rousseauian decision-making procedure and setting rests solely upon the arguments that only under these conditions can we guarantee truly authoritative practices and rules and, at the same time, make most likely the development and maintenance of truly just practices and rules. In fact, however, there is an additional, and again Rousseauian, argument here: *"True consensus reconciles liberty with authority"* (268; emphasis added). As with Rousseau, this argument or claim cannot be understood apart from the conception of freedom underlying it. In this section I will briefly describe Sibley's view of freedom in order to explicate "the relation of authority to freedom" which he develops.

Sibley considers at some length the concept of freedom in *Nature and Civilization,* distinguishing several meanings of the term none of which he completely rejects. Despite this (characteristic) eclecticism, however, Sibley does stress the distinction between negative and positive freedom, referring to the former as denoting the "opportunity to do what one desires" and to the latter as "consisting in doing what is desirable" (83, 86). His position is that both conceptions of freedom are meaningful and valuable—"both negative and positive freedom must be taken into account as we seek to build the just society" (89)—but he explicitly favors, and gives priority to, positive freedom.[9] As a result, individuals in his utopia are rightly concerned about their negative freedom, but they recognize that giving up some negative liberties in order to gain positive freedom is often both necessary and justified. They do so on the understanding that the constraints of

law and legislation may not only not be restraints on true freedom but may assist positively in the process of liberation: Insofar as the constraints are on my "lower" (or primitively natural) self, they may be doing me a service by assisting me in discovering and giving expression to my higher and true self (86).[10]

Sibley's language in this passage is conditional because the laws to which an individual is subject *may* be corrupt; in these cases, the laws can hardly be said to assist in "the process of liberation" or, as he says elsewhere, in "perfecting the true self." But should the laws be based on or embody justice, they will by definition contribute directly or indirectly to the (positive) freedom of the individual. Since a person "is free when...one knows what one ought to do and does it" (85), just laws contribute to freedom because they prescribe actions that ought to be performed, or proscribe actions that ought not be performed, or facilitate or protect conditions beneficial to the flourishing of human reason and virtue.

The coincidence of just legislation and positive freedom cannot ordinarily be guaranteed because individuals may mistakenly regard as just unjust laws, or regard as unjust just laws. Under the utopian conditions described earlier, however, this problem is effectively eliminated. When authoritative laws representing the will of all are promulgated and enforced, all citizens "know" that these laws are just. It is true that this "knowledge" may be mistaken since even genuine consensus cannot guarantee the justice of decisions made. But here it must be emphasized that, in deciding what one ought to do, the individual must in the final analysis consult his or her considered intuitions and judgments—and it is precisely this which the indivdiual has done when he or she participated in the making of, and consented to the passage of, the laws in question. From this it follows that laws based on genuine consensus—fully authoritative laws—are in fact compatible with, and indeed contribute to, positive freedom.

Authoritative laws cannot, however, be reconciled with negative freedom. Anarchists are correct, Sibley admits, when they point out that even authoritative and just laws "inhibit human freedom in its negative sense." But if the laws prescribe the desirable or proscribe the undesirable the individual's loss of his or her freedom to do what is desired is hardly to be lamented. In utopia, moreover, although a genuinely authoritative law may well check the individual's "momentary impulses," they "are checked in the name of one's own rational standards"—because one's own standards are embodied in the law, that law having been consented to and developed by oneself in the legislative process (94).

It should be noted here, if only in passing, that Sibley's acceptance of the concept of positive freedom does not open him to the charge that citizens might be "forced to be free." He is quite clear that positive freedom consists, not in doing what is desirable, but in willingly doing what is desirable. Should a citizen deviate from genuinely authoritative and just laws, and be punished for that, the community, and presumably the individual citizen as well, will know that such punishment is justified; but no one will pretend that the citizen has been forced to be free or set on the path to virtue. One must choose freedom. "The self-governing fully aware personality is the goal" (87).

We can now summarize Sibley's position on the relationship between political authority and individual freedom. Laws and rules, policies and directives, sanctioned institutions and processes, often constrain individual behavior and/or opportunity. Should those laws (etc.) be genuinely authoritative, however, they will constrain the individual for reasons and in ways which the individual rightly, or wisely, regards as just. Just constraints may conflict with negative freedom but they necessarily contribute, either directly or indirectly, to positive freedom. The citizens of Sibley's utopia, therefore, insofar as they are subject to and constrained by genuinely authoritative laws, are nevertheless free in the positive sense. Most laws made and enforced at the neighborhood level are of this variety.

A Defense and Clarification. In the remainder of this paper, I want to present—and rebut—some objections to Sibley's theory of authority that I take to be especially troublesome and challenging, or helpful in further clarifying Sibley's position, or both. Since my focus will be selective, and limited as well (for instance, objections directed at the concept of positive freedom will be ignored), the defense I construct must be understood as both tentative and incomplete.

All of the objections I shall consider are related to one central feature of Sibley's theory: his claim that genuine authority must reflect or presuppose a genuine consensus on the desirability, righteousness, or justice of that which is alleged to be authoritative. Although some theorists (notably some positivists) have rejected altogether such a normative formula, I want to focus our attention on those who would object to Sibley's application of this conception of authority to the level of substantive law and policy. It is, after all, not uncommon for political theorists and social scientists to claim that the authority of any political or legal system does in fact presuppose some kind of consensus, or at least acceptance, on the part of citizens (or subjects)—but rarely are they willing to extend this claim to the substantive level of law and public policy in the way Mulford Sibley does.

There are a number of reasons for this reluctance. Probably the most common is the fear that, if individuals were to regard as authoritative only those decisions, rules, and commands with which they individually agreed, social order and unity would be impossible. Expressed in this way, the fear is probably justified; but it is not really applicable to Sibley's position. Although Sibley contends that most political decisions, rules, and practices—and all political systems as well—are not genuinely or "fully" authoritative, he also maintains that they are, typically, at least "partially" authoritative. Essentially this is because they will typically reflect or "appeal to a common ordering of values and to reason" *to some extent* (94). "Even in despotisms," Sibley thinks, legislation always appeals, "in however small degree, to standards which are widely if sometimes thoughtlessly accepted" (90).

Sibley thus conceives of authority as almost always a *matter of degree.* Our goal or ideal ought to be the achievement of genuine authority, but the fact that we fall short of this ideal does not mean that political authority does not exist. On the contrary, most political systems, and many institutions, laws, and policies, are at least partially authoritative and for this reason impose on citizens a *prima facie* duty to obey. (This position, implicit in *Nature and Civilization,* Sibley develops at length in *The Obligation to Disobey.*[11] I shall return to it below.) Such a position does not serve only to defuse the fear expressed above. It serves also to underscore the fact that whenever a conscientious citizen decides to obey anything but a fully just, genuinely authoritative law, "he will be doing so in full recognition that his obedience sanctions some [degree of] injustice" (128). In an imperfect world characterized by "impure authorities," our duties and actions will be correspondingly imperfect and impure (96).

A related objection to Sibley's contention that laws and decisions are fully authoritative if and only if they reflect a genuine consensus is that such a position demands the impossible. Although some kind of broad consensus on the basic norms or fundamental standards underlying a regime or political/legal system may well be attainable (and even necessary to authority), achieving a substantive consensus on specific decisions, rules, and policies is, quite simply, an unrealizable dream. Given the diverse and constantly changing interests, values, needs, wants, and beliefs of individuals, disagreements on the demands of justice, on morally acceptable conduct and desirable social goals, will be the rule—and consensus an exceedingly "scarce resource."[12]

This objection, while not without force, is I believe adequately handled by Sibley. As already indicated, Sibley treats consensus as an ideal to be sought; he does not suppose that it can be easily achieved. One purpose of his utopian sketch is to describe those conditions—cultural, social, economic, political, educational, and psychological—which, if met, would make the achievement of consensus more likely; and even then he explicitly recognizes that consensus cannot always be realized. To this should be added the observation that, in his utopian world, substantial room is made for diverse forms of life so that individuals may choose to live in those neighborhoods, cities, or regions most suited to their personality— or, indeed, may choose to live outside of any community whatsoever as a kind of "voluntary exile" (269). Thus, for example, in the economic realm, certain worldwide standards and rules are uniformly imposed, but "regions, provinces, and cities have a wide latitude as to how, in specific terms, they are to regulate their economic life" (280-281).

Social diversity coupled to freedom of movement is thus another feature making consensus more likely. Of greater importance, however, is the fact that the utopians limit the scope of authority, of law and legislation, as much as possible, thereby reducing the very need for consensus. "The general movement of utopian society is in the direction of indirect rather than direct constraints on human beings" (289). Since the expansion of positive freedom, and even negative freedom, is a central goal of utopia, the operative principle or understanding is that "attempts to regulate minutely all aspects of life [can only] frustrate the quest for positive freedom and constitute an intolerable burden on negative liberty" (129). In general, the goal in utopia—as in any just society—is to regulate (to the degree necessary) the realm of material necessity, and to expand (to the degree possible) civil, political, religious, intellectual, and "life-style" (e.g., sexual) freedoms.

Assuming, then, that the degree of consensus expected in a just society is plausible and not an empty dream—assuming, in other words, that the quest for consensus, justice, and authority at the substantive level of law and public policy is not altogether impractical—a quite different objection to Sibley's theory would argue that this quest indicates a serious conceptual confusion or mistake on his part regarding the nature or function of political authority. According to this argument, the essential "function" or "point" of political authority is to make possible social unity and collective action in the face of dissensus, and to do so without recourse to violence, force, or bribery. This can be done, so the argument goes, by supposing that citizens have a duty to obey those rules and commands issuing (in an authoritative or "valid" way) from an authoritative *system*, and that an authoritative system is one that embodies substantive and/or procedural norms which all (or most) citizens accept. The point, of course, is that assuming such a general consensus is in place, rules and commands promulgated and enforced in accordance with systemic norms are authoritative and binding—despite the fact that disagreements over the substantive merits of these rules and commands will be a fairly common occurrence.

The third objection I want to consider, then, is this: Any theory of authority that seeks to connect authority to a substantive consensus on specific rules and policies is self-defeating. For if laws invariably commanded citizens to do what they believe they ought to do, what would be the point of saying that these laws or commands are "authoritative"? The purpose of political authority is precisely to make possible collective action in the face of dissensus, to make possible unity in the midst of disunity, and to do these things by giving citizens a reason (other than fear) to obey laws and commands despite their (likely) disagreements over the merits of these laws and commands. But in Sibley's theory—under ideal conditions at least—dissensus, disunity, and disagreement are eliminated. Although the intent is to reconcile liberty and authority, the actual effect is to eliminate the need for authority. Sibley's theory undercuts and makes superfluous political authority; it *replaces authority with consensus.*

This argument regarding the alleged point of political authority—traceable to Hobbes[13]—has been most recently pressed by Richard Flathman. Flathman's position is that wise citizens— and theorists—must remain wary of political authority precisely because its point or function is to get individuals to do what they may on occasion feel they ought not to do. An implication of this is that those theorists—Rousseau, for instance—who have sought to escape this problem by making consensus a necessary condition of authority, have succeeded only in eliminating authority. Authority

has a role to play in our affairs [only] when we disagree concerning the merits of the actions we should and should not take.... Where there is consensus concerning what should and should not be done, authority has no role (or no more than a narrowly technical role) to play. We simply act or refrain from acting on reasons specific to the actions considered. But if we disagree or are uncertain concerning the merits of the proposed actions...authority may enter, may be invoked, as a reason for accepting or acceding to a particular course or decision adopted. Thus as a logical matter...either authority has no work to do or it works to give us a reason for an action that we would not otherwise...take, or for refraining from an action that we would otherwise take.[14]

Probably the best way to defeat this criticism is to argue that authority *does* have an important role to play in the presence of consensus. Such a counter-argument is presented, at least implicitly, in Sibley's discussion of his utopian society. The crux of this counter-argument is that the citizens of utopia are (at the neighborhood level most of the time) subject only to laws they think they ought to obey but that this does not guarantee that they *will* obey them. Given the nature of men and women, Sibley argues, "momentary impulses" may conflict with their sense of right and, being weak, they may do what they think they ought not to do. One important function of authority, therefore, is to remind such weak-willed or wayward citizens of their duty to justice, and (especially) to justify the community in holding them responsible, if necessary, for failing to do what they agree they ought to do. Authority, in short, does have a role to play even in the presence of unanimous consensus: it serves to reinforce the conscience of citizens and to justify community-imposed constraints on the wayward.

This argument, it should be noted, is important to Sibley's utopian vision. In order for that vision to serve as a plausible alternative to present-day politics, Sibley can not and does not offer an image the major features of which are altogether contrary to human experience. Thus he actually emphasizes the "weak" and "wicked" side of human nature, and uses precisely this assumption to explain the need for law and police—i.e., authority—in utopia. The utopians have "retained law, since they believe that men cannot be trusted to act justly without the guidance of previously established legal norms" (292). And the utopians retain a police force because its presence

is a constant reminder to men and women that, while they may will the good in all sincerity, they sometimes revolt against what they know to be right. The police are a visible embodiment of the general will of most human beings to do justice, even though at times they depart from that way (290).

Sibley's position, then, is that even when consensus on the merits of specific decisions is achieved, authority—and its embodiment in laws and police—has an important function to perform. That function, essentially, is to justify the use of coercion. As I have repeatedly pointed out, however, Sibley also recognizes that consensus at the substantive level of decision-making is not easily achieved, even under ideal conditions. The attainment of consensus is only an ideal. But this very fact provides the basis for another objection to his theory of authority.

Since in utopia a unanimous, genuine consensus is not always possible, majority rule is sometimes permitted and practiced. Earlier I indicated that Sibley's utopians regard the use of majority rule as an "unhappy expedient." It needs now to be explained more fully how this expediency is justified:

To be sure, the utopians are quite aware that consensus is unlikely to be attained on all occasions—hence the provisions, under certain circumstances, for a majority vote. They are quite aware that if no deliberate decision is reached within a reasonable period of time, then the decision is in effect made by events or "fortune"—and, according to their priorities, this is an extremely undesirable outcome (285).

This argument is important, and problematic, for the following reason. Since majority rule is under certain conditions permitted, it must be the case that decisions made by majorities under such conditions are authoritative. But the authoritative status of majority decisions obviously cannot be based on the claim that they reflect a genuine consensus on the part of all citizens that they are meritorious decisions. On what, then, is their authority based? Surely it must be the case that the citizens have agreed to regard as authoritative a purely procedural norm—and to abide by decisions made in accordance with this norm. If this is so, Sibley appears to hold an inconsistent position by maintaining, on the one hand, that genuine authority must reflect a genuine consensus and, on the other, that decisions not reflecting a genuine consensus are also (sometimes) authoritative.

The best way to respond to this criticism, and clear up this alleged inconsistency, is to begin by explaining precisely why majority rule is regarded by the utopians as an "unhappy expedient." Part of the explanation is based on the premise that the central goal of any polity, real or imagined, ought to be the creation and maintenance of justice—of just institutions, rules, policies, conditions of life, etc. Given Sibley's view that what justice is is best known or established through continuous dialogue and the forging of a genuine consensus, it follows that a central goal *and procedural norm* of any polity ought to be that all political decisions should be based on such a consensus. Only decisions made in this way can be said to be truly just—or more accurately, as just as circumstances and human ignorance allows. Now if we are to take seriously the commonplace understanding that authoritative decisions have a *right* to *bind* us, we should accept as *fully* authoritative, and as *absolutely* binding, only those decisions that are in this sense just— because "My only absolute obligation is to righteousness, as I see it at my highest possible level of consciousness."[15]

Decisions based on majority rule, therefore, are undesirable for two reasons. Since they do not express a genuine consensus, since they do not reflect a truly *common* ordering of values and reason, they cannot be regarded as altogether just. And since they are not altogether just, they cannot be reconciled with positive freedom.

Nonetheless, because a genuine consensus is not always attainable, especially under the pressure of events, procedures like majority rule that permit less than unanimous decisions, ought to be allowed. To not accept such procedures is to give up the search for justice altogether, to be ruled by events rather than by reason, and to threaten social order and collective action. The procedure of majority rule is a defensible, albeit deficient, form of collective decision-making; though authoritative, it can produce only partially authoritative results. It can do no better since it cannot generate decisions based on a genuine consensus.

What are the implications or consequences of this position? The two most significant are, I trust, obvious. First, utopian citizens will regard laws made by majorities as relatively just, partially authoritative, and, therefore, as deserving of serious respect and— probably—obedience. But, secondly, no citizen will regard these laws as absolutely just, genuinely authoritative, and, therefore, as absolutely binding. Utopian citizens will for these reasons express their dissatisfaction with such laws, and will try to replace them with genuinely authoritative laws by seeking to establish a genuine consensus. When the effect of majority rule is the creation of "seriously disaffected minorities" (as sometimes happens even in utopia) (268), the search for a genuine consensus is presumably intensified and may even require, on the part of conscientious minorities, a form of civil disobedience that respects "the *principle* of lawfulness by accepting the sanctions attached to violation of the law."[16] Disobedience of this kind is another route, not lightly taken, of "enhancing righteousness," of "carrying on [the] dialogue" in order to establish genuine authority.[17]

The utopians' beliefs and actions represent, of course, models or ideals for us to emulate. Sibley recommends that we regard ourselves as absolutely bound only to justice, and that we connect authority to justice in the way his utopians do. If we follow this advice, we will become more sensitive to the injustice permeating the systems under which we live, and be more willing to take an active role in the collective determination of our fate, in the search for justice, and in the improvement of authority. At the same time, we will be more likely to recognize the relative justice present in those same systems, and thereby avoid taking the kind of precipitious action that is likely to undermine the very possibility of authority. It is in this way that Sibley's theory of political authority balances the demands of a just conscience with the need for social order and collective action.

III
The Nature of Political Theory

Twelve

To Interpret or Change the World? Theses on Marx and Philosophy*

David Spitz

Doing moral and political philosophy has traditionally meant engaging in but three of four possible activities.[1] The first is to describe, that is, interpret, the world. The second is to formulate principles and arrangements allegedly superior to those that exist in this world, and to urge their adoption. The third, a critical activity, takes two forms. One is to criticize the values and practices of this world in terms of standards appropriate to the prescribed alternative. This mode of criticism, as Professor Mulford Sibley reminds us, is particularly exemplifed in the writing of utopias, where the intent or expectation is not to remake an existing society in accord with a perfectionist image but to condemn, by comparison, prevailing and patently unjust (or at least inferior) practices and arrangements. The other is to interpret and critically to evaluate other (especially earlier) theorists, movements, and ideas, and thus other conceptions of the world, in an effort to enrich moral and political understanding and to clear the ground of errors and limitations that would otherwise hinder or undermine new constructions.

A fourth activity, rarely undertaken by moral and political philosophers, is to set forth a program of action that provides for the effective transition from the world that is to the world that ought to be, or that, more modestly, ensures the translation of crucial moral and political remedies into law and social conduct. This is not to say that moral or political philosophers do not intend their principles to

. . . .

*This paper is an abbreviated version of a larger and more copiously documented essay. It has been revised by the editors with the assistance of Elaine Spitz of Cornell Univerity. The editors wish to thank Elaine for her aid and cooperation.

162

serve as a guide to practice. Even one who conceives of his effort as a theoretical enterprise, whose proper end is knowledge and not practice, recognizes that what he is aiming at is a theoretical knowledge of practical principles.[2] It is rather to argue that such theoretical knowledge must somehow be yoked to power if it is to be socially and politically effectual. That, by and large, this has not been done, that political and especially moral philosophers have played little more than a spectator's or critic's or moralist's game, is why Bacon caustically remarked that the books of the old philosophers can talk but cannot generate; they have been "fruitful of controversies but barren of works."[3]

Whether philosophers can or should break through this traditional division of labor and attempt, like nuclear physicists and geneticists, not merely to interpret but actually to change the world is of course contestable. In one sense they may be said unavoidably to do so, for interpretation and prescriptions are themselves forms of action that in one way or another alter the perceptions and behavior of individuals and groups, and through them the world. But in the sense articulated here, the philosopher is called upon to do far more. He is asked to recognize and come to terms with the constellations of power in the real world—either by adapting and mediating his doctrines to accord with those power factors or, where possible, by controlling and directing them. He is asked not to leave the implementation of his teaching to the ad hoc or prudential judgments of political activists and statesmen but to accept responsibility for that implementation himself—at the very least through a general theory of action, but more importantly through specific policies that attend to programmatic details. For

while theories and principles may be general all activity is particularized. Each act is done by a particular individual, at some specific time and place, and under a given set of conditions. Action, to be successful, must be cognizant of the uniquely individual character of the situation in which it occurs. A moral philosophy whose end is action cannot help but take note of the pecularities and particularities of each individual moral agent and of his situation.[4]

The philosopher, moreover, cannot be unaware of the fact that his new morality, however valid, threatens established interests and practices and will thus engender resistance; and also, what is more disturbing, that even those who ostensibly embrace his teaching will in some measure subvert it. In order to win the acceptance (or at least acquiescence) of individuals and groups already committed or habituated to other creeds and interests, those who seek power in the service of his new morality will find it necessary to compromise and thereby alter some of its central tenets. For this reason, the philosopher who wishes to change not merely thought but also law and social behavior in maximum conformity to his doctrines must formulate not only a theory of the morally and politically good but also a general (even better, a programmatic) theory of practical activity.

It was one of the more important contributions of Karl Marx that he recognized and gave urgent emphasis to this twofold task, though that recognition cannot of course be said to have originated with him. This "philosophy of the act," the replacement of speculative philosophy (that looked, with Hegel, to the past) by a philosophy of practical activity (praxis) that would change the world in the future, was the dominant view of the Young Hegelians and had first been articulated by August Graf von Cieszkowski in his *Prolegomena to Historiography* (1838) and later, within Marx's own circle, by Moses Hess, though in a subjective form, i.e., the activity of man's will.[5]

Whether Marx's claim to have performed this task successfully is warranted, is another matter. It turns, in the first instance, on the adequacy of his moral theory, and second, and more crucially, on his notion of praxis, in particular on his resolution of the question whether men can effectively determine, or are determined by, their circumstances.

Concerning the first of these matters, little need or can be said. For Marx, quite simply, was not an ethical theorist or moral philosopher. He attended to none of the traditional problems: the elucidation of moral terms; the articulation of rules and criteria by which individuals can resolve their everyday moral dilemmas; the distinction, logical and empirical, between goods (or the good) and evils, or between moral and other demands, or between private and public interests; the consideration of moral "obligation" and moral "justification;" and the like. On these and related issues Marx said little or nothing, and what he said was often contradictory and confused. It is true that Marx rejected the dualism of "is" and "ought" and explicitly claimed to be a scientific, not a utopian or ethical, socialist. Hence he could, with some warrant, neglect the traditional concerns of moral philosophy and argue instead in terms of causal (or internal) relations. Yet in condemning the servility and dehumanization of the individual in history, in retaining the idea of historical "progress" as a normative concept, and in pleading for freedom (as the liberation of human creativity) and for rationality (as something which one *ought* to support), he clearly committed himself to certain ethical values. He was, if not a moral philosopher, at least a moralist, certainly a social critic or sociologist of morals—

describing or explaining normative principles as "rationalizations" or ideologies, i.e., reflections of economic or class interest.

The question of the content and adequacy of Marx's moral theory—to whatever extent he may be said to have had one—is of less consequence here, however, than the question whether he offered valid directions as to the implementation of that theory. For even if we were to concede that Marx had a coherent, and compelling, moral theory, this would still leave open the problem of converting that theory into practice.

Here Marx was more than confident. He believed that through praxis—the union of (philosophical) theory and (political) practice—he had grasped the true (dialectical or interrelated) nature and destiny of man and society, that he had communicated this understanding to others, and that, most crucially, he had provided for a mode of political action that would effectively transform both man and society in the desired (perhaps necessary) way. But Marx's confidence was misplaced. A careful examination of his account of the relationship between theory and practice points to the inescapable conclusion that he failed to articulate a coherent account of "praxis." What is more—and worse—this failure, given his own pretensions, gives him some measure of responsibility for the way in which Marxist political practice actually developed.

I

In his Eleventh Thesis on Feuerbach, Marx expressed a certain contempt for philosophers because they had only *interpreted* the world. The point, he said, is to *change* it. But the point is indeed to interpret the world, for how else are we to understand it; to know why and in what respects we ought to change it; how and when and in what order we may most effectively proceed; what forces and powers, and of what magnitude and skill, will be brought in array against us, and what resources they will be able to tap to reinforce their effort; which leaders and organizations, at what costs and to what limits, and which strategies and weapons, can be mobilized and employed to overcome that opposition; what consequences are likely to follow from such an engagement, and what is to be done with respect to those and many other anticipated (not to speak of unanticipated) consequences?

Merely to state these obvious requirements is to explain why it is a first axiom, indeed a truism, that we can never hope fully to grasp or to understand all these things. We can never completely command and sensibly integrate all the external and internal facts that (separately or dialectically) constitute "the world," that make up "reality." Those facts are always too numerous.

Now, it would be foolish to assert that Marx was oblivious to this consideration. In fact, it can be—as it has been[6]—argued that his complaint was not that previous philosophers had interpreted the world but that they had been content to interpret the world, that they had not sought to realize that philosophy by transcending it. There is no antithesis, that is to say, between knowing and changing the world; no one is to be reprimanded for having philosophized. What is at issue, rather, is the restriction of that knowledge to scholastic or inert contemplation. Marx is contemptuous of philosophers who have confined themselves to interpreting the world, or who have thought that a different interpretation of that world would in itself—through self-awareness or self-consciousness—revolutionize it; and who have not, consequently, gone beyond—negated—previous (traditional and speculative) philosophy to seek and pursue a more activist philosophic role.

But this is not a complete and wholly accurate rendering of Marx's argument. On the one hand, while Marx does indeed reject philosophy as mere contemplation, he proclaims a conception of the world that remains philosophical. He is not (at this point in his intellectual development) a "scientist" or "positivist;" he does not (or so it has been argued) accept the notion that "objective" thinking furnishes a ready guide to practical conclusions.[7] On the other hand, as he argued in the Second and Eighth Theses, it is impossible to know the "objective truth" of human thinking by contemplation alone; the acquisition of such knowledge is not, in his view, a theoretical but a practical question and can be resolved only in human practice.

Because he believed that the question of truth is a practical rather than a theoretical matter, Marx went further and held, with Feuerbach,[8] that for philosophy to realize its aims (as he conceived them) philosophy must become practical and must therefore in some sense cease to be philosophy. One "cannot transcend philosophy without actualizing it."[9] Philosophy must become the theory (and part of the praxis) of revolution. Moreover, that activist role, Marx argued, had to be pursued not by the philosopher but by the ordinary man. As he wrote in *The German Ideology:* "One has to 'leave philosophy aside,' one has to leap out of it and devote oneself like an ordinary man to the study of actuality, for which there exists also an enormous amount of literary material, unknown, of course, to the philosophers."[10] Unknown, that is, except to Marx. For it was somehow given to Marx (whether as philosopher or as ordinary man is not altogether clear) to seek, and also to find, not truth for truth's sake but truth for the sake of transforming the world in a revolutionary and total manner. In this way, and only in this way, he thought, could change be directed rather than chaotic, directed toward the realm of freedom.[11]

But despite all his talk of relating philosophic knowledge to political activity, of demonstrating the truth of a theorem by applying it to and in social reality, Marx did not in fact address himself to these things, certainly not in the requisite details, and especially not (to take a crucial problem) with respect to the period of transition to, and the subsequent character of, his classless and stateless society. His own research, most obviously in his earlier works but also in the *Grundrisse* and *Capital,* was primarily theoretical, not practical; and his practical activities, not to speak of his concrete predictions, reflected less his philosophical understanding (or the necessary outcomes of his philosophical system) than they did his ad hoc tactical judgments (so often misjudgments) of men and events. There is all too little correspondence between Marx's criticisms and exhortations, interpretations and major theories, on the one hand, and the concrete evidences drawn from experience, whether actual or potential, on the other. His alleged union of theory and practice is never adequately demonstrated and is certainly never proven.

No less consequential is Marx's understanding of what is entailed by interpretation. He conceives of it as "mere" or "idle" contemplation. But this is surely no more than a half-truth. Interpretation is very often itself a form of action; for through interpretation individuals do more than conceive abstractions, they create and thereby establish general and particular images of the world, which then become a part of—indeed, they not only constitute, they change—the very reality those images are designed to portray. Those images, of course, are always in some measure subjective, but they are nonetheless "real;" they are the closest approximation to and thus the only "real" "objective" images of the world that individuals can hope to attain. They are also of course partial, which despite Marx's pretension to the contrary is all that he himself achieved. Yet, like Hegel, he supposed that he had in fact comprehended the "totality" of history; that his image of the world was rooted not in his partial and subjective understanding but, by the genius of his mind and his "unsurpassed" ability to grasp connections,[12] in absolute or at least sufficient knowledge to justify taking the world into his own hands; that he had fulfilled the Arthurian legend and come into possession of the Holy Grail.

II

There are always certain things that cannot be changed immediately. There are other things that ought not to be changed, for not all things of this world are evil—as Marx well knew but in incautious moments was all too prone to suggest. The Marx who revered Aeschylus, Shakespeare, and Goethe, and who in *The Communist Manifesto* celebrated the many achievements of capitalism, would have been the first to insist that some things, perhaps many things, are good, or at least pleasant and not harmful. It is then necessary to discriminate among the things of this world: to modify or eliminate practices and arrangements that are oppressively harmful or evil and that can in fact be changed—always with a due concern for sequence, time, and the receptivity of public opinion—but also to identify and then to preserve and promote those things that merit retention.

Marx, it may be said, was self-consciously a part of Western culture and wished to carry over certain of its central values and achievements into the "higher stage" of which he dreamed and anticipated. Obvioulsy, too, some of those values and achievements had to be carried over. The revolution cannot remake the world out of nothing; the new can but grow in the womb of the old. But if values are no more than rationalizations of class interests, if achievements are the consequences of particular modes of production and the relations of production to which those modes give rise, and if both values and achievements are thus historically bound—the diverse outcomes of past and present (varying) modes of production—and will necessarily change with changes in that historical process, which values and achievements are (or ought) to be retained, and by what criteria are we to know? It is a signal fact that Marx did not discriminate between the things of this and some future world, certainly not in any systematic way; nor did he provide standards or criteria by which we might determine what merits retention.

By failing to discriminate and to lay out appropriate criteria for such judgment, by insisting (as he so often did) on total, revolutionary, change that will remake "the world," without logical or empirical demonstration that the change (or changes) will be for the better rather than the worse, Marx left a legacy of ambiguity, not a directive or a theory of intelligible and intelligent action.

III

There are always limits to what we can or wish to do. Those limits are set in part by external circumstances over which we may have little or no control, and in part by our own selves.

It has been aptly said that even Chairman Mao's thoughts are not so powerful as to render a mule fertile. There are forces and conditions, not simply physical and economic, but also racial, religious, political, and ideological; there are emotions—the passions of prejudice, the lusts of the body, the fantasies of mind—that enter into any confrontation between what is and what ought to be, and that cannot be ignored or dismissed (at least in morals and politics) simply because they are deemed unworthy or irrational. These forces, conditions, and emotions set limits to human action. Recognition of those forces rules certain acts out of the realm of immediate or foreseeable possibility, at least among a given people in a particular time and place.

It cannot be said that Marx ignored those limits, that he pretended that anything is possible, that he had no sense of varying circumstances, and consequently of varying possibilities, among diverse societies. And yet, in treating the problem of social change, it also cannot be said that he adequately resolved the central issue: whether men make or can intentionally make their circumstances or whether circumstances make men.

IV

In his Third Thesis on Feuerbach, Marx directed attention to the (hitherto existing) materialist doctrine that men are the products of circumstances and upbringing, but argued against this view that men can and do change those circumstances and that it is therefore essential to educate the educators.

By this Marx did not of course mean to reject the materialist doctrine *in toto*; that remained a necessary aspect of the correct explanation. But by itself materialism "up to now"—especially as developed by Hobbes, Descartes, and certain French philosophers of the eighteenth century—was not sufficient. Its mistake, Marx argued, was to divide society into two parts, willed (or conscious) activity and given (or unintended) circumstances, one of which was then rendered superior to the other. But insofar as one can distinguish between men and circumstances, so that it is possible to describe men as products or makers of, or as standing in some sort of dialectical or internal relationship to, those circumstances, there *are* two parts, no matter how linked those parts may be in social reality.

This distinction Marx did recognize and repeatedly employ, as indeed he was required to do if he was to speak of competing interests and antagonistic relations. Thus, in describing man's alienation from his labor, his fellow men, and his species, he routinely invoked language that termed such labor "an object, an external existence,...that...exists outside him, independently, as something alien to him,...it becomes a power on its own confronting him." And just as this product is "an alien, hostile, powerful object independent of him," so is "the master of this object, someone who is alien, hostile, powerful, and independent of him."[13]

So too with the relations between men and circumstances. They are indeed parts or aspects of the same whole. But they are differentiated parts. Consequently, the question is to determine, not generally but precisely, how those parts or aspects of the whole relate to and affect or include each other. Marx himself recognized the centrality of this question, writing in *The Holy Family* that:

Proletariat and wealth are opposites; as such, they form a single whole. They are both creations of the world of private property. *The question is exactly what place each occupies in the antithesis. It is not sufficient to declare them two sides of a single whole.*[14]

Hence we must ask: Which changes in the one produce, or can produce, which changes in the other, under what circumstances or conditions, in what particular ways and to what extent? How are such changes introduced in the one in the first place, by who, or what and in what ways? Which, if either, may be said to have a controlling or decisive influence over the other? Or if, as Marx argued in the Third Thesis, "the coincidence of the changing of circumstances and of human activity can be conceived and rationally understood only as *revolutionizing practice,*" what are we to comprehend by "coincidence" (or concurrence) and how does any practice (or critical activity) yield that understanding? How, finally, on the basis of what empirical evidence, can we be certain that the answer to any or all of these questions is a matter of concrete or practical knowledge rather than of speculative opinion?

For such answers we must look not to the *Theses on Feuerbach*—they are not there—but to Marx's other writings, notably *The German Ideology*, where he argues that "circumstances make men as much as [not decisively or more than] men make circumstances."[15] If this is true, then men are clearly limited in what they can be or do, though it is not immediately apparent to what extent and in what ways they are so limited. But if men also make circumstances, they are indeed free to modify the world, though again it is not immediately apparent to what extent and in what ways they are able to do so. Obviously they cannot change circumstances at will, in any way they please; for history is not solely a matter of "self-consciousness." There is a realm of "necessity" that sets historical limitations on human freedom. "At each state stage there is found a material result: a sum of productive forces, a historically created relation of individuals to nature and to one another, which is handed down to each generation from its predecessor;...[it] is indeed modified by the new generation, but also...prescribes for it its conditions of life and gives it a definite development, a special character."[16] But if each generation both modifies and prescribes for its successor, yet each is in turn bound in some way by that inheritance, in what sense, in what specific ways and degrees, can it be said that circumstances determine men or men determine circumstances? All the more so when human needs are social and historical, that is, a product of man's historical development and of the cultural values achieved by preceding generations: in short, when human needs are determined by man himself, though often blindly, as a consequence of unintended or irrational (as well as rational) actions.

Marx is anything but specific. In fact, the argument smacks of circularity. For now it no longer matters—indeed, it is irrelevant even to ask—whether changes in men precede and cause changes in circumstances, or the reverse; for if individuals and societies do not exist as entities distinct from and independent of each other, then change in either men or circumstances is in itself change in the other. But what, then, is the point of speaking of man and society at all? Why speak of circumstances determining men or men determining circumstances if men and circumstances are so intertwined as to negate, or make it impossible to "individuate," the differences between them?

If Marx is correct in this postulated union of the individual and the external world, so that (under communism at any rate) there is no longer any conflict between man and society—since man's *natural* existence has become his *human* existence, i.e., nature has become man[17]—he articulates, at best, a tautology. At worst, when we look at man not in communist but in capitalist society, where his nature and his humanity are severed to the point that Marx can speak of the alienated person as an "abstraction," all we can gather from this "hierarchy of nonsense"—if we may apply to Marx what Marx said of Stirner[18]—is that men and circumstances stand in some sort of historical and continuing relationship to each other. But precisely what that relationship is, in what precise ways particular things operate and are tied together within that system (if it is a system) of relationship, and precisely what Marx has contributed to its understanding—as a theory of action (as praxis) for the present and future, as distinct from descriptive accounts of that relationship in certain historical situations, e.g., as Marx depicted them in *The Eighteenth Brumaire of Louis Bonaparte*—remains obscure.[19]

Has Marx himself done no more than, or as much as, Feuerbach did: develop only a new interpretation of a contemplated, even if more empirically grounded, world, not a replacement of theory by praxis?

V

It is necessary now to raise the difficult question: Who will educate the educators when it is the educators who reproduce themselves? In what ways, in what kind of education and for what ends, shall those educators be educated, and if not by other (presumably non-determined and non-alienated) educators, by whom and how? I say difficult because nowhere in Marx, or in the writings of his disciples or commentators, is there an adequate answer.[20]

If it is said that the answer is patent, that Marx and the Marxists will educate the educators, the question is merely moved to another level: What other than self-arrogation establishes his and their legitimacy as educators? Which circumstances, and on the basis of what evidence, have so molded or made them that they, and they alone, are competent to make not only new circumstances but also new men? The answer cannot be that they, unlike alienated men who need educating, stand "outside alienated society;" for if "society" is alienated those who stand outside stand nowhere. It can only be that they define themselves as non-alienated men, as practical beings "in practical opposition to the actual trends of alienation in the existing society." Possessing "true self-consciousness as a *practical programme,*" they can thus supersede "the historically concrete content and form of alienation."[21] But why their self-definition and assumed true self-consciousness are warranted, and should consequently bind others, remains unclear.

It may also be contended that the subject of the historical process is not educated by others but educates himself in the course of his activity, which is but the progressive unfolding of his own being.[22] But if education is personal and internal, then clearly the conundrum is abandoned rather than solved; for then attention is diverted from the education of the educators, who are no longer needed despite the fact that Marx had termed them "essential," to man's alleged ability through his own activity to rearrange the world of which he is a part. But is "any" activity or only the "right" activity required? In what way, and to what degree, can a part rearrange the whole, and how can that part effectively do so if it has not been educated properly?

Unlike Pilate, we yet stay for an answer.

VI

If we are limited in what we can do by our circumstances, we are also limited by our own selves, by what we are in this and not some ideal or future world. It is a fact, perhaps unfortunate, that men simply will not do all that they should—not merely what we think they ought to do but what they themselves, in their infrequent nobler moments, recognize they ought to do. This is why the major religions prudently provide for recurrent sin, confession, and repentance, knowing full well that those same men will sin again.

This is as true of Marx and his disciples as it is of all men. It is notorious that Marx himself often failed to behave according to his own moral principles—not only in his close personal relationships, as in his insensitive response to Engels when the latter wrote to him (in January 1863) of the death of his long-time companion Mary Burns,[23] but also, and quite inexcusably, in a variety of deceitful intellectual and political practices and above all in his calumnies against his political opponents, e.g., Bakunin and Lassalle.[24] What is worse, those who have allegedly acted in his name, or in the service of his teaching, have where they have come to power produced not what he recommended but precisely what he denounced: the dehumanization of the individual. In the fury of their fanaticism, in the corrupting effects of their power, they have deprived men and women of the one thing Marx professed above all others to seek—their liberty, i.e., their self-realization as non-alienated human beings. Those disciples have reduced man to animal, exactly as Marx had depicted that animal condition in his *1844 Manuscripts*.[25] Most shamefully, they—and their apologists—have then celebrated this achievement as the conquest of bread. They have yet to learn that the choice is never between bread and liberty: for without liberty there will be little bread, nor any way for men to protest that they do not have it or to share in determining the conditions under which they might hope to secure it; without liberty even the bread they may have will turn out to be bitter and unsatisfying; and without liberty that bread even if physically appeasing can provide but a portion of a person's needs, not realize the whole individual whom Marx sought to bring into being.

It is said, with some justice, that Marx's social and political theory should not be judged by the cruel and ruthless policies of Lenin and Stalin and Mao, no more (or less) than any other philosopher's doctrines should be judged by the uses to which others have put them. But this can only be maintained with some, not complete, justice, and only if one is prepared to deny any relevant connection between Marx (or his teachings) and those men. This, I think, would be difficult: For those men believed that as Marxists they understood the nature of man, of society, and of history; they believed, or at any rate professed to believe, too, that their understanding coincided with Marx's understanding; they consequently acted in what they took to be the spirit, though obviously not (always) the letter, of Marx's teaching.

It can, of course, easily be shown—though a neo-Marxist like Louis Althusser will obviously dispute this (and thereby confirm rather than refute the point)—that such men deliberately or ignorantly falsified their adherence to Marx's views, that they (in Trotsky's terms) "betrayed," or drastically modified, Marx's philosophical views and revolutionary principles.[26] Still, there is so much in Marx's writings and intellectual temper—not the least the insistence on changing *the world*, accompanied by the arrogance that can lead Marxists to say: "There is no further truth, there is no other"[27]—that while Lenin and Stalin and Mao may properly be said to have stood Marxism on its head, they were also able, at times with some semblance of plausibility, to insert their revisionist doctrines into the Marxian framework, especially as that framework was (after Marx's death) elaborated and crucially transformed by Engels.[28] Hence Marx (and especially Engels) cannot wholly be exempted from responsibility for the disastrous consequences of their disciples' acts,[29] all the more so when we recall Bakunin's prescient remarks concerning Marx himself:

> Marx is an authoritarian and centralizing communist. He wants what we want: the complete triumph of economic and social equality, but he wants it in the State and through the State power, through the dictatorship of a very strong and, so to say, despotic provisional government, that is, by the negation of liberty. His economic ideal is the State as sole owner of the land and of all kinds of capital, cultivating the land through well-paid agricultural associations under the management of State engineers, and controlling all industrial and commercial associations with State capital.[30]

Let it not be thought that in these respects any of us is different from, and superior to, Marx and the Marxists. None of us is what he fully wants, or once wanted, to be. None of us has achieved all that he desired, or behaved always as he should. And none of us ever will. Moreover, what is true of us as individuals is true also of our social entities, whether groups, classes, religious associations, political parties, or nations. And the world, that lonely planet hurtling from nowhere to nowhere, is but a feverish maelstrom where nations and would-be nations clamor and scramble for what they take to be higher and better places, often in the process converting citizens to subjects, pilgrims, refugees, and pirate bands, each of them struggling in turn—for what? To become full-fledged citizens again, or anew? To build a just world? To found a new tyranny of their own? Or simply to survive?

To suppose that among such confused and tormented men in such a disorganized, even deranged, world it is possible to bring about, much less impose, an ordered and correct pattern of practices and arrangements without first understanding, by interpreting, the nature of that (otherwise) chaotic reality, requires an act of faith that ill becomes a philosopher—least of all a determinist, of whatever sort and however that determinism may be qualified. To suppose that a philosopher can effect all these changes according to some rational scheme is to attribute to him a measure of wisdom and power—of human control over men, events, and institutions—that no philosopher, or any other man (not even a Moses or Solomon, not even a Jesus or a Mohammed) has previously possessed, or ever should possess; for no one, not even the wisest and most virtuous man, can live up to his intentions and promises completely.

VII

Unless men resort to violence, politics and morality entail a process of accommodation. If they resort to violence they may lose, and—as the case of the Soviet Union only too well demonstrates—lose even if they seemingly win. If they accept the principle of accommodation, they must compromise, and this alone precludes changing the world as any one man or group might wish it to become, presently or ultimately. Politics is argumentation leading, one hopes, to accommodation. It is in this sense that pacifists—prominent among them the man whom we honor in this volume—are preeminently political people. Repudiating the anti-political vocation of violence, Mulford Sibley reminds us that the line between theory and practice is to be found in living one's life among, and for, our fellows.

VIII

Is it really necessary, at this point in history or even in Marx's time, to emphasize that one cannot change the world as a totality, cannot abolish an entire system (or complex of systems) and long-established traditions, and construct a totally new set of human relationships? One can only change particular things within that world. And if we claim the ability to anticipate many of the consequences of our actions, we can scarcely foreclose the possibility of human error, the play of accident or chance, and the emergence of unknown or unforeseen reactions and events, to each of which surprises we in turn respond by new inventions that transform the problem (or problems) anew. The world in any case is much too big and diverse a subject (or object) for directed and simplistic control. We can effectively address ourselves only to piecemeal reforms in limited areas, whether or not our design is to bring about total or limited change.

The impossibility of total change is a result of the uncertainty of human knowledge. Precisely because our knowledge both of ourselves and of the external world is always partial and inexact, we can never be sure that what we think we know we really know. This should make for a large measure of humility. It should make us aware, too, of the importance of attending to ideas and experiences other than our own and of the need for corrective mechanisms, such as representative government and elections. To dismiss or interpret such mechanisms as mere forms that mask unseemly realities is to ignore the utility of those forms in promoting both civility and deliberation.

IX

Always some men have yearned for, and some have ventured to depict, a harmonious rather than tension-ridden system. They have seized on the obvious fact that cooperation, not competition, is the supreme law; for without cooperation men could have accomplished nothing. Recognition of this social nature of man is doubtless the key to the oft-quoted sentence in *The Communist Manifesto* that alone deals directly with future society: "In place of the old bourgeois society, with its classes and class antagonisms, we shall have an *association*, in which the free development of each is the condition for the free development of all."[31]

But whatever the solidarity that may characterize this future (hypothetical) association, and however deep and wide the feeling (or consciousness) of mutual interdependence, some polarization, some separation of individuals from each other and from the collectivity, will always remain.

Of course man is a social being; how can he be otherwise? But he is also an individual, a unique being who differentiates himself, and wants to differentiate himself, from others. Indeed, it can well be argued that even while society seeks to mold his character and impose conventional uniformities of behavior upon him, it accentuates the differences between him and others. For no man's social environment is exactly the same as another's, and each man experiences society's treatment of him differently. Consequently he will often find himself at odds even with those he esteems. He is and will remain a "private" as well as a "public" person.[32]

Hence, however much Marx may insist that man and society are the same thing, two aspects of the same phenomenon (which is why for Marx one cannot be a "product" of the other), disagreements, and consequently divisiveness, will continue to play a crucial role in social life. This is why there will always be a need for a political and social process by which conflicts among individuals, groups, and classes may be rationally resolved—not merely peacefully (for who but a madman wishes an untimely death?) but with a measure of respect for human dignity.

But Marx will have nothing to do with programmatic considerations of this kind. He means to resolve conflicts, to be sure, even to eliminate them by eliminating social antagonisms, but through a utopia; or, since he denied that his communist society is a utopia or ideal, through a "real" (i.e., political) movement, a "world-historical" existence,[33] whose mid-wife—at least in non-democratic states[34]—is revolution.

Now revolution, however warranted it may be (or may have been) in particular historical situations, is in many ways incompatible with, if not Marx's desire for (or belief in the inevitability of) fundamental change, certainly his concern for freedom and human dignity. For though revolution, in particular Marx's proletarian revolution, appeals to universal rights and universal dignity, it actually begins with and feeds and grows on what divides men, not on what unites them. It cleaves the human race into higher and lower orders—the chosen and the rejected—and fosters hatred between them as a necessary prelude to the overthrow of the one by the other. Thus Marx writes:

For a popular revolution and the emancipation of a particular class to coincide, for one class to stand for the whole of society, another class must...concentrate in itself all the defects of society, must be the class of universal offense and the embodiment of universal limits. A particular social sphere must stand for the notorious crime of the whole society, so that liberation from this sphere appears to be universal liberation. For one class to be the class *par excellence* of liberation, another class must...be openly the subjugating class.[35]

This deceit—that a "particular class" must stand for the "crime of the whole," in order that liberation from that particular may appear to be liberation from the whole—is an affront to the dignity of its author and to those to whom it is addressed. What is worse, it forgets that

it is not merely inhuman to kill, it is dehumanizing to resort to violence. Violence corrupts both the user and those against whom it is employed. It corrupts the user by making him a different man than he was before: consumed by passion and convinced of the rightness of his cause, he soon loses the capacity to draw distinctions; all who are not with him are against him, all are the enemy; and in the crudity of his monolithic rage he turns into a weapon of destruction. He becomes an extension of his gun, and [those who use] guns know neither tolerance nor decency.... So it is with those who must now unleash their own guns against him. From the civilized world of moral discourse we thus move into the jungle.... Revolution, even the "success" of the revolution, destroys both the revolutionaries and the cause for which the revolution was ostensibly begun.

[Further], it ought never to be forgotten that revolution, even in the name of reason, is *always* an attack upon reason and that one of the terrible consequences of revolution is the inflammation of the passions, the governance of might rather than right. And who can say whether the might that prevails is truly in the service of the right cause, or whether that right cause will not itself be corrupted by the new strong men who, rather than the revolutionary idealists, come to power and impose repressive policies of their own?[36]

That these are real and not imaginary consequences of Marx's argument is attested both by his imputation of stupidity to, and thus his assault on the dignity of, men other than himself (and of course his disciples) and by the denial of freedom to those and other ordinary men under his socialist state. He imputes stupidity to those who view neither themselves nor the system they respect as despicable, for in his judgment their thoughts, unlike his, but reflect their class status and interests; their thoughts are a product of "false consciousness." He also imputes this "false consciousness" to those proletarians who fail to mobilize, though in their case he compassionately argues that they are but the victims of their oppressed status. Because of this Marx and his Party are required to tutor them, and Lenin and the party to lead them—even, if need be, against their will.

The new dictatorship, however, will provide neither equality nor liberty; for it is still a form of state, and as such must remain an instrument of class oppression—in the service, to be sure, of ultimate liberation. When will that moment of liberation arrive? Only when the state disappears, only when (as Engels, but not Marx put it) the state withers away. Concerning this process and time Marx is not totally silent but certainly restrained, refusing, as he expressed it, to write recipes "for the cook-shops of the future."[37] But he was fully aware of the problem and did not hesitate to castigate others for a similar refusal to speak out in detail. Thus he wrote in his *Critique of the Gotha Program* (1875):

The question then arises: what transformation will the state undergo in communist society?... This question can only be answered scientifically.... Between capitalist and communist society lies the period of the revolutionary transformation of the one into the other. There corresponds to this also a political transition period in which the state can be nothing but *the revolutionary dictatorship of the proletariat.* Now the [Gotha] program does not deal with this nor with the future state of communist society.[38]

Despite this rebuke of the Gotha program, one will look in vain (here or in other writings by Marx) for his own treatment, scientific or otherwise, of the transitional period to, or future state of, communist society.[39]

Unlike Marx, Lenin later did essay an answer to this question. He asserted that only habit will cause the state to disappear. In *The State and Revolution* (1917), Lenin argued:

> Only in communist society, when the resistance of the capitalists has been completely crushed, when the capitalists have disappeared, when there are no classes...*only* then "the state...ceases to exist," and it *"becomes possible to speak of freedom."*... [Freed] from capitalist slavery...people will gradually *become accustomed* to observing the elementary rules of social intercourse...*without the special apparatus* for compulsion which is called the state. The expression "the state *withers away"* is very well chosen, for it indicates both the gradual and the spontaneous nature of the process. Only habit can, and undoubtedly will, have such an effect.[40]

But clearly the habits cultivated in making a revolution and living under a dictatorship are not those of independent judgment by free men voluntarily joined in a free association but those of command (by an elite) and subservience (on the part of the controlled masses). This is why even one who believes that revolutions are "true as movements" can also say they are "false as regimes."[41]

Whatever may be said of the difference between Marx and Lenin—who on this question but followed Engels[42]—it is difficult to understand how any of this may be termed the union of theory and practice, or how any of this adequately explains or portends the dissolution of the state, the emergence of freedom, and the attainment of human dignity.

X

This is all the more clear when we consider Marx's depiction of life in that future stateless and classless society. There, he says, free men will be able "to hunt in the morning, fish in the afternoon, rear cattle in the evening, [and] criticize after dinner," only to take on a new set of diverse activities the following day.[43]

But if that society is to function at all, if it is to produce the goods and services requisite for the maintenance of life, and perhaps of a commodious life, such freedom is simply impossible. Work must be done, and some work requires not only long and intensive training but also, and precisely because that society rests on mutual interdependence, regular performance. The doctor must be there when needed, and not when it suits his inclination. The engine-driver must move his train out of and into designated stations according to a fixed schedule; he may not, midway in his journey, stop the train to gambol in the fields on a lovely Spring day; his freedom to do as he may please, whenever it fits his fancy, must give way to his duty to his fellow-men, his passengers.

Social men must participate in social regulation; they must plan, organize and carry through all sorts of necessary tasks, those that are arduous or tedious or irksome as well as those that are pleasant and intrinsically satisfying. Thus it is simply not true that men may be free to do whatever they please. Some work requires not merely regular—dutiful—performance but also special competence, which excludes many from doing what they might perhaps have a desire but not a capacity to do. The life even of a communist man will remain in some measure as demanding as his previous life.[44]

XI

The question here is not whether Marx held a right or wrong moral and political theory but whether he did or did not attend to the programmatic requirements and consequences of that theory. It is my contention that he did not. He extracted general propositions from his reading of the unique circumstances of his own and past times, and derived from these general propositions what he took to be appropriate future projections, in ways not unlike those of the English utilitarian philosophers he criticized. He sought to mobilize men behind his theory rather than fit his theory to the world of actual men.[45] Yet that theory can hardly be said to have yielded precise "decision-rules" in concrete situations.

It is correct to say, with Avineri, that Marx held "that an end cannot be divorced from the historical means of its realization. It cannot be consciously realized by means that negate it—not on moralistic grounds, but on simple empirical grounds."[46] But there is all too little in Marx's writings that relates means to ends in that empirical fashion, almost nothing that pursues in careful detail the intimate relationships between his theories (e.g., alienation, class struggle, and revolution) and what is actually required for their realization.

It would be somewhat misleading to say of Marx what may be said of many another social philosopher: that he deluded himself into believing that to refute an idea is to impose a death sentence upon it, or that to establish the truth of an idea is itself sufficient to cause men to embrace and act upon it. Or to attribute to Marx the notion that it is not even necessary to "establish" that truth, since men will accept and act upon correct ideas *malgré eux,* simply because objective conditions compel them to do so. Marx clearly took into account both the objective and the subjective elements in the historical process. Revolution, for example, is possible because of objective conditions; it becomes inevitable only when to those objective conditions is added the revolutionary consciousness of the proletariat.[47]

But somewhat misleading statements often contain important kernels of truth. Consider, for example, Marx's expectation that this revolutionary consciousness would emerge as a matter of self-change, as an achievement of self-discovery by the workers themselves through association, economic struggle, and political activity. Through their own (dialectical) engagement with the external world, Marx thought, the subjective aspect of consciousness would be united with the objective aspect of social conditions. As he put it in *The Holy Family:* "It is not a question of what this proletarian, or even the whole proletariat, at the moment *regards* as its aim. It is a question of *what the proletariat is,* and what, in accordance with this being, it will historically be compelled to do."[48] Unfortunately, history after Marx did not fulfill this expectation.

This is why Karl Kautsky—in this respect commended (and echoed) by Lenin for his "profoundly just and important utterances"—sought to explain that class consciousness (i.e., socialist ideology) and revolutionary activity did not and could not emerge spontaneously (i.e., without real choice) from the objective conditions of men's lives. Instead, he argued, socialist consciousness was something that had to be "introduced into the proletarian class struggle from without," from above, by those with scientific knowledge, i.e., Marxist philosophers. That those philosophers (in this construction) were and are but the alienated children of the bourgeoisie; that they were and are (what Karl Mannheim was later to call free-floating) bourgeois intellectuals detached from and outside of the deterministic forces that allegedly compel class divisions and class consciousness; and that without those "classless" intellectuals the very ideas of class conflict and socialist (as distinct from job or trade-union) consciousness could not be introduced into "the proletarian class struggle"—all these, among other things, render the scientific pretensions of Marx's praxis less than tenable.[49] Indeed, that metamorphosis of bourgeois intellectuals into a classless and truly scientific elite constitutes, from the standpoint of Marx's own social theory, nothing less than a miracle.

XII

The conclusion, I think, is inescapable. Marx talked about but did not solve the crucial problems entailed by the unity of theory and practice; nor—though I will not attempt to show this here—have Marxist writers or activists done so after him. Marx's (and Marxist) theory thus but poses a continuing query concerning the role of the intellectual and his moral and political responsibility for the programmatic implementation of his teaching.

The conclusion, too, is that the problem is not so much to change the world as properly to interpret it. Then, indeed, we may be able to change, not "the world" but those specific practices and arrangements that lend themselves, in the immediate situation, to correction, to praxis. Only when we hold in hand and move in accordance with either a general theory of action or (better) a particular theory rooted in specific programmatic requirements and consequences, can we hope effectively to translate theory into practice in a historical situation beset by conflicting constellations of power. Only then can morality unite and work with, and in this limited sense transcend, control, and give direction to, the otherwise implacable forces that foster and hinder social change in the real world.

Thirteen

On Political Philosophy
and the Study of Politics

J. Donald Moon

In the period following World War II students of politics tended to see a radical disjunction between the empirical or scientific study of politics and traditional political theory or political philosophy. On the "scientific" side, political philosophy was often dismissed as ideology or political doctrine,[1] while political theorists frequently argued that the "scientific study of politics" was deeply wrong-headed. In the words of one critic, the "new political science...fiddles while Rome burns," and it does not even "know that it fiddles," nor "that Rome burns."[2] In the face of these often vitriolic polemics, Mulford Sibley contributed a balanced and thoughtful analysis of the relationship between empirical political science and political philosophy. In a series of papers he articulated a conception of the role of traditional political theory in the study of politics, and set out both the value and the limits of the "new political science."[3] His arguments effectively defended the unity of political inquiry against those who would enforce a strict dichotomy between political philosophy and political science.

My primary interest in this essay is to continue in the direction Sibley has pointed, to show the close and complementary relationships between political philosophy and political science. My main thesis is that one central task of political philosophy is the articulation of fundamental conceptualizations of what it is to be a person, including not only an account of human needs and capacities, but also a view of how a person is related to others. These fundamental conceptualizations serve two functions.[4] On the one hand, they underlie the analyses which political philosophers provide of the basic concepts and practices of their societies—concepts such as authority, freedom, law, representation, and "politics" itself. On the other hand, they serve as the basic paradigms, conceptual frameworks, or research programs for any systematic study of political and social life. If this characterization of political philosophy is accurate, it follows that the relationship between political science and political philosophy is very close: to study politics one must also do political philosophy, and in doing political philosophy one must also do political science.

In making this argument I will be opposing two widely held positions regarding political philosophy, and I will develop my view in opposition to these two positions. The first position I will discuss opposes any attempt to distill "timeless truths" from the writings of political philosophers, holding that a political thinker must be understood in the context of the particular society within which he or she wrote, and that his or her voice can never carry beyond that context. Our interest in political philosophy, according to this perspective, can only be historical in the sense that the study of political philosophy can only be the study of isolated particulars from which no general lessons or conclusions can be drawn. At best it may have some pragmatic value in teaching us of the possibility of alternative ways of living, and so providing us with some "distance" from our own society.

The second view I will be opposing is one that sees a radical break between political philosophy and the empirical study of politics. According to this view, philosophy is a "second-order" activity, consisting of an examination of the kinds of issues which arise in the study of some subject—especially conceptual issues. Hence, political philosophy must be a "meta" activity: it does not teach us about politics, but about how we would study politics. It does not explain political life, but tells us what can count as an explanation of political phenomena. In short, political philosophy provides us with the tools to clarify the conceptual issues which arise in the study of politics. I will argue that political philosophy does raise these "meta" questions, but I will insist that its scope is not confined to such issues.

By setting forth the views that I will be opposing I do not mean to suggest that my intention is polemical. On the contrary, both of these positions are correct in a number of important respects, but each is one-sided in other ways. In this paper I do not intend to set forth anything like a complete account of the nature of political philosophy. On the contrary, I shall only defend the rather general thesis stated above against these two alternative views, and I will illustrate my argument with a brief examination of Hobbes and what may be called the "Hobbesian paradigm" in political inquiry.

1. Political Philosophy and Timeless Truths
At least since Hegel thinkers have understood that "every

individual is a child of his time," and many have drawn the conclusion that "philosophy too is its own time apprehended in thoughts," and so is unable to "transcend its contemporary world."[5] Notoriously, Hegel was not entirely faithful to these words, but in recent years a position akin to his has been vigorously defended by a new school of historians of political ideas. One of the principal theses of this school is that political theory is "radically situated," in that it is completely bound to the context in which it was written. Several years ago Quentin Skinner provided a particularly forceful statement of this position in a widely celebrated (and criticized) essay, "Meaning and Understanding in the History of Ideas."[6] Although Skinner has changed his views in some particulars, this essay is such an important statement of the conception of political philosophy I am opposing that I will develop my own ideas from an examination of its central argument.

Skinner's argument for the radically situated character of political theory grows out of post-Wittgensteinian accounts of language and human action. According to Skinner, to understand a text, or a statement of any sort, we must grasp not only the meaning of the utterance, but also "the intended force of the utterance itself in the mind of the agent who uttered it...." (p. 46) That is, to understand what someone says we must grasp the meaning of what he says *and* his intention or what he was doing in saying it—"*how* what was said was meant...." (p. 47).

To reconstruct the author's intention, we must understand the linguistic context within which the author wrote. The linguistic context, particularly the conventions of the speaker's language community, determines both the meaning of a particular statement, and the kind of action one performs in making that statement on a particular occasion. To clarify this point, Skinner offers the example of a policeman's calling out to someone skating on a dangerous pond, "The ice over there is very thin."[7] In this situation, given the conventions of ordinary English this utterance constitutes the action of "warning the skater." We are able to grasp the meaning and the intended force of the utterance because we know the conventions of ordinary English. And knowing these conventions, we can see that the same utterance in a different situation might have counted as a (mere) assertion, or perhaps even as a command or a threat.

Because the meaning of an utterance depends upon the linguistic context in which it is uttered, and because this context is necessarily particular to a specific period of time and a specific group of people, the study of an historical political theory must focus upon the reconstruction of its linguistic context. In studying any given text, we must determine "what its author, in writing at the time he did write for the audience he intended to address, could in practice have been intending to communicate by the utterance of this given utterance." (p. 49) A political text is necessarily situated in a particular linguistic context, and it "is inescapably the embodiment of a particular intention, on a particular occasion, addressed to the solution of a particular problem, and thus specific to its situation in a way that it can only be naive to try to transcend." This means not only that "the classic texts cannot be concerned with our questions and answers, but only with their own," but it also implies that "there simply are no perennial problems in philosophy: there are only individual answers to individual questions, and as many different questions as there are questioners."(p.50)

Skinner is correct in claiming that the meaning and the intended force of a statement depends upon the broad linguistic context in which it is made. But it does not follow from this that a text in political theory cannot have implications which transcend the occasion of its composition. While it is true, as Sibley points out, that a text may contain notions that are "peculiar expressions of the way of life of a given region and time and which deal with particular issues that may disappear in another age," it may also include "propositions which might conceivably have more universal applicability."[8] Of course, the author may not have understood the ways in which a statement may transcend his or her own time, and we may even suppose that sometimes political theorists would find the implications of their ideas abhorrent. While they often could not have imagined, let alone intended, that their ideas be taken in certain ways, their ideas may nonetheless have such implications.

In part, as Ricoeur has argued, the possibility of a text going beyond the intentions of its author results from the difference between spoken and written language. Speech occurs in a dialogical situation, in which one can confront the speaker about the meaning of his or her words, and the implications of what has been said. And the speaker, in response to such questions, can elaborate, amend, clarify, and even retract what has been said, to bring about a congruence between his or her intended meaning and the meaning of his or her discourse. This is not possible with a written text.

With written discourse...the author's intention and the meaning of the text cease to coincide. The dissociation of the verbal meaning of the text and the mental intention of the author gives to the concept of inscription its decisive significance, beyond the mere fixation of previously oral discourse. Inscription becomes synonymous with the semantic autonomy of the text, which results from the disconnection of the mental intention of the author from the verbal meaning of the text, of what the author meant and what the text means. The text's career escapes the finite horizon lived by its author. What the text means now matters more than what the author meant when he wrote it.[9]

In response to this argument, one might agree that a text can have a range of meanings that go far beyond the intentions of the author, but argue that its implications cannot reach beyond the author's age and form of life. One might claim that each language community is unique in the sense that it is constituted by a set of basic concepts and self-understandings which are not shared by other language communities. Hence, speakers of one language can express ideas and talk about things which speakers of another language cannot. This is not to say that we cannot translate what they say into our own language, or that what they say must forever be unintelligible to us. But it is to say that a condition of translation or intelligibility is that we consciously learn the practices, forms of actions, and basic self-understandings in terms of which their language makes sense. But because each society and each age enjoys a unique form of life, political philosophers reflecting on the political and social life of their own communities will have nothing to say to each other. Although they will be able to understand what other political philosophers have said if they make the effort to understand, their ideas and arguments will be of no use or interest in dealing with the issues relevant to the philosopher's own community. Each philosopher will be referring to different issues and doing so in terms of fundamentally different concepts and principles. Although the theoretical structure of a philosopher's argument can be explicated, and his or her theory can be shown to have implications for issues he or she didn't discuss, the theory will not have implications for issues that *we* discuss since our issues arise within a system of concepts and principles which is radically different from the system underlying his or her political philosophy. Just as a medieval treatise on astrology has no import for issues in modern thermodynamics, so Plato's *Republic* has no relevance to contemporary politics.

Anyone who has tried to teach Plato to undergraduates will recognize the doubts this argument expresses. In fact, the argument can be extended to call into question one of the most cherished ideals of modern political science: the idea of a general, comparative theory of politics. For the actions of people differ from the movements of things in that human action is constituted in part by the intentions of the actor, and the conventions of his or her society. Hence, even the identification or description of a particular action is possible only against the background of a set of social practices and self-understandings which give the action its specific character and "point." One cannot make promises in a society lacking the institutions of promise-making, nor give an order in a society lacking the concepts of authority or command. So when the background of practices and self-understanding changes, the range of behavior available to members of the society also changes, along with the choices and issues which this range poses. If one of the tasks of political philosophy is to investigate and articulate the presuppositions and constitutive meanings of a social order, then this task must be performed anew for every form of life, and the interpretation of one form of life cannot help us in understanding novel forms, except perhaps in a pragmatic sense, by sharpening our conceptions and interpretative capabilities.

This argument seems to me to be essentially sound, but it is considerably overdrawn: the differences among societies are not so sharp as it suggests. There are, after all, certain universal features of the human condition. We all have basic survival needs, and so we all must wrest our livings from nature. We must recognize the finitude of our own existence as individuals, the fact that we are born and will die and the fact that we reproduce ourselves sexually. As language-users, we must at least implicitly have some conception of rationality or intelligibility that marks the sense of what we say. And as social beings we experience ourselves in relation to others. No doubt many other things could be mentioned, but what is important is that all humans do face a set of common circumstances. Moreover, since we are self-conscious beings, we not only live, but we are also aware that we live, we have *conceptions* of ourselves and our lives. These conceptions, naturally, may not be explicitly formulated; they may only be implicit in our institutions and practices, providing the contexts of meaning which give our practices their "points," and which give significance to our lives. Part of the task of political philosophy is to articulate these underlying conceptualizations of the human being and society, to explicate the "constitutive meanings" which define the forms of life in a community. And since all societies confront at least the issues I mentioned above, those issues constitute a set of what Winch calls "limiting notions," which serve as "points of contact" at which different political philosophies meet.[10] Even though the conceptions of work, life, death, rationality, sexuality, and privacy of different societies will not be the same, these different conceptions can be seen as distinct answers to a common set of questions. And so in this way we can say that there is a theoretical level at which political philosophers from different times and places may be said to meet.

Of course, not all political philosophers have seen themselves as only articulating the basic self-understandings of their own societies. Rather, many (if not most) have attempted to set forth general theories of political life that will not be bound by the limits of one particular society, or one particular age. When Plato discusses "justice," for example, he does not intend merely to explain what is involved in a particular set of practices and self-understandings which prevailed in the Greek city-state, but to make an argument which he considered to be universally valid. And, from the opposite end of the philosophical spectrum, when Hobbes discusses political obligation and law, he does not see himself as articulating the "limiting notions" of English society in the seventeenth century, but as enunciating a general theory of political life which will hold for all times and all places.

According to Skinner, this project of developing a general theory of politics is inherently impossible, and so their authors must be fundamentally confused about what they are doing. I do not wish to defend the particular visions which any philosopher might have offered, but I will maintain that this enterprise is not, or need not be, incoherent. I have already argued that reflection on the self-understandings of particular forms of life leads to the articulation of the basic conceptualization of the human being and society that is implicit in a set of social practices and concepts, and that these basic conceptualizations express "limiting notions" of the human condition, issues which are common to all forms of society. Similarly, the general theories which political philosophers advance must also be based on, and give expression to, a conception of the person and society which transcends the particular context in which the philosopher is writing. Hence there are two senses in which we can point to a level of theoretical discourse about politics at which political philosophers can meet: in terms of their interpretations of the "limiting notions" which constitute a particular form of life, and in terms of the fundamental conceptions of the person and society which they adopt, and which may serve as a basis for a general account of political life, and for a desirable form of political and social order.

Their meeting at this theoretical level is not only an abstract possibililty—it is also realized in the history of western philosophy. Although, as Skinner argues, there may be serious difficulties in tracing the careers of particular concepts or in examining the influence of one thinker upon another, the existence of identifiable traditions of political discourse is less open to doubt. Traditions can be defined in terms of shared or similar conceptualizations of these basic dimensions of the person and society, as Hobbes and Bentham may be said to share a conception of the person as a calculating, self-regarding, want-satisfying animal. On the other hand, a tradition could be defined in terms of its opposition to another tradition, and in terms of certain formal similarities in its fundamental conceptualizations of the human being and society. Rousseau, Hegel, and Marx, for example, share a common opposition to the Hobbesian-Benthamite tradition, and they are all committed to a genuinely historical view of humanity and society, rather than to a view of human nature as fixed and unchanging. Undoubtedly, the identification of traditions involves pragmatic considerations and depends in part upon the purposes of the scholar. This is because the ideas and arguments of different political philosophers resemble and draw upon each other in different ways, and so there is room to highlight now this, and now another area of comparison. Such variability does not mean that these traditions "exist" only in the imaginations of scholars. It should be obvious that when we organize the writings of different political philosophers into traditions on the basis of similarities and differences in the structures of their arguments, we will generally be going beyond the intentions of the writers we are studying. Locke could not have intended to contribute to the liberal tradition or to anticipate Berkeley's metaphysics, (p. 29) but in saying that he did these things we are simply calling attention to certain similarities between the positions he developed and those which were articulated later. One may, of course, confine one's studies to discovering "what genuine historical thinkers did think," (p. 29) but if we are interested in doing philosophy we shall also be concerned with the arguments and claims these thinkers advanced, with the objections which could be made to these claims, and with how these objections could be answered. And since these objections and counter-arguments frequently appear in the writings of later philosophers, we come to see these writers as part of on-going traditions of political and social thought.

I have been arguing that the statements of political philosophy are in some ways general, and not confined to the situation of their utterance. Not only are there certain universal dimensions of the human condition which all societies must face, but there are also traditions of political discourse at the theoretical level. I will also argue that there are standards which can be used to evaluate and to criticize the claims of political philosophy. These standards include the coherence or internal consistency of a political philosophy, and its explanatory power. Coherence, obviously, is a regulative ideal not only in intellectual pursuits, but also in other aspects of life, for it is a condition of the intelligibility of a belief or practice. In attempting to understand a political philosopher we are committed to trying to see how his or her ideas "hang together," for that is what is involved in making them intelligible. And in criticizing a political philosophy one of our principal tools, as in all areas of philosophy, is the *reductio:* we show the inadequacy of a system by showing that and how it is internally incoherent. No doubt this may lead to the "mythology of coherence," to the discovery of "coherence" in a writer that isn't there, but this does not mean that we can abandon the ideal of coherence—either as a regulative principle in interpreting texts, or as a critical principle in evaluating arguments. Just because we *can* make mistakes, it does not mean that we must do so, or that we should abandon the attempt to get things right.

The explanatory power of political philosophy is a little harder to characterize than its internal consistency, for it involves two different ideas. In the first place, viewing a political philosopher as providing an account of the basic concepts which inform the political and social life of his or her society, the explanatory power of his or her theory will depend on the adequacy of his or her interpretation. For example, we can ask whether Marx's account of the fundamental self-understandings of capitalist society is correct. This would involve, *inter alia,* determining whether his interpretation of the bourgeois doctrine of human rights (as presented, e.g., in his writings *On the Jewish Question*) provides an adequate explication of the meaning of this doctrine. In the second place, the explanatory power of a political philosophy can be evaluated in terms of its ability to account for (or to generate theories which account for) those features of social and political life which are not the intended results of actions, including processes of social and institutional change, patterns of political instability and violence, and recurring features of social structures such as trade cycles in capitalist economies. These two kinds of explanation are not generally distinguished in the writings of political philosophers, at least prior to Rousseau, but they can be distinguished and the contributions of a particular thinker can be assessed in these terms. Obviously, the point of such "assessments" is not to "grade" political philosophers (Plato, A; Hooker, C-; Burke, B-; etc.). Rather, these standards can be used to criticize and develop the arguments which political philosophers offer, thereby making it possible for deeper and richer theories to be developed. Because of the existence of certain "limiting notions" which all societies share, political philosophers have points of contact at which they speak to each other, and because of the existence of the standards of coherence and explanatory power, these discussions need not amount to simply "comparing notes," but can involve criticism, change, and progress. Political philosophy may not give us "timeless truths," but it is not, or at least not necessarily, radically situated. Sometimes political theorists pose questions that we too wish to answer, and sometimes they offer interpretative and explanatory accounts that are sufficiently general to have implications going beyond their own age.

In developing a critique of Skinner's conception of political philosophy I have been setting forth the essential elements of my own viewpoint. In the next section I will develop my views further by contrasting them with another conception of political philosophy. In this way I hope that part of what must have seemed obscure or dogmatic in the preceding argument will become clear.

2. Political Philosophy as Metapolitics

One popular conception of political philosophy sees it, along with other branches of philosophy, as a "second-order" activity. It does not "add to our factual knowledge of the 'real world' but aims rather at increasing our critical understanding of the body of knowledge which (political science is) providing." To this end it "deals with the logical analysis of descriptive concepts, particular statements, and general hypotheses about political phenomena."[11] In a similar vein, Gregor writes, "Philosophy is today generally recognized as a critical and analytic activity that performs a variety of metafunctions—it is a serious and insistent analysis of the language of inquiry." This involves encouraging "participants in the knowledge enterprise to sort out, catalogue, and characterize the truth conditions governing the kinds of claims advanced by rational agents." So, he concludes, philosophy is "a special order of cognitive activity—a second-order concern with first-order questions. Engaged in this kind of pursuit, men ask questions about questions and they talk about talk."[12]

This view of philosophy as "talk about talk" is based on some very persuasive considerations. It begins with the idea that empirical inquiry is the province of "science," for in order to find out about the world we must engage in controlled observation and experimentation: we cannot decide the truth about matters of fact through *a priori* reasoning. On the other hand, in order to conduct empirical inquiry and report on our investigations we must develop concepts and procedures which are satisfactory for these purposes, and this requires reflection on, and reasoning about the concepts and methods of science. Since philosophy, as opposed to science, does not engage in empirical inquiry, the only kind of "knowledge" it can give us is an analysis of the process of empirical inquiry. What philosophers can do is to provide conceptual analyses of the "language of political inquiry," refining and sharpening that language so that it is a better instrument for purposes of scientific explanation, theory construction, and manipulative control.

This argument obviously turns on a particular view of the relationship between language and the world. Specifically, it presupposes that the phenomena we wish to describe and explain are independent of the concepts and theories we use to describe and explain them. The behavior of lightning does not depend on whether we call it "lightning" or "Zeus's thunderbolts." Hence, what we must do is to frame our concepts in such a way that we can formulate scientific laws and theories which are precise, yet broad in scope, and to eliminate language which is vague, ambiguous, or tautological. Physical science began with a vocabulary and set of basic notions drawn from ordinary language and progressively refined or abandoned them in accordance with its own need for explanation and description. Similarly, political science must begin with ordinary language, but it

cannot effectively use the language of everyday life as it stands. To adapt ordinary discourse for scientific purposes, it is necessary to make explicit the rules for governing the use of its concepts, to sharpen the criteria of their application, to reduce their vagueness and eliminate their ambiguity, and hence sometimes to modify their meaning.[13]

The idea that the world is independent of the language in which we describe and explain it is plausible when applied to natural science and natural phenomena, but it is problematic when applied to the human sciences, for the possibility of certain forms of behavior is *constituted* by the language of social life. The concepts we use to describe what we do are not introduced in order to have a convenient way of referring to behavior that could exist apart from these concepts, since at least some of the actions in question are in part constituted by rules which define them. The concept of "playing chess," to use a familiar example, is not introduced so that we can describe what people are doing when they move odd shaped figures around on a checkerboard, nor is "marriage" a term social scientists might invent to designate certain living-cum-sexual arrangements. To play chess or be married requires that the actors involved have and follow the conventions of chess or marriage, and so it is with virtually all of the concepts employed by political science.

We can readily accept the idea that a crucial role of political philosophy is the analysis of the concepts that figure in political inquiry. But because of the mutual dependence of the language of political life and the patterns of political behavior, political philosophy cannot simply be a "meta" activity, sharply distinguished from empirical political inquiry. Because many of the concepts the political philosopher must explicate are in part constitutive of political reality, the analysis of these concepts is not simply a second-order "talk about talk," for it also provides a kind of knowledge of the social world.

Analyzing social concepts involves two kinds of activities: explicating the relationships which hold between one concept and others, and drawing out the presuppositions of a concept—the fundamental ideas and beliefs which give the concept its sense. An analysis of the concept "law," for example, would involve tracing its relationships to such notions as "rule," "command," "liberty," and "legal system." Secondly, it should provide an account of what is presupposed by the non-defective use of the concept: what assumptions must we make in order for the concept to have a "point" or "sense"? Among these presuppositions are the kinds of constraints on what can count as law, such as those which Hart and Fuller discuss. Depending on the specific conception of law developed, the interpretation must also provide an account of those features of the human condition which make acting according to laws possible and (perhaps) necessary. Whatever the analysis of "law" a philosopher gives, the results of her or his reasoning are not, in at least one sense, *a priori* truths, for it is not necessary that a society have the institution or concept of law at all. Although the philosopher is engaged in a conceptual inquiry, it is an inquiry into the concepts and associated practices of a particular society, and so in clarifying these concepts he or she is also rendering those practices intelligible. And that is because the forms of social life, unlike the patterns of natural phenomena, are constituted by the beliefs and self-understandings of social actors. Because the language of social life is part of the social world, the analysis of that language is not a "second-order activity," an activity at best preliminary to discovering the "facts" about the social world. On the contrary, philosophical analysis is an integral part of social inquiry.

As I pointed out in section 1, in addition to analyzing the language of political life, political philosophers may also develop a conception of the person, a fundamental conceptualization of the individual and society, which may serve as the basis for a general theory of politics. In articulating such conceptualizations, political philosophers are advancing "research programs" or "paradigms" which are essential to any systematic study of politics, and so this is a second way in which political philosophy is not a "meta" activity, divorced from the actual process of political inquiry. This function of political philosophy is reasonably familiar, and it highlights a second misunderstanding regarding the relationship between language and the world which appears to underlie the conception of political philosophy as involving simply "talk about talk." Nowadays virtually no one argues that empirical inquiry can be conducted in any field of investigation without some kind of conceptual framework which guides and structures research. But there are still those who view the function of such a framework as essentially "heuristic," as only suggestive of how research might proceed, but which can be dispensed with as the science in question develops formalized theories which are confirmed (or not refuted by) "protocol utterances" or "observational statements."[14] Perhaps some areas of scientific inquiry have developed in this way, but it is a mistake to suppose that these theoretical structures stand independently of their initial (i.e., logically primary) conceptual frameworks. That is because even our "rock-bottom" observational statements, those which supposedly involve a minimum of interpretative content, are nonetheless part of a system of concepts which constitutes a conceptualization of the phenomena at hand, and which is therefore subject to criticism and change. The idea that our language can "picture" reality is simply incoherent. To think of statements as true because they correspond to some set of entities called the "facts" is, as Scheffler argues, to "...beg the very question of truth and project our language gratuitously upon the world...."[15]

Recognizing the fact that there are no "rock-bottom" observational or protocol statements on which we can ground our knowledge claims means that we must revise our conception of empirical knowledge.[16] Instead of saying that a theory or putative generalization is "refuted" by the facts, we should now come to say that what we have is an inconsistency between a statement based on a particular theory and another statement that, given the conventions of our language and the particular observations we have made, we also accept. The question then becomes, what are we to do in the face of this inconsistency? We could change our theory and so make the "theoretical" statement consistent with the "observational" statement, or we could alter the theoretical assumptions underlying our "observational" statement, and so change the observational statement to make it cohere with the "theoretical" statement. The problem is to determine what standards should govern these theoretical adjustments.

I do not have the space to develop even the outlines of an adequate treatment of this topic here, so what I shall do is to propose the two criteria that Lakatos develops. His first criterion is that only those theoretical adjustments are admissible which increase the empirical content of our theories. Whether we decide to make adjustments in the particular theory under investigation or in the theories which underlie our observation statements, only those adjustments should be made which enable us to explain hitherto unexplained and (hopefully even) unexpected facts. And until some such adjustment is found, we reject neither the theory, nor the observation statement, for all of our theories are born into an "ocean of anomalies" and if we allowed every disconfirming instance to destroy our theories, we should never have any theories, nor any scientific progress either.

This criterion alone is inadequate, however, for it would permit adjustments to be made in our theories which would not advance the scientific enterprise at all. In particular, it would not prevent the "growth" of scientific knowledge by the agglomeration of unrelated hypotheses, so that the "theory" constructed from the conjunction of two totally unrelated theories would be considered a progressive development. But that would be completely contrary to the purpose of *science* as an organized, coherent body of knowledge. In order to prevent such theoretical adjustments Lakatos proposes an additional criterion: that changes in a theory be made only in accordance with the underlying "research program" of which the theory is a part. A research program, according to Lakatos, defines the basic conceptual structure and fundamental principles in terms of which theories may be constructed. Given a research program, we can determine whether a particular alteration in a theory is *ad hoc*, since we can see whether the proposed change is expressed in terms of the basic conceptualization of the subject-matter which the research program presents. Moreover, a research program enables us to judge whether a particular theoretical adjustment increases the empirical content of a theory, for this judgment can be made only against the background of a single conceptual framework. Finally, the research program not only structures research and theory building, but it also provides a rationale for not abandoning a theory in the face of well-confirmed empirical evidence which is inconsistent with it, since we are no longer concerned about any particular theory, but with the series of theories which a research program generates. And so, if the research program has demonstrated its heuristic power, we can be confident that we will be able to account for the anomalous findings without abandoning the program itself.

It follows from this argument that the basic conceptualization of a field which a research program or paradigm[17] represents is not simply a heuristic construct which may facilitate the advance of knowledge, but which has no place in what is called the "context of justification." On the contrary, research programs become the fundamental "unit" of scientific work, a presupposition of any process of theory testing or explanation at all. Far from inhabiting the context of discovery, they are part of the logic of justification in empirical inquiry. Hence, to the extent that political philosophers articulate basic conceptualizations of the individual and society which can serve as research programs in political and social inquiry, political philosophy is continuous with political science, and not a sharply distinguished "meta" activity.

At this point one might object that the "theories" which political philosophers offer (or which can be constructed using the conceptualizations of the individual and society they develop) have little in common with the kinds of theories which are developed in accordance with research programs in the natural sciences. Political theories, it could be argued, are either normative or interpretative: they either make prescriptions about desirable political arrangements, or they interpret the political practices of a particular society. In neither case do they enable us to explain or predict facts in the way that theories in the natural sciences do. How are we to test the empirical content of Plato's "theory" of justice, or Hegel's interpretation of the modern state? Since a normative theory is intended to be critical, it cannot be tested against the "facts," while an interpretative theory, by providing an account of the meanings of a particular set of practices or forms of life, cannot be tested in terms of the predictions it makes in the way that natural science theories are tested. In either case, the methodology of scientific research programs is inapplicable to political and social theories, and so the alleged continuity between political philosophy and political science is shown to be baseless.

The mistake underlying this objection is the tacit supposition that all political and social phenomena are intentional, and so can only be understood in terms of the meanings they express, or perhaps evaluated in terms of some set of standards. There are, however, social phenomena which can and must be explained in what might be called a "quasi-causal" or a "quasi-nomological" manner. Such phenomena include the unintended consequences of intentional action, recurrent features of social structures, patterns of political instability or violence, or the progress of arms races. Large-scale social and institutional change, particularly as this involves changes in a society's fundamental self-understandings, may also require quasi-nomological explanation. Because these phenomena are not the intended results of anyone's actions, they obviously cannot be explained in terms of the meanings they express—at least not without committing oneself to a rather extreme form of idealism. In the next section I will outline a theory which provides quasi-nomological explanations, but familiar examples of such theories include Plato's account of a pattern of social change in the *Republic*, Aristotle's celebrated analysis of revolution in the *Politics*, or Rousseau's explanation of the transition from the advanced state of "nature" to the state of "civil society" in Part 2 of the *Second Discourse*. In all of these cases, a particular pattern of social or political phenomena is explained by showing how some social conditions provide a reason for action on the part of certain actors, whose actions alter the situation in a determinate way, thereby creating an occasion for action on the part of other actors—the chain being continued until the pattern has been accounted for. The motivational assumptions, or the generalizations linking conditions and actions, are provided by the basic conception of the person that the philosopher adopts. And because these accounts are not offered simply as interpretations of the actions of a particular, identifiable group of people, but are generalized over a potentially unrestricted class of instances, the explanations in question are quasi-nomological and not simply interpretative.

3. The Hobbesian Conceptualization of the Individual and Society

In the preceding sections of this paper I have offered one kind of justification for my view of political philosophy, a justification that consists in showing how this view can be used to meet the difficulties which plague alternative conceptions. If we conceive of political philosophy as involving the articulation of fundamental conceptualizations of what it is to be a person, we can recognize that some of the ideas of political philosophers are contextually bound by the self-understandings of their own societies, but we can also recognize the ways in which their arguments can transcend the situations of their utterance. To the extent that political philosophers reflect upon and interpret the self-understandings of their own societies, the questions they ask and the answers they give are likely to be specific to their own situations. But because all societies face a common human condition, an interpretation of the self-understandings of one society may have important implications for another. Moreover, and perhaps more important, political philosophers may go beyond providing interpretative accounts of a particular form of life by offering conceptualizations which can provide the frameworks for theories of politics. These theories, in turn, can be used to criticize or justify particular practices or institutions. Finally, this view of political philosophy does not exclude a concern with methodological issues, with "meta-politics," but it shows how political philosophy goes beyond second-order "talk about talk" and raises first-order questions regarding political life. In the rest of this chapter I will try to add to the verisimilitude of the ideas I have been developing by showing how they can be applied to the political thought of Hobbes, and to the tradition of political inquiry that he "launched." I will first outline Hobbes's conception of a person and show how he uses it to demonstrate that conflict or war is inevitable outside of political society. I will then briefly present a modern version of Hobbes's conceptualization, and show how it is used to develop theories of political processes that Hobbes could never have imagined.

3.1 Hobbes

Hobbes begins the *Leviathan* by setting out his conception of a person and its philosophical presuppositions.[18] He posits a thorough-going materialism: everything is but matter in motion. Sensation, e.g., is only motion within the brain (and heart) caused by the "pressure" exerted by external objects upon the body. Thought, imagination, and memory, similarly, are "nothing but decaying sense," the continued motions of previous sensory experience, and a train of thoughts is simply the succession of motions inside one's brain which was, at one time or another, a series of motions that were produced by our senses. A train of thoughts, however, can be guided or "regulated by some desire, and designs." (p.9) From our desire for something "ariseth Thought of some means we have seen produce the like of that which we ayme at; and from the thought of that, the thought of means to that mean; and so continually, till we come to some beginning within our own power." (p.9) Hence, we can come to find the causes and effects of things even without the use of speech! Moreover, people can be said to be "rational" in the sense that they can discover the means to the ends they seek. This conception of reason as instrumental rationality is central to Hobbes's view of the person.

Having described the structure of this marvelous, human

machine, Hobbes must now show us how it runs. Voluntary bodily motion begins with the imagination:

And because *going, speaking,* and the like Voluntary motions, depend always upon a precedent thought of *whither, which way,* and *what;* it is evident, that the Imagination is the first internal beginning of all Voluntary Motion. (p.23)

Hobbes calls the motions of the imagination "endeavor," and points out that endeavor may be toward some object, in which case it is called appetite or desire, or away from some object, in which case it is called aversion. Some appetites and aversions, Hobbes continues, "are born with men," and others we acquire through experience as we come to associate some objects with our original desires. But since

...the constitution of man's Body, is in continual mutation; it is impossible that all the same things should always cause in him the same Appetites, and Aversions: much lesse can all men consent, in the Desire of almost any one and the same Object. (p.24)

This is a fundamental aspect of Hobbes's conception of the person: all people share the same passions—they are motivated by the same kinds of causes, but the particular objects they seek vary from person to person and from time to time. Hence, to explain how people act we must develop a way of classifying and describing their passions such that determinate statements can be made about human behavior without making reference to the specific objects particular individuals seek.

When a person is subject to more than one desire, the resulting successions of conflicting passions is called "deliberation." The action one actually performs under these circumstances will be that one which the individual believes will realize the greatest good, that is, the greatest satisfaction of his or her appetites or desires. In this way Hobbes applies the concept of reason as instrumental rationality which he developed in an epistemological context to the sphere of action.

The last feature of Hobbes's conception is really just a corollary of what has gone before. Given that our actions are caused by our passions—our appetites and aversions—and given that the passions are continuously being excited by the action of the environment on us, it follows that "there is no...utmost ayme nor...greatest Good" of a person. On the contrary, felicity in this life can be nothing more than "Continual successe in obtaining those things which a man from time to time desireth, that is to say, continually prospering...." (p.29) To be alive means to have desires and so to be continuously striving to satisfy them. The good of a person, then, can be nothing but uninterrupted success in satisfying the desires one happens to have.

On these simple principles Hobbes is able to erect an entire theory of political and social life. I will mention only one part of his theory: his demonstration that the state of nature is a state of war. His argument begins with the conception of felicity that I have just presented. If the good of a person consists in constantly getting what one wants, then one will strive to satisfy not only the desires one has at a certain moment, "but to assure forever, the way of his future desire." (p.47) This follows from the fact that we are continually subject to the development of new desires, and from the fact that we are rational beings in the sense that we can see, and act in accordance with, what is required in order to achieve the maximum satisfaction of our wants. And this striving means that everyone must constantly be trying to increase his or her power— "his present means, to obtain some future apparent Good...." (p.41)

And the cause of this, is not always that a man hopes for a more intensive delight, than he has already attained to; or that he cannot be content with a moderate power: but because he cannot assure the power and means to live well, which he hath present, without the acquisition of more. (p.47)

The basic sources of power which an individual can try to control are wealth and reputation, for these can be used to obtain what one wants, or to enlist the aid of others in attaining it. Hence, people will inevitably find themselves in a state of competition and conflict, since both riches and reputation are scarce commodities. And since all are approximately equal, according to Hobbes, they can all entertain the hope of attaining their ends, and so this conflict is transformed into war:

...there is no way for any man to secure himselfe, so reasonable, as Anticipation; that is, by force, or wiles, to master the persons of all men he can, so long, till he sees no other power great enough to endanger him: And this is no more than his own conservation requireth.... (p.61)

People are brought to engage each other for gain, for safety, and for reputation, and these causes of quarrel are inherent in their very being.

3.2 Hobbes Today: The Rational Choice Research Program

Modern political and social scientists differ from Hobbes in not founding their conceptions of the individual and society on basic metaphysical and epistemological theories, but many do accept Hobbes's basic model. Although they show little interest in reducing human action to the behavior of particles of matter in motion, they agree with Hobbes in attempting to reduce all social phenomena to the actions of atomistic individuals each pursuing his or her own private goals. Like Hobbes, they recognize that the specific objects that different individuals pursue will differ, and so they strive to explain behavior by making generalized assumptions about the kinds of wants or preferences individuals have. Finally, like Hobbes, they conceive of people as having a capacity for instrumental rationality, a capacity to calculate the most efficacious or efficient means to their goals, but not as capable of recognizing and respecting principles in their conduct.

Anthony Downs's *Economic Theory of Democracy* may be the most widely known work in political science that is based on the conception of the person as a calculating, self-regarding, want-satisfying animal. Downs recognizes and clearly affirms each of these elements of the Hobbesian conceptualization of the person. Indeed he begins his study by noting that most previous attempts (at least by economists) to develop a theory of government action have been deficient precisely because they have violated these basic presuppositions:

...most welfare economists and many public finance theorists implicitly assume that the "proper" function of government is to maximize social welfare. Insofar as they face the problem of government decision-making at all, they nearly all subscribe to some approximation of this normative rule.

But, Downs goes on to argue,

Even if social welfare could be defined, and methods of maximizing it could be agreed upon, what reason is there to believe that the men who run the government would be motivated to maximize it? To state that they "should" do so does not mean that they will.

What this amounts to, Downs continues, is that economists

do not really treat the government as part of the division of labor. [For] every...agent in the division of labor carries out his social functon primarily as a means of attaining his own private ends: the enjoyment of income, prestige, or power.

Finally, a few paragraphs later Downs adds, "Every agent...behaves rationally at all times; that is: it proceeds towards its goals with a minimal use of scarce resources...."[19]

In the space of a couple of pages, then, Downs accepts the basic elements of the Hobbesian model—even down to the assumption that the ends of human action can be summed up as "income, prestige, and power" or, to use Hobbes's terms, "gain, safety, and reputation." Like Hobbes, Downs sets out to account for social phenomena by explaining them in terms of the actions of individuals each out to achieve his or her own private ends. Like Hobbes, Downs recognizes that the particular desires of different individuals will differ, and so he sets out to explain their actions by making general assumptions about the kinds of desires they have. Finally, Downs specifically rejects the idea that people might act in accordance with general rules or principles, and insists that they act only to maximize the satisfaction of their own self-regarding wants. So familiar have these ideas become that Downs does not even have to present a serious argument for them, but can invoke them almost as self-evident truths. And he can do so, of course, since they have comprised one of the most widely accepted research programs in the social sciences at least since Bentham, and whose first exponent was Hobbes.

On the basis of this framework Downs proceeds to develop a theory of government behavior by adding a number of particular assumptions characterizing the institutional framework of a democratic government. He does not try to show the conditions under which democratic government will exist, or that such governments are the most desirable. Rather, assuming that parties are motivated "to attain the income, power, and prestige of being in office," and that each citizen views "elections strictly as means of selecting the government most beneficial to him," Downs sets out to explain the kinds of policies a government will follow, the conditions under which ideologies will develop, the conditions under which parties will agree on their programs, patterns of the political activity of citizens, and so forth.

Because Downs presupposes an institutional framework that is very different from anything in Hobbes's experience or imagination, and because Downs does not attempt to explain the framework itself, the theories that Downs and Hobbes offer appear to have very little in common. Nonetheless, because their theories are based on the same conceptualization of the person and society, they can be seen as belonging to the same intellectual tradition. And because they are related in this way, we can learn from Hobbes's solution to his own problems, and from the criticisms to which Hobbes's views have been subjected. If, for example, Hobbes's model is fundamentally incoherent, or if it is only a partial, one-sided account, applicable only to those social contexts (such as a market economy) in which people see themselves in instrumental terms, then these limitations or criticisms should apply to contemporary theories erected on Hobbesian presuppositions. No doubt, as Skinner argues, we have to do our own thinking for ourselves. But we are in the fortunate position of being heirs to a number of intellectual traditions from which our thinking may begin. We need not hope, nor even have a use for "timeless truths," but political philosophy can help us achieve a deeper and more enlightened self-understanding. Far from being limited to the specific contexts in which they are written, or confined to dealing with "second-order questions," with talk about talk, the works of political philosophy are integral to the study of politics.

Fourteen

Human Nature and Forms of Government: The Case of Original Sin

Samuel DuBois Cook

Conceptions of human nature, whether moral or psychological, seem always to influence men's thinking about the organization, uses, and process of political power. "All theories of politics," Benjamin F. Wright observes, "are based upon a set of presuppositions concerning the nature of man."[1] Merle Curti asserts that one's "concept of human nature is closely related to his social attitudes and his world-view, and to the decisions he makes in his day by day activities."[2] And Mulford Sibley, whose study of political ideas and ideologies lends some support to these claims, makes a conception of human nature central to his own political views in *Nature and Civilization*.[3]

But the degree and the manner in which doctrines of human nature influence political thought and behavior is an issue on which there are wide and sharp divergences. Are views of the nature of man decisive, for example, in the determination of fundamental choices like the form or system of political order? This is the basic question to which this inquiry is addressed. Gooch voices a widely held position when he observes that,

Our political views are determined in the last resort by the estimate we have of human nature. Those who think meanly of it naturally cry aloud for autocracy and the strong hand. Those who think highly of it inevitably desire the maximum of self-determination and self-realization and a minimum of constraint.[4]

In terms of the history of ideas, the identification of "optimistic" or "honorific" beliefs about man with democracy and "pessimistic" or "cynical" beliefs about him with authoritarianism is not, of course, without warrant, as Hobbes and Luther, on the one hand, and Rousseau and Locke, on the other, make clear.

205

But it is a curious fact that men who hold a common view of human nature sometimes arrive at opposing political and social positions, e.g., Aquinas and Maritain; while men who hold to different views of human nature sometimes arrive at a similar political and social position, e.g., John Dewey and Reinhold Niebuhr. This suggests that perhaps there is no necessary relationship, no one-to-one correspondence, between conceptions of human nature and forms of government.

Original sin is a psychological and moral along with a religious approach to the human condition. Perhaps, then, an inquiry into some selected political theories based on that framework may illuminate the problem of the relation of conceptions of human nature to rival systems of political order. Original sin is, indeed, a complicated doctrine of multiple meanings.[5] But whether interpreted ontologically, biologically, symbolically, essentially, institutionally or otherwise, it seems to possess a generic meaning. That core of meaning, expressed in one way or another, suggests an inherited or inevitable corruption, bias toward evil, an enslaved or morally defective will, a depraved self. Moral affliction or depravity is found in the essence of the self. Running through various formulations of original sin is a thread of emphasis on man's self-centeredness, self-love (*superbia*), pride (*hubris*), and pretensions which are said to disclose the moral defects, infirmities, and limitations of the human fabric. Accordingly, man is caught up in the grip and prison of self-love. Perspectives of original sin stress, in varying degrees and forms, not only man's estrangement from God but also his constant rebellion against God and his cosmic imperialism in trying to usurp the place of God. Generally speaking, the social dimension of the universality of sin is, according to its interpreters, the will to pride and power, collective self-worship, egocentricity, and the inclination to injustice, exploitation, domination, and other corporate evils. In spite of all the differences among exponents of this doctrine, therefore, it seems to possess a certain unified kernel of meaning.

The purpose of this paper is threefold. First, it seeks to show that belief in original sin, as Protestant thinkers have conceived of original sin, does not dictate a single political preference but is compatible with any one of three possible positions — authoritarianism, democracy, or neutrality with respect to the form of government.[6] Second, this paper attempts to probe the question of why belief in original sin is logically neutral to the form of government. Finally, it seeks, by implication at least, to shed a measure of light on the broader question of conceptions of human nature in relation to social and political attitudes and choices.

I have selected belief in orginal sin as a standpoint from which to test the validity of the widely held view that conceptions of human nature are decisive in the determination of the form of government for three reasons. It is a moral and psychological as well as a religious doctrine and thus has inclusive bearing and implication. Original sin, moreover, clearly falls within the category of thought of which Gooch's observation quoted above typifies. Also, original sin is more than one of the master ideas and recurrent themes of Western history; it has wide currency today. For a variety of reasons, this conceptual scheme has been a leading principle for the interpretation of contemporary life and culture since Karl Barth detonated his theological bomb in the wake of World War I. And the influence of neo-Reformation thought is by no means limited to theological and religious systems of value and meaning; Niebuhr and Tillich in particular have a wide secular following.

A critic may well argue that original sin is too ambiguous a doctrine to evaluate the thesis that there is a necessary relation between ideas of human nature and various systems of governance. That the anthropology of original sin contains ambiguities and other perplexities cannot be gainsaid. But no account of human nature is exempt from these perils for conceptual analysis. Consider, for example, hedonism, conceptions of man as a rational or social being, or constructions of human nature as mutable or as immutable. In all these, the same difficulties that beset a consideration of original sin are encountered. In fact, inherent in the very notion of human nature itself are ambiguities and related problems of analysis. Thus, there is no compelling objection to the selection of belief in original sin as the frame of reference. For if alternative approaches offer similar problems from which there is no escape, these problems cannot be any more a ground on which to exclude original sin than to exclude any other formulation.

In any event, this paper, while dealing with a broad and perennial problem, moves within quite narrow limits. Its purpose is preliminary and suggestive rather than final and exhaustive. Of necessity, my treatment both of schools of thought and of representative thinkers will be brief, sketchy, and to a degree, superficial.

Original Sin and Anti-Democratic Thought

Historically, doctrines of original sin have fostered and nourished a fundamental distrust of democracy. More than this,

they have spawned absolutist as well as other anti-democratic
political philosophies. Interpreting the human estate in terms of an
afflicted predicament—bondage to selfishness, pride, and greed—
orthodox Protestant thinkers had little difficulty denying the
capacity of democracy to maintain order, peace, and justice; and
asserting the efficacy of authoritarian regimes to curb sinners and
punish evil-doers. Government was conceived almost exclusively as
a dyke against the flood of egoism of citizens, individually and
collectively. Orthodox Protestantism, both Calvinistic and
Lutheran, Niebuhr notes, "gave government and the principle of
order an absolute preference over rebellion and political chaos.... It
tended to ally the Christian church too uncritically with the centers
of power in political life and tempted it to forget that government is
frequently the primary source of injustice and oppressison."[7]

Like Augustine, who knew the psychology of power and the
consequent greed, pride, and temptations of the rulers of *civitas
terrena,* Luther sanctioned monarchy, and, again like Augustine,
Luther offered no institutional means by which citizens could check
the power of rulers.[8] Still worse, in spite of his intense commitment
to religious freedom and individualism, Luther's involvement in
historic controversy led him to provide a weighty transcendent
justification of political interference and coercion in the realm of
opinion and belief, including the privacy of conscience.[9] The prince,
he held, ought to have the power and right to restrain and punish
"sinners" everywhere. This is, of course, the ground on which rests
the linkage of Luther with absolutism.

True, there is another side of Luther. He insisted on normative
limitations of political power, such as Biblical authority, the law of
nature, and the welfare of the community. This facet of his thought,
along with the doctrines of the "priesthood of all believers" and the
right of private judgment, is the source of the association of Luther
with the genesis of modern democracy.[10] So long as this view is
restricted to the exoneration of Luther from the charge of consistent
absolutism, it is not without merit. But political absolutism is not
the only alternative to democracy. And while there are elements in
Luther's thought congenial to democracy, it does not follow that we
are justified in identifying him with the sunrise of the modern
democratic state. Even A.D. Lindsay, who has waxed eloquent on
the democratic bearings of the idea of the spiritual priesthood of all
believers, observed that "Luther taught a doctrine of the relation
between Church and State which has made Lutheranism either
completely indifferent to forms of government or definitely anti-
democratic."[11]

Calvin's political thought is more ambivalent than Luther's. Beyond his normative limitations of political power was his important distinction between the authority of office and the office-holder, as well as the doctrine of the "elect," and passive resistance to civil authorities. In the hands of neo-Calvinists, there is a measure of evidence for associating the Calvinist tradition with the emergence of modern democracy.[12] Even so, it is perilous and misleading to identify Calvin himself with democracy, as indeed it is to make any simple and easy historical association between neo-Calvinists and democracy. The evidence is ambiguous. Recent discussions, particularly those issuing from neo-Calvinists, tend to exaggerate the differences between Luther and Calvin on human nature and the process of government.[13] In addition—and apart from the basic problem of the criteria, interpretation, and application of Calvin's normative considerations—there were no institutional safeguards against the tyranny of power of which Calvin's own Genevan experiment is a grim and haunting reminder. In fact, the hazards of arbitrary and irresponsible power were aggravated and heightened by the claim that he and his little oligarchy had special contact with a transcendent and ultimate norm and reality. Baffling indeed is the attempt today in certain quarters to make democrats of Luther and Calvin. As Walter Rauschenbush observed, "Neither Luther nor Calvin was by nature or conviction a democrat."[14]

The anti-democratic tendencies of Protestant political theories based on a belief in original sin persisted, I believe, in the American political tradition. Two frames of reference are relevant here: the Puritans and the "Founding Fathers."

Democracy and the Puritan Tradition. Original sin, all agree, was dear to the heart of Puritans.[15] And much has been written about democracy and Puritanism.[16] The Puritan heritage, it should be emphasized, is not one; it is many, varied, and complex. Yet numerous writers give Puritanism a great deal of credit for the advent of American democracy. F. Ernest Johnson expresses a typical view:

Interestingly enough, among the Puritans the notion that all men are sinners, that they are in a "fallen" state, supported democratic ideas by enabling the Puritan to insist that, since every man is a sinner, none was good enough to lord it over any other man. Macaulay in his *Essay on Milton* said that the Puritan "groveled in dust before his Maker, but he set his foot upon the neck of his king."[17]

There is some warrant for the claim that some forms of the Puritan communion, along with a few individual Puritans, contributed to the origin, growth, and development of democracy. Particularly significant were the conceptions of ecclesiastical polity, the sovereignty of God, and individual salvation. Perhaps in some situations these ideas and practices made a contribution, if only indirectly, to the evolution of democratic institutions. But, for several reasons, the ground is insufficient to connect democracy and original sin via Puritanism. That entails the master assumption that Puritanism itself was democratic. At best, this assumption contains only a small fragment of validity.

Consider first the internal structure and practices of Puritan church bodies. Some writers stress the alleged democratic character of these congregations, a quality, it is held, that flowed into the political stream so that a democratic church helped to beget a democratic state and society. There is a modicum of truth in that argument. But Puritan ecclesiastical structures, like its theology, often were authoritarian. Ecclesiastical autocracy flourished.[18] It took two forms: the local congregations themselves and the power exercised and attempted by key religious groups and leading clergymen. With respect to the first of these, it is fallacious to assume that the mere investiture of power and authority in local congregations guaranteed democracy. Religious authoritarianism is not limited to a centralized and hierarchical church. Local ecclesiastical bodies, like political institutions, may be tyrannical. Owing to their strategic position, many Puritan ministers and elders exercised unlimited and irresponsible power.[19] A fundamental distrust of "the people" characterized religious as well as secular society in colonial America. Indeed, the Puritan theocracy was largely responsible. For not only did it control the reins of power; it also provided divine sanction for it.[20]

The second form of ecclesiastical authoritarianism lay in the power wielded and sought by clergymen and associations outside the local congregations. According to the original form and motive of congregationalism, the power of local bodies—formed by a covenant—was independent and autonomous and therefore not responsible to outside organs—the presbytery, synod, convention, association, episcopacy, etc. In principle, independency reigned. But the practice was otherwise. "Although the congregational form of church organization was inherently democratic, the divines of the first generation were able to stifle this local democracy in favor of central control."[21] Even in the waning years of the Puritan theocracy, when it had lost control of other roads to power, the leading divines made a final attempt to entrench their control over local churches.[22] For these reasons, then, it is largely misleading to speak of "church democracy" under the Puritans.

A second objection to the contention that the Puritans were generally democratic is more obvious. As is well known, the Puritans engaged in practices hardly compatible with the spirit of democracy: they were generally intolerant; they persecuted Baptists, Quakers, Catholics, and other dissenters from the established creed; moral regimentation and censorship were common; and, in many instances, they made political participation, including the right to vote, dependent upon membership in the "right" church.

Finally, and most important, it is clear that Puritan political theories and practices were, with few exceptions, authoritarian.[23] Of the Puritan divines, Cotton and Winthrop are representative. They were intensely and unabashedly anti-democratic. In the following passage, John Cotton lucidly voices the substance of Puritan political theory.

It is better that the commonwealth be fashioned to the setting forth of God's house, which is his church: than to accommodate the church frame to the civil state. Democracy, I do not conceive that ever God did ordain as a fit government either for church or commonwealth. If the people be governors, who shall be governed? As for monarchy, and aristocracy, they are both of them clearly approved, and directed in scripture, yet so as referreth the sovereignty to himself, and setteth up Theocracy in both, as the best form of government in the commonwealth, as well as in the church.[24]

The overriding meaning and implication of all this are not far to seek. Democracy was repudiated in terms of the will of God and Biblical history. But authoritarian power is always more offensive, dangerous, and insensitive when it is exercised in the name of God, some other high order of reality, or the absolute truth. For it then brooks no criticism, no challenge, and no external correction. The Puritan divines sometimes identified the Kingdom of God with their own will-to-power and love of God, goodness, and righteousness.

In the light of the foregoing observations, then, we are justified in denying the claim that Puritanism was, for all its possibilities, the historic bearer of democracy. With rare exceptions, the Puritans were ecclesiastically, theologically, and politically, overwhelmingly authoritarian. Puritanism cannot be used as a leaven for uniting democracy and original sin.

The Founding Fathers. In an effort to link doctrines of original sin and American democracy, some writers appeal to the moral, psychological, and religious beliefs of the architects of the Constitution.[25] Perhaps this appeal is plausible. Decades ago, the perceptive James Bryce asserted that a "hearty Puritanism" informs the Constitution of 1787, and that it was framed by believers in original sin.[26] Doubltess the framers, or at least most of them, had a firm grasp of the evil possibilities of human nature and the consequent perils of unchecked and arbitrary power, especially when the "power structure" is in the hands of certain individuals and classes. Even so, the main contention, connecting the history of American democracy with original sin, is unconvincing. Two objections stand out.

First, in the light of the Constitution itself, our very fragmentary knowledge of the moral, religious, psychological, and political ideas of the framers, and the special historical conditions out of which the document was born, the extent to which the "Founding Fathers" were guided by belief in original sin is an open question. Uncertainty lurks here. Authorities differ. All sorts of conflicting religious and moral ideas have been attributed to the authors of the Constitution. They have been labeled free-thinkers, deists, theists, atheists, agnostics, scholastics, etc.[27] In particular, there are diametrically opposed views concerning the doctrine of man to which the Constitutional formulators ascribed. In a recent inquiry into their religious and moral ideas, one writer, representing a typical approach, concludes that they "believed in the natural goodness of man and in the capacity of the human to build tall edifices of nobility and decency."[28] Opposed to this view, Hofstadter echoes Bryce. The Constitutional framers, he insists, "had a vivid Calvinistic sense of human evil and damnation and believed with Hobbes that men are selfish and contentious."[29] Of these differences of opinion, no conclusive answer can be given because of the absence of sufficient information. Building on the fragmentary deposits of data, however, I am inclined toward the latter view.[30] *The Federalist* is a major clue.

In any event, the attitude of the "Fathers" to democracy is much clearer and nearer to sight than are their views of the nature of man. And their views on democracy loom with significance. For even if it were demonstrated conclusively that they, all of them, were committed to belief in original sin, it would still be necessary, if the two concepts are to be joined, to establish their espousal of democracy.

Now, whether the "Fathers" were essentially friends or foes of democracy is, of course, an issue of endless debate.[31] Deep is the disagreement. Different minds, looking at the same facts, often arrive at opposing inferences and meanings. The evidence is mixed. There is no clear-cut and conclusive answer. The fact that each commentator is a bearer of preconceptions and values adds fuel to the flame. All the same, while neither side can be conclusive, the weight of evidence does not seem to be equally distributed.

Proponents of the view that the "Fathers" were primarily anti-democratic usually point to such things as the Electoral College, the initial method of selecting Senators, equal representation of states in the Senate regardless of population, perpetuation through silence of various restrictions upon suffrage, the difficulty of the amending process, and the sanctioning of the institution of slavery. To these, some add the power of judicial review.

True, the argument continues, the members of the Constitutional Convention meant for at least one organ of government to be responsive to public desires and pressures: the House of Representatives. But consider both the then existing limitations upon suffrage and the superior power and status given to the Senate. For these and other reasons, I agree with those who argue that the "Fathers" desired to stem the tide of democracy and to perpetuate oligarchy.

Significantly, Hofstadter relates the anti-democratic sentiments of the "Fathers" to their particular interpretation of human nature. He suggests that their commitment to the anthropology of original sin affected them in the same manner in which it did the political philosophy of their ideological forerunners: distrust of the "common man." Throughout "the secret discussions at the Constitutional Conveniton," Hofstadter holds, "it was clear that this distrust of man was first and foremost a distrust of the common man and democratic rule."[32] This indicates that the authors of the American Constitution were the offspring of the anti-democratic lineage of doctrines of original sin. As with Augustine, Luther, and Calvin, for all their differences, the overriding object of distrust was not *man,* but *some* men, not power in the hands of all persons and groups, but power in the hands of specified individuals and groups. The basic distrust of power found expression not in universalism but in particularism. It was not so much the "classes," men of wealth, status, "culture," and birth, but the "masses," the common people, the multitude. Key sections of *The Federalist* will demonstrate the point.

Conclusion. In terms of the broad perspective of history, exponents of original sin have been foes, not friends, of democracy. They have been "partisans" of various anti-democratic ways of governing. Their main object of distrust was the "masses," the so-called common or average man rather than certain other wielders of political power. To be sure, they insisted that "all men are sinners." But this proposition was not construed to mean that no man or group is wise or good enough to rule others without their consent. On the contrary, original sin was interpreted to give special sanction to particular oligarchies over against the general population. So, in many instances, instead of belief in original sin countenancing institutional humility through checks upon the exercise of power, believers in the doctrine virtually identified those who controlled the reins of government with the divine order of creation. Thus anti-democratic principles and practices became an article of faith, a divine imperative. Even when particular kings and monarchs were denounced, the principles on which their power rested were not.

Thus, the growing conviction in certain quarters today that belief in original sin or "pessimism" about the human fabric is essential to democracy is, from the perspective of the history of ideas, strange music. For, historically, political theories cut from the cloth of original sin were authoritarian. Glorifying order *qua* order, exponents of this doctrine looked upon the multitude as a source of disorder and chaos and consequently were not to be entrusted with the "decision-making" process. They tended to identify the principle of order with a particular kind of order—authoritarianism or at least some small, narrow, oligarchic ruling class. And this was compounded and cushioned by the theory of the divine ordination of government that buttressed anti-democratic political systems by alleged eternal and transcendent sanctions. Thus, in terms of the structure and process of power and social control, doctrines of original sin have spawned *selective* perceptions and applications. They bred distrust only of some men of power. By the same token, inordinate faith was placed in other men of power, particular classes were assumed to have special wisdom and virtue in the exercise of power. Accordingly, particular governing classes or specific individuals, within the interpretive framework of doctrines of original sin, were given monopolistic, arbitrary, and irresponsible power.

Today, however, we are counseled by certain thinkers that belief in original sin or its secular equivalent is indispensable to the justification and preservation of democracy. This is strange music. History echoes the opposite. "The new partisans of original sin tell us that pessimism about human nature will prevent the placing of too much power in the hands of a few leaders; but in the eighteenth and nineteenth centuries, it was usually pessimism about human nature that was used to justify keeping power in the hands of a few."[33] The New Conservatism and its ideological, intellectual, and spiritual ancestors are a classic example of this historical paradox and conceptual reversal of meaning.[34]

Original Sin and Political Neutralism

Ideas, like culture and civilization, rise and fall. They bloom and wither. Belief in original sin was largely eroded under the impact of modern culture. Theological liberalism flourished. It was in the ascendancy during much of the nineteenth, as well as the early decades of the twentieth century. The fortunes of different schools of theology have waxed and waned with the fortunes and tenets of modern culture. Thus the lot and influence of theological liberalism have declined rapidly and those of "neo-Reformation" theology have increased at a swift pace. "Neo-orthodoxy," wrote Dean Sperry, "is the theological fashion of the day."[35] Within Protestantism today, the most influential theologians, in varying degrees and emphases, derive much of their inspiration and content from the Reformers themselves, particularly Luther. In their view, they are seeking to rediscover the "pure gold" of the Reformation which, they insist, has been evaporated by the attempt to cast "Biblical faith" in the mold of modern culture.

Since World War I, and for a variety of reasons, Protestant "neo-orthodox" theology has resurrected original sin and elevated it into one of the most influential perspectives for the interpretation of contemporary life and culture. Indeed, one of the primary motives of this frame of reference is to demonstrate the relevance and compelling significance of the ancient theme of *man as sinner* to the plight of contemporary human existence. Emphasizing man's pride, self-centeredness, self-love, and flattering image of himself, this school has touched, in one way and degree or another, virtually every sector of human thought. It has not ignored political theory. In this section, I propose to show how and why three leading and typical Protestant theologians (Karl Barth, Emil Brunner, and Paul Tillich) deny that there is one best political system. For all three, of course, the universality of human sinfulness is a master article of their theological formulations.

Karl Barth has been called the greatest Protestant thinker since Schleiermacher. His treatment of political and social issues is minimal. This, in itself, drips with meaning and significance. Its deeper meaning is his profound attachment to the Pauline tradition of submission to the "powers that be." (Barth, of course, vigorously opposed Hitler.) Undergirding this doctrine of uncritical obedience to political power and authority is the notion of the divine ordination of government.

The substance of Barth's political theory is indifference to forms of government, so long as particular governments abstain from interference with the freedom of the Church to preach the

Word—justification by faith, etc.[36] True, there have been at least two occasions on which Barth suggested an affinity between democracy and the New Testament.[37] All the same, his consistent emphasis and basic theological commitment are neutrality to alternative political systems. Since Christianity has no particular doctrine of the just state, he holds, the Christian community "will beware of playing off one political concept—even the 'democratic' concept—as the Christian concept."[38] Against those who insist that democracy is rooted in Christianity or that the democratic state is closest to the Christian view, Barth's rejoinder is that "such a State may equally well assume the form of a monarchy or aristocracy, or occasionally that of a dictatorship."[39]

Barth's political neutralism is anchored in two related assumptions: Lutheran dualism and human depravity. The legacy of Lutheran dualism in his thought prompts a sharp separation between the realm of grace and the realm of culture. The former is maximized, the latter minimized. Culture is evaluated in terms of grace. In consequence, the criterion of a good or just state is almost solely whether or not it permits the church the freedom to exercise its priestly function. Hitler's cardinal sin, then, was not his dictatorship, according to Barth, but rather his unforgivable interference with the life of the church.[40] This position is typical of Lutheranism, particularly in Germany.[41] Moreover, so great is Barth's emphasis on the ultimate religious perspective, the yawning and endless gulf between God and man, and the sinful character of human history, that he is betrayed into a position of virtually ignoring the qualitative differences between rival political institutions. Failing to come to grips with the gradations of good and evil of which alternative forms of state and government are capable and are likely to embody, Barth is perilously close to insisting on the qualitative equivalence of competing organizations of political power. His only criterion of criticism, discrimination and choice, is religious and ecclesiastical.

In comparison to Barth, Emil Brunner has given systematic and comprehensive consideration to social and political issues. Like Barth, however, he is essentially indifferent to forms of government.[42] In *The Divine Imperative,* this neutrality is expressed in terms of an indeterminate empiricism, according to which there are no a priori principles for the evaluation of rival systems of order.[43] In *Justice and the Social Order,* oddly enough, this indifference to alternative political systems is expressed in terms of an ambiguous formalism, according to which institutional means and power structures are secondary questions.

Brunner offers an imposing exposition of the principles of absolute justice anchored in the divine order of creation. With him, however, the end, justice, is the all-important question: "The question of just or unjust laws and government is more important than the question of democracy or not democracy."[44] Once more, according to Brunner, the form of state is a secondary question, no form of state is a bulwark against totalitarianism, and the source of the sovereignty of the state is a "subordinate, if not unimportant question."[45] But apart from the meaning, criteria, and application of Brunner's philosophy of absolute justice, he, in substance, provides no affirmative direction and institutional means for the realization of a just social order except federalism of which his native Switzerland is the model.

In addition to Brunner's stress on the end of the state, he is neutral to the form of government because of his preoccupation with the need for order. Doubting the ability of democracy to maintain order, Brunner at once echoes the authoritarian bias of the tradition of original sin and buttresses his own indifference to competing systems of governance. The *kind* of order is not for him a major question.[46] If order is possible "in the democratic form," he holds, "so much the better; if it is not possible in that form, then any other form in which it is possible is preferable, even if it were the dictatorship of an individual."[47]

Paul Tillich has been called a "theologian of culture." It is interesting and significant, however, that he does not give ethical primacy to any particular form of political order.[48] He distinguishes between democracy as a system of government and as a way of life—an ethical and religious framework.[49] Minimizing the former, the latter is, he holds, the fundamental principle of political ethics because it predicates the dignity of man. Tillich is not clear on the relation between democracy as a way of life and as a political system. Indeed, he seems to imply tension between them. Democracy as a constitutional principle is desirable, he maintains, only if it works successfully, the criterion of which appears to be the fulfillment of democracy as a way of life.[50] Thus, he concludes, while Christianity must support the democratic way of life, i.e., belief in the value of human personality, it "must not identify itself with any particular form, whether feudalism or bureaucratic patriarchalism or democracy..."[51] But this is a paradox indeed. Is there in principle a better or an equivalent way to protect and fulfill the dignity of man than by the constitutional and institutional safeguards of democracy? After all, they are bulwarks against the tyranny of power. Significantly, Tillich once asserted the impossibility of democracy and the inevitability of oligarchy.[52]

Tillich's political neutralism appears based on his conception of the "Protestant principle." Universal and eternal, this principle is, he holds, a framework for the comprehension, evaluation, integration, and transformation of all historic forms and cultural artifacts, including Protestanism itself.[53] Although the principle is, in his view, creative (in terms of the "Gestalt of grace" which combines protest and formation), it is, above all, a prophetic protest against all historic forms, particularly all alleged absolutisms. Tillich, therefore, stresses the omnipresent gulf and tension between the fragmentary and conditioned character of all human, institutional, and historic realities and the "Unconditioned," God.[54]

The "Protestant principle," then, seems to be the fundamental reason why Tillich asserts that Christianity must not be identified with any particular organization of political power. There is, however, a touch of irony or paradox in this. In the first place, is not democracy a corollary of the "Protestant principle"? Democracy is institutionalized humility. Of all systems of government it alone recognizes that we are all men and not God. Human fallibility and frailty is the cognitive structure on which democracy builds. This is why democracy is largely self-corrective. It is so aware of human finitude and human pretension to infallibility that it contains built-in procedures to accommodate conflicting opinions, changing perspectives, and deeper insights. It prevents certain abuses of power as well as provides curative procedures—including the exposure of errors, folly and human pretensions. Apart from the conditions of its own existence, democracy makes no alleged truth or good normative and absolute. And even here, difference and dissent are not only tolerated but encouraged. In this sense, then, democracy appears to be the political translation of Tillich's own Protestant principle. Democracy nurtures, sustains, and thrives on "protest."

In the second place, Tillich's political neutralism invites some obvious questions. If it is true that no system of political power can claim divine sanction, does it follow that all political systems are equidistant from the "Unconditional"? What of the problem of comparative evaluation and moral risk within the contingencies and uncertainties of existence? Tillich emphasizes the integral linkage of religion (issues of "ultimate concern") and culture. But are not basic political choices, e.g., between democracy and dictatorship, significant for both religion and culture? Since they affect the range and quality of human alternatives, do they not make a difference for the human predicament?

Original Sin and Democracy

Reinhold Niebuhr reverses the main tradition of political theory issuing from the perspective of original sin. Neither authoritarianism nor lack of appreciation of the comparative value of rival political systems characterizes his thought.[55] Largely because of his influence, there is a rapidly growing body of literature which uses, in varying degrees, doctrines of original sin to justify democracy.

Niebuhr links democracy and original sin so intimately that the greater his emphasis on sin, the stronger is his affirmation of democracy.[56] Perhaps more than any other contemporary theologian, he understands the problems, psychology, and processes of power. Luther and Hobbes, he argues, were not realistic enough. "They saw the dangers of anarchy in the egotism of the citizens but failed to perceive the dangers of tyranny in the selfishness of the ruler. Therefore, they obscured the consequent necessity of placing checks upon the ruler's self-will."[57] Irresponsible power, he asserts, aggravates man's inclination to take advantage of his fellows and is the greatest source of injustice. Democracy arms citizens with constitutional safeguards against the pride, pretension, and evil propensities of rulers.

In justifying democracy in these terms, Niebuhr's contribution to political theory is original and significant. It is no longer true that the framework of original sin goes by default to political authoritarianism or neutralism. Niebuhr cannot be ignored. Moreover, his formulation may well foster a deeper appreciation of the institutions of a free society.

In this brief paper, I cannot attempt a comprehensive evaluation of the validity of Niebuhr's vindication of democracy. It may be fruitful, however, to suggest the two basic counts on which his construction is vulnerable. They are the *possibility* and the *desirability* of democracy in the context of his analysis of human nature.

First, so great is Niebuhr's stress of man's will-to-power and inclination of injustice, especially in collective relationships, that it is difficult to see how democracy can achieve even relative stability and efficiency. The root of evil is, he holds, at the very center of human personality: the will. The human will is depraved. But what of the creative and constructive components of the will? Democracy requires a freely-given consensus, a genuine will to cooperate, and loyalty to its normative procedures no matter who wins the day. It involves a dimension beyond self-absorption and the lust for power. As such, democracy presupposes rational self-restraint in the form of the painful and endless search for more inclusive interests, compromise, renunciation, and sacrifice. Rare, indeed, are resolutions of conflicts of interests whereby all disputants get all they want. Why, on Niebuhr's terms, do majorities obey the principles of democracy?

Democracy, then, entails the will for democracy, a profound and pervasive will to make government the function of consent and an agency of the general community. Niebuhr's emphasis on the balance of power as a condition of justice would be of no avail without a sense of, and will to, justice. An equilibrium of power is possible only because men desire it and consider it essential to the realization of justice. Thus, unless man's creative resources— ethical, rational, and social—are considerably greater than Niebuhr concedes,' the conclusion is virtually inescapable that belief in democracy is, as he says of the guiding tenets of modern liberal culture, "a sentimental illusion."

Second, Niebuhr's doctrine of the "ideological taint" in all knowledge and belief is a double-edged weapon and can be used with equal force against his own constructive efforts. His evaluative illumination seems to be exhausted in the counsel of humility—to avoid absolute and final claims. His imperative is this: "Whatever you claim, don't claim finality for it." For all claims are rooted in the fragmentary, finite, and contingent character of historical existence. But Niebuhr provides no objective criteria for the evaluation and adjudication of conflicting claims. Consequently, he does little to illumine the problem of comparative evaluation and justification.

If it is true, as Niebuhr insists, that, on the one hand, no claim is altogether justified and, on the other, alternative positions are not qualitatively equivalent, then it is imperative for him to offer principles and criteria for the determination of the degree and extent to which rival claims are justified. The absence of such principles and criteria is Niebuhr's Achilles' heel. But, in a profound sense, this inadequacy is inherent in his sweeping approach, which involves him in a dilemma. For if he gives principles and criteria of discrimination and choice, even they, on his terms, would be infected by ideological distortion and pretension. Niebuhr's justification of democracy in terms of the universality of sin, then, is objectively wanting.

Conclusion

This brief survey demonstrates that political theories informed by belief in original sin may be authoritarian, democratic, or indifferent to forms of government. It also indicates that, in view of the marriage of original sin and democracy in Niebuhr and others, Gooch's quoted remark, which is representative of a wide body of opinion, must be rejected except in terms of past tendencies and associations.

We are brought afresh face to face with the initial question posed in this paper. While it is true that political theories ultimately depend upon conceptions of human nature, it is equally true that common views of the human fabric sometimes yield opposing political constructions and *vice versa*. Why? Have our selected theorists failed to think through their positions? Are some of them inconsistent? Can it be said that the authoritarians, the democrats, or the neutrals stand condemned under the critique of logic and evidence?

At first blush and in the light of historical association, it may seem that some of our representative thinkers have failed to grasp the implications of their position. But how are we to identify the correct implications and inferences? What are the criteria? It is impossible, without standards, to establish the proposition that one of the three positions is valid or more valid than the others. Selection involves rejection. But norms there must be to select and reject interpretations and applications. Who is to say that the authoritarians, the neutralists, or the democrats have the mighty weight of logic on their side? In the history of political thought, it is true, there has been a tendency to identify "optimistic" accounts of man with democracy and "pessimistic" views with anti-democratic systems. But this is psychological, traditional, and prejudicial, not logical. From the fact that many have followed this line of reasoning, it is a *non sequitur* to infer that they were justified in doing so. In any event, there appears to be no evidence that our writers have failed to think through their positions. From the perspective of *man as sinner,* all formulations make an equal claim to validity, and there is no *logical* way of choosing between them.

It is perilous to make any suggestions on so vast, complicated and perennial a subject in this brief paper. Even so, I hazard the observation that there is, perhaps, no necessary relation, no direct causal chain of reasoning, between doctrines of original sin and alternative forms of political order, or, for that matter, between any other conception of human nature and rival political systems. By themselves, logical operations cannot establish such a kinship. The problem here is roughly analogous to that of the alleged necessary connections between metaphysical positions or worldviews and various organizations of political power. The issue cannot be reduced to a mechanistic exercise in logical deduction, implication, and inference. Nor can it be divorced from the question of the interpreters themselves—their total scheme of values and their orientation in culture and in time.

The clue to the inability to derive particular forms of government or specific views on public policy from doctrines of human nature is to be found in the character of such propositions. In the very nature of the case, these propositions about the quality of human nature are large, sweeping, ambiguous, and lacking in material content. Put differently, they are usually purely formal, with no clear-cut empirical element. Hence these propositions rarely carry for diverse interpreters the same material content of meaning and value. When we try to winnow from them concrete meanings, practical applications, and determinate implications, abstract and general agreement fades into sharp cleavages. Indeed, the same facts about the human estate often carry different meanings and implications for different thinkers.

General propositions, as some logicians insist, do not decide concrete cases. The assertion "do good and avoid evil" does not illumine the problem of what is good and evil in particular situations just as the proposition that justice means giving each his due tells us nothing about what is due. Similarly, the proposition that man is inherently evil, good, or neither is not instructive of what kind of government is best or of which course of political action is wiser. And the same is true of other general propositions about the nature of man—such as man is inherently rational or irrational, social or anti-social, or intrinsically valuable.

In arguing, then, from conceptions of human nature to systems of political order, logical analysis is not decisive. Purely formal propositions do not yield material conclusions. Logical operations have to work with material premises supplied by the whole system of values of the interpreter, the "existential" context, the spirit of the time, and the ideological and other priorities of a given culture. Of special significance is the value system of the theorist. If he gives undue weight to order, he is likely to be authoritarian or neutral to forms of government, neutral in the sense that any government that establishes and maintains order is desirable. On the other hand, if he cherishes both freedom and order and tries to reconcile and balance them, as in the case of Niebuhr, he is likely to be found in the democratic camp. It may well be argued, of course, that the values selected—e.g., order—are often selected on the basis of a theory of human nature—e.g., Hobbes; hence a reciprocal relationship. The controlling point, however, is that conceptions of human nature are ultimately normative, qualitative, or evaluative.

Values, time, place, and culture—the whole context of human experience, conceptual and perceptual—endow the formal propositions about human nature with material constituents and "answer" the question of the preferred kind of government. This, then, is why there is no logical affinity between views of human nature and the variety of political systems or programs. Until these formal propositions are elaborated and spelled out in terms of material content, there is no direct, immediate, and sure sequence of thought which, in reference to human nature, gives one system priority over others.

Fifteen

The Structure of Argument in Political Theory

Arthur L. Kalleberg

Logic, as the science of the objective through formal conditions of valid inference, or as the science of the weight of evidence in all fields,[1] does not exhaust the meaning of philosophy. Aside from logic, epistemology, ontology, ethics, and esthetics, philosophers may be interested in applying ethical standards in evaluating policy options, clarifying the meaning of basic political concepts, both normative and empirical, or analyzing methodological problems. These are the activities I have in mind when I use the terms "philosophy of politics." It is, as it were, epistemology or meta-ethics applied to a substantive field, as in the philosophy of science or religion.

Political theory, however, is not to be equated with the philosophy of politics any more than it can be reduced to scientific theory.[2] Political theory is an attempt to illuminate practical questions; it takes place in practice, grows out of practice, and is reflection upon practice. This in turn means that the soundness of argument in political theory is always inherently substantive, always dependent to some degree upon the content rather than only the logical form of its argument. Many have stressed a relationship between theory and practice in the theoretical analysis of politics, but the implication of this for the way in which one argues in developing theories of politics has not been made explicit.

This is exactly why so many thinkers, when they get to the point of trying to describe just *how* one gives reasons or justifies at some ultimate level of argument, like Paul Taylor at the point of describing how one can be said to make a rational choice among ways of life, are forced to have recourse to terms that refer to existential conditions, such as conditions of freedom, enlightenment, and impartiality. This would also seem to be why more discursive writers, such as Arendt, find it necessary to use value-laden, existential terms when defining basic political words, as when she states that the *"raison d'etre* of politics" is freedom.[3]

A. The Polemic of Self-Reference and Other Forms of Philosophical Controversy

The nature of both political life and argument—practice and theory—can be seen *in relation to* philosophy, but not if political theory is considered as an integral or subordinate *part of* philosophy or identified only with the "philosophy of politics." If one examines argumentation not from *within* a particular philosophical perspective or set of assumptions, or restricted to logical criteria alone, but the kind of argumentation that is only occasionally engaged in by philosophers arguing *between* complete philosophical perspectives, one can achieve a better understanding of the nature of political argument. This is the question of the nature of philosophical *controversy*, rather than the question of the nature of the logical validity of arguments within a school based on shared assumptions.

In discussing the nature of philosophical controversy, Johnstone suggests that an assessment of such controversy cannot be made on cognitive, only on what he believes are non-cognitive grounds—although in my judgment they become cognitive in Searle's sense.

> The doctrine I wish to elaborate is that controversy is one of the channels through which a person may seek power. And one important feature of the kind of power that philosophical argumentation attempts to secure is that it is bilateral. It is power that one can possess only by granting it to others. For there is no dispute at all unless each party to it is willing to be corrected by precisely the same principles he uses to correct the others. If *I* condemn *your* philosophy for violating the Law of Contradiction, or the Principle of Parsimony, I must be prepared to meet *your* charge that my view itself fails to satisfy these standards.[4]

There is no logical necessity that requires one to accept the critical principles used to correct others. It seems to be a matter of will, or willingness; it seems to be a psychological condition, and therefore non-cognitive from the narrow positivist perspective. In my judgment, however, it is still possible to be cognitive in a broad Toulminian sense at this level of argument. The obvious logical compulsion that can be recognized among a group of persons who accept the principle of identity and the "laws" of contradiction and of excluded middle depends upon reciprocal acceptance. Similarly, a group's acceptance of the norms undergirding the process of scientific inquiry facilitates debate within that framework regarding the reliability or validity of specific studies or procedures.

But, if to be rational is merely to be logical in the narrow, formal sense, there are no rational grounds for choosing even a way of life that encompasses the norms of logic or science themselves. Argumentation across ways of life, or between fundamentally different philosophical perspectives is based on reciprocal acceptance of critical principles. If a critic tries to remain immune to his own criticism that criticism will fail to achieve "that general effectiveness which any critical principle, to be valid, must have," as Johnstone puts it. This requirement of reciprocity, moreover, implies other values such as sincerity and corresponding forms of action—and those are not types of logical argument but an attitude and a condition of bilateral power.[5]

Bilateral power occurs in other areas of activity, such as in the acquisition of empirical knowledge. Impartiality, for example, is one of several shared values essential to the scientific enterprise. Unlike empirical knowledge, however, no fact by itself has ever overturned a philosophical point of view or a way of life. Indeed, a philosopher's point of view will involve or imply a definition of factuality.[6] Thus the power sought in philosophical controversy is different from the kind of bilateral power available to those who mutually accept the standards of scientific inquiry where disputes, when they arise, take place within the context of reciprocal acceptance of methodological principles and usually a number of substantive assumptions.

Genuine controversy, as opposed to logical criticism, arises when positions are genuinely exclusive of one another, and yet the parties involved have some hope of persuading each other. Such hope is not warranted by the criticisms characteristic of logical analysis and empirical inquiry. That is, such criticisms are certainly not irrelevant to controversy, but by themselves they do not allow one to develop significant communication between fundamentally opposed philosophies or to bridge the gaps between ways of life.[7] Facts and logic are external to the point of view attacked, inasmuch as a philosophical perspective can always reformulate itself to cope with alleged inconsistency and what is a fact is defined by the philosophy. There must be another kind of criticism which is internal to each radically opposed philosophical position or there could be no hope for persuasiveness.

When external polemic is used to attack a given philosophy, the objective will be to defeat that philosophy through considerations alien to it. Internal polemic, on the other hand, would attempt to show that the philosophy defeats its *own* purpose. Whatever it exposed would of necessity fall within that philosophy itself, and could be construed as a defect only with respect to the motives that had given rise to the outlook in question.[8]

Rational persuasiveness across the gulf of fundamentally opposed positions requires internal polemic, requires that one ultimately defend his philosophy or way of life against challenges "through the disclosure of a consequence incoherent with its own principles or motives...."[9]

A philosophy that does not permit its own responsible utterance is an instance of "self-referential refutation." But according to Johnstone many will hold that "to conclude the falsity of a position merely from the predicament of its advocate is...only an *argumentum ad hominem*." Johnstone does not deny that the polemic of self-reference as often used is that type of argument.

Instead, we shall attempt to distinguish a valid employment of this device from its customary invalid uses. We shall try to show not only that self-referential refutation exemplifies this valid use, but also that many other types of philosophical argumentation belong to the same category, and indeed that no genuine *argumentum ad rem* is available for philosophical controversy.[10]

Argumentum ad hominem certainly can be fallaciously applied, as Johnstone suggests with a number of examples. The point of the examples is to support his position that a temporarily confused mind is one that is "unable to identify an act as falling under a rule it has itself proposed."[11] When a person feels an unconditional obligation to do something, or states this in terms of a categorical imperative, and then fails to so act, he violates no logical principle or *argumentum ad rem,* but can be validly criticized in terms of *argumentum ad hominem.* Similarly, when a philosopher attempts to exempt himself from his own viewpoint, as has often happened according to Johnstone, his position is fundamentally confused and *argumentum ad hominem* is a proper type of polemical argument against the philosophy as such, not just the particular exponent of it.[12] A consideration of philosophical *polemic,* then, points directly to conditions of existence. In Johnstone's terms, it appeals to "nothing except the purpose of the utterer;" that is to say, not social conditions but the psychological condition of the person who defends a position. Now, academic or professional philosophers seldom function at this level of discourse. They are usually concerned with elaborating answers to such questions as "How do we come to know anything?" or "How do we justify ethical statements?" from *within* a special perspective or set of assumptions. Philosophers have seldom seriously considered the nature of controversy *between* philosophies.

228 Dissent and Affirmation

A political theory, however, must always operate at this level because politics itself always involves persons who have commitments to fundamentally opposed ways of life, either explicitly or, relative to everyday policy or administrative decisions, implicitly. The alternatives to politics are war, repression or "persuasion" through propaganda. One philosopher can always ignore another's entire philosophy, concentrate on peripheral problems, or play at dispute; but one citizen of a given country *must* existentially accommodate himself with or among other citizens. If he makes an Epicurean withdrawal from politics he will be governed by them and their values without opposition. A political theory is related to politics in a manner similar to the way a scientific theory is a part of a developing science, or a theology is an aspect of a religion. None is the same as philosophy of politics, science or religion.

This is not to say, of course, that there cannot be or that there should not be a "meta-political theory" or philosophizing about the meaning of political terms, only that there is a difference between what Conal Condren terms *political* theory and political *theory*.[13] Such disparate students of the history of political thought as the Humeian George Sabine and the Platonist Leo Strauss, among others, recognize that the *political* theories that comprise the objects of their studies arise from, and are a part of, political life. They differ as to what it is that the political theorist can accomplish from that point on, but in no case is it merely logical or conceptual analysis. It is only recently, under the impact of positivism and linguistic analysis, that some have endeavored to philosophize about political terms without developing a *political* theory.

B. The Structure of Political Argument

If one accepts, at least tentatively, the different types of argument that I have discussed here and elsewhere[14] as potentially capable of being used in a sound manner, one is left with the problem of how they might be linked together. I suggest that a normative political theory may well include deduction, some types of induction, conduction (or moving from a variety of evidence, including facts, to a value conclusion), variations of the practical syllogism, self-referential polemic against opposing views, and other arguments *ad hominem* in form. Of course, some theories will exhibit more arguments of one type than another. But if these specific forms of argument are always inherently unsound then past political theories are mostly meaningless, as positivists and emotivists have suggested. Even assuming that the non-deductive forms of argument can be sound, this melange of arguments makes the development of a political theory difficult at best, and certainly puzzling to many. Can better sense be made of these specific forms of argument by relating them to a process of argumentation?

It seems to me that with regard to the process of argumentation, Toulmin's analysis of practical reason and his terminology can both encompass the views of Taylor and other proponents of the "good reasons" or conductive approach and also provide a workable identification of the steps that have to be taken in non-formal argumentation.

The structure of practical reasoning developed by Toulmin is well known, so I will only sketch it below and briefly indicate where some of the specific forms of argument might fit into the process. But let me first add one caveat. In developing normative political argument I believe one might begin at any stage and work both backwards and forwards, but I also believe that in practice most political theorists usually begin where Paul Taylor ends, with at least a vague choice of a way of life. Toulmin and Taylor in effect create "reconstructed logics" that in my judgment enhance our understanding of the complexities of practical reasoning, but the actual development of a political theory probably does not proceed in the same order. Perhaps one starts with what Wolin called a "vision" of a way of life and then, through extended argument along Toulmin's lines, one comes around full circle to what Taylor terms a "rational choice" of what is essentially the same way of life, but clarified and grounded in supporting reasons.

The structure of Toulmin's process of practical reasoning might be illustrated as follows, including some indication of the place of the various arguments in the process (Fig. 1). The specifics are Toulmin's from an argument regarding voting rights at a New England town meeting.[15] The warrant "authorizes" taking the step from G to C, and the kinds of general statements that may be appealed to as providing the "rational authority" needed to connect G to C vary according to the contexts of different human enterprises. In science and engineering, for example, warrants are largely exact mathematical formulas, with the help of which scientists "calculate the values of unknown magnitudes from the values of other related variables that they already know." In the legal field, however, if the facts in a case are not in dispute, a lawyer will be concerned with statutes and sometimes judicial decisions as warrants for his legal opinions or conclusions.

Indeed, much of the knowledge that legal students master during their professional training has to do with learning to recognize what general statements of law will

FIGURE 1

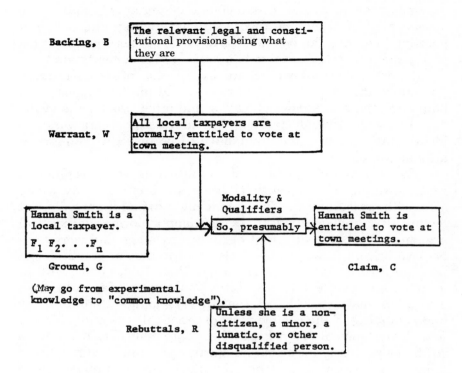

serve as satisfactory warrants to legitimate—or alternatively refute—some particular legal claim, C, given a particular set of specific facts, G. [And in many everyday ethical situations, the] role of 'moral principles' in ethical discussion is similar to that of legal statutes and roles in judicial argument.... [16]

Of course, conclusions in ethics, politics, and esthetics are more presumptive and subject to rebuttal than well-grounded conclusions in science. But, it is important to note that the structure and procedures of argument in ethics, science and law are the same. The involvement of values does not prevent ethical and political claims from being rationally debated and defended. Of course, after centuries of effort, certain sectors of natural science have become highly developed and permit systematic presentation in a deductive form, but the history of scientific discovery probably exemplifies informal logic more often.

Although the type of warrants differ substantially from one area of existence to another, probably the greatest difference occurs at the level of the backing provided for warrants. Backing does not refer to the factual basis (G) for the claim (C). The questions related to backing have to do with the facts supporting one's *way of arguing,* the warrant (W). Warrants are not self-validating, and require substantial supporting considerations or reasons. Backing is highly diverse. It involves giving content to the phrase, "Given general experience in the field concerned,.." and this varies greatly according to the field of action we are talking about. It may involve vast accumulations of scientific theory and experimental data relevant to the claim; facts about the history and intent of legislation or judicial precedent; or, in ethics, current understandings of what the demands of equity in human relations require, or perhaps widely accepted principles such as universalizability and impartiality.[17]

Systematic and thorough application of this procedure to questions and claims that typify political theory has not yet been done and deserves a separate paper. I will here only sketch an example based upon Rawls' theory (Fig. 2). Furthermore, what Toulmin terms the "modality" of arguments, or the degree of qualifications, or certainty/uncertainty, that characterizes fields such as ethics, esthetics and politics is much greater than, say, in science, and the corresponding variety of "rebuttals" requires in my judgment prior attention to the specific types of argument used in the history of political thought. And any form of argument, from deduction to *argumentum ad hominem,* may appear at any of Toulmin's levels from backing to rebuttal, as can be seen in examples from the history of political thought.

Finally, before turning to the classics, we should recognize that in the political realm, as in the esthetic, there is a multiplicity of interpretations—of a work of art or of social justice—that are within the range of legitimacy, i.e., of relatively sound argument. They never achieve what Toulmin terms either the degree of consensus possible in science or the adversarial definiteness of judicial proceedings. It has been this multiplicity of interpretations that has led many to condemn political theory as well as ethical and esthetic theory as "subjective." The implication is that everyone can make any interpretation he chooses; that there is no "right or wrong" or "rationality" involved in the choice of interpretations. This is too strong. Interpretations of politics and art can be subjected to critical analysis to avoid misleading or perverse views, although there is no possibility of "demonstration" in the strict sense. Usually, though, it is easier to establish that interpretations are plainly wrong. And this is not a matter of arbitrary emotional response.

The rationality of the resulting aesthetic arguments may not be the rationality of law and science. But it may nonetheless be the product of experience, reflective thought, careful deliberation, and well-chosen language—and so, in short, be a characteristic

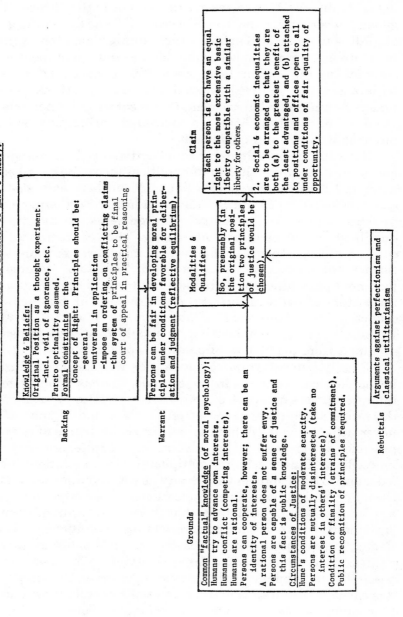

FIGURE 2

Toulmin's Structure Tentatively Applied to Elements of Rawl's Theory:

Backing

Knowledge & Beliefs:
Original Position as a thought experiment.
  —incl. veil of ignorance, etc.
Pareto optimality assumed.
Formal constraints on the
Concept of Right: Principles should be:
  —general
  —universal in application
  —impose an ordering on conflicting claims
  —the system of principles to be final
    court of appeal in practical reasoning

Warrant

Persons can be fair in developing moral principles under conditions favorable for deliberation and judgment (reflective equilibrium).

Grounds

Common "factual" knowledge (of moral psychology):
Humans try to advance own interests.
Humans conflict (competing interests).
Humans are rational,
Persons can cooperate, however; there can be an
  identity of interests.
A rational person does not suffer envy.
Persons are capable of a sense of justice and
  this fact is public knowledge.
Circumstances of Justice:
Hume's conditions of moderate scarcity.
Persons are mutually disinterested (take no
  interest in others' interests).
Condition of finality (strains of commitment).
Public recognition of principles required.

Modalities & Qualifiers

So, presumably (in the original position two principles of justice would be chosen).

Claim

1. Each person is to have an equal right to the most extensive basic liberty compatible with a similar liberty for others.

2. Social & economic inequalities are to be arranged so that they are both (a) to the greatest benefit of the least advantaged, and (b) attached to positions and offices open to all under conditions of fair equality of opportunity.

Rebuttals

Arguments against perfectionism and classical utilitarianism work of reason.... In art criticism, though the temptation to search for uniquely 'right' interpretations or 'correct' procedures may rest on a delusion, the weeding out of worthless, defective, misguided treatments and points of view continues in a rational manner.[18]

What Toulmin writes regarding art criticism applies to political theory as well. Ethics and politics certainly involve the way we feel about choices and actions, but we can always ask whether our feelings were appropriate or our reactions justifiable. "And once these questions have been stated, the whole machinery of rational criticism and practical argumentation can immediately be called into play all over again."[19]

The cognitive/non-cognitive issue thus becomes relatively insignificant. Short of taking an extreme reductionist emotivist stand, rational criticism can be applied to the entire gamut of human endeavors, from the precise and deductive arguments of mathematics to the merely presumptive and multifaceted arguments of esthetics, where several interpretations of a work of art can provide enriching insights and thus be more or less "right" at the same time.

In respect to the arts, a kaleidoscopic and eclectic appreciation of their many forms and expressions of meaning may lead to a richer and more fulfilling life. Unlike politics and political theory, commitment to manifold artistic values poses no problems for practice, unless one is an artist in some respect. Then, of course, one must choose a "way of life" of a specific type (involving a certain form of expression), at least for a period of time.

The matter is quite different in political life, however. Although a pluralist society might enjoy a great variety of ethical, esthetic, and noetic forms of life, its polity will necessarily have a specific structure. That system, or an alternative to it if one is critical of that system, is necessarily exclusive because of its integrative function. Because of this necessary exclusivity, argument in political theory is undoubtedly even more difficult than argument in ethical theory.

Politics, which is analogous especially to the art of clinical medicine, as Socrates saw, falls somewhere in between mathematics and esthetics, utilizing some empirical evidence, some historical data, and some values and normative principles. Both medicine and politics also *require* practical decision under conditions of uncertainty. Like medicine, in synthesizing empirical and historical fact with values, normative political theory can be cognitive or rational to a degree. Unlike esthetics, the *necessity* of singular commitment, the *necessity* of always dealing in real, existential alternatives, provides not only the major problem but also the major opportunity in politics and political theory. Argumentation across ways of life necessitates reciprocal acceptance of critical principles. This begins the creation of a theoretical or actual political accomodation or community based upon a special kind of bilateral power, where "the power of a given disputant is enhanced by his subjection to it, because that subjection serves to increase the number of critical principles available for his own use." In this way normative political theory strives for political community through rational practical criticism, and is intrinsically opposed to forms of unilateral domination.

C. The Complexity of Argumentation: Illustrations from the Classics

The way political theorizing has been done in the past cannot validate a particular "method." This is true even when that "method" is sufficiently comprehensive to allow for the possibility that there may be legitimate modes of inference other than the strict deductive or inductive forms. Nevertheless, an examination of past theorizing about politics can suggest a certain answer to a Kantian type of question: namely, what must the world be like for the political theorist's "knowledge" to be possible?[20] At the very least, we might determine whether a part of historical reality—the structure of past political theories—exhibits types of argument other than induction and deduction. If this is so, the perennial reassertion in intellectual history of implied claims to validity by the constant reappearance of variations of the complex form of argumentation we have isolated would seem to indicate that the social world must be so constituted as to provide a continual challenge to some minds to raise questions regarding political life that cannot be dealt with adequately solely through deductive and inductive argument.

Political theorizing, I have argued, is a form of practical reasoning that is especially complex, involving as it does not only attitudes, as is true of the traditional "practical syllogism," and conduction and the analysis of "good reasons," but even more important an "inventive function," as John Dewey termed it. The latter is not just persuasion and criticism, but results in new attitudes and experience, the creation of a new paradigm of social and personal meaning, "a transformation in symbolic expression."[21] It is this latter aspect, this "vision of a way of life" that is at the heart of political theory. The theorist is creative or transforming in that he literally "sees a different world," as Walzer puts it, and this means he has to invent a partially new language, which means a different interpretation of rational conduct. It seems to me that the major political theorists have utilized the many forms of argumentation we have discussed, sometimes grounding, often surrounding and buttressing their respective visions with many forms of practical reasoning. A few examples from major political theorists will illustrate the common use of non-deductive argument.

Plato. Let us begin with the initiator of systematic political theory. Plato develops a variety of arguments that, as a whole, can only be considered conductive and *ad hominem*. Without going into detail unnecessary for illustrative purposes, the argument of the *Republic* exhibits the "third pattern" of conduction. That is, a conclusion is drawn from both positive and negative considerations.[22] For example, the arguments (usually by analogy, which is a type of argument that is itself neither deductive nor inductive) in the early part of the *Republic* directed against Polemarchus, and especially Thrasymachus, are often felt by students first exposed to them to be unsatisfactory, at the minimum frustratingly incomplete. And, of course, if one is expecting a systematic, thoroughgoing presentation of a Thrasymachean position, they are unsatisfactory. But Plato is endeavoring, through various types of negative and positive arguments—deductive, inductive, analogical and conductive—to lead into the development of his vision of an entirely different way of looking at politics.

The first two arguments against Thrasymachus, for example, are essentially analogical. The first is based on an analogy between the art of conduct in general and the nature of any art—such as the practice of the art of medicine or music. That is, Thrasymachean injustice, or overreaching everyone, is contrary to the nature of any art. Socrates argues that "competitors" in any art do not try to go beyond anyone who practices the art perfectly. In medicine, if one doctor prescribes a correct dosage, a "rival" doctor does not seek excellence in the practice of medicine by prescribing more. A "wise" artist of any sort tries to achieve a goal that all practitioners of a specific art recognize as constitutive of successful practice. The analogy is between the component arts and the art of conduct in life as a whole, and the implication is that it is wiser, more "intelligent" to seek the limit or measure proper to any art, including the art of living in general.

The second argument against Thrasymachus is especially interesting because although like the first it is founded on an argument by analogy it includes a second form of argument. The analogy is between the internal relationships among members of a band of thieves and the relationships that obtain among members of a viable society. Its point is that if the group of thieves wants to over-reach everyone else in society *as a group* they must be capable of self-restraint, or no effective concerted action would be possible. But this implication shows that this argument, though based on an analogy, also involves a type of *argumentum ad hominem*. That is, the Thrasymachean position is fundamentally incoherent because, in Johnstone's terms, it commits the error of "self-disqualification." Socrates shows that the Thrasymachean position is intelligible only on grounds alien to it, for if the band of thieves is to act in a Thrasymachean fashion towards others, each individual thief must operate on non-Thrasymachean principles *vis-a-vis* his fellow thieves. It is a matter of the position existentially defeating its own purpose in one sense or another, an *argumentum ad hominem*. From Socrates' perspective, the consistently unjust (in Thrasymachus' sense) are actually incapable of common action.

Immediately after the confrontation with Thrasymachus Socrates offers the additional intriguing suggestion that "injustice" or unrestrained overreaching will produce individual as well as societal discord and inefficacy. This is a type of inductive argument, although it is not developed to the point of being supported with evidence. The psychological thesis that the price of "unjust" power is a divided mind, or the political thesis that legitimacy must ultimately come from sources other than force, are both capable of being supported or undermined by empirical or historical evidence and are therefore inductive in principle.

These are illustrations taken from one brief section of the *Republic,* but the only way in which they can be combined with similar arguments developed elsewhere by Plato, together with what I can only term Plato's "vision" which informs the entire remainder of the dialog, is by conduction. Plato's "positive vision" of the ideal polity is particularly difficult to "combine" with the various "negative" arguments intended to discredit opposing views, unless the utility and potential soundness of conductive argumentation is recognized. The connection between various kinds of argument and the "vision" that structures Plato's own position is certainly not logical in the deductive sense. But even images can be a part of conductive argumentation.[23] The whole is a complex conductive argument, often poetic, leading towards a transformation in symbolic expression.

Hobbes. A seventeenth century Epicurean like Thomas Hobbes is far removed from Plato in regard to virtually all substantive philosophical views. Nevertheless, in regard to types of argument Hobbes' political theory has much in common with Plato's. The paradigmatic science for Hobbes was geometry, so it is not surprising to note the frequency of deductive or ostensibly deductive argument throughout the *Leviathan,* but his political theory provides examples of other forms as well.

The most crucial type of argument for Hobbes, as for all social contract theorists, is the "mental experiment." But he leads into his "mental experiment" with prior analyses of "facts"—what I'd prefer calling empirical presuppositions—about human nature and the human condition. As a rationalist, Hobbes assumes that "by taking thought" one can know something about the existing world. The appearance of the argument is inductive, its use conductive.

In the *Leviathan,* for example, Hobbes states that he will *describe* the nature of the artificial man, the State, by first analyzing the "matter" and the "artificer" of that State, both of which is man. Man creates the State out of himself and others, and we must understand human psychology in order to understand the origin of law, ethics and politics. Aside from his sensationalist and nominalistic epistemology, law and politics are undergirded with a materialistic and deterministic psychology. General terms, such as good and evil, are reduced to the objects of appetite or aversion—physical movements towards or away from an object.

At first glance, Hobbes seems to be presenting arbitrary definitions of words. Hobbes is actually reacting to the tendency in the universities of his time of scholars to define their terms on the authority of Aristotle. Instead, he would define his terms on the basis of experience rationally analyzed, upon common usage properly cleansed of Scholastic bias. The type of argument is nonempirical induction,[24] or at least would be were examples given.

More importantly, Hobbes' analysis "of man," of the many aspects of human nature treated in Chapters One through Twelve of Part One of *Leviathan,* form a definitional foundation for his presentation "of the natural condition of mankind" at the end of Part One. The absence of references to historical cases or empirical data, which characterizes both his earlier philosophical psychology as well as his concept of the state of nature, is consistent with both Hobbes' own methodological paradigm, geometry, and with the nature of a "thought experiment" as a type of argument.

The fact that it is a bit of reasoning explains why the thought experimenter need not produce any actual case. Reasoning need not begin with true premises; one can reason just as well from merely postulated premises. Therefore a possible case will do as well as an actual one. The fact that a thought experiment is an argument also explains why no appeal to experience is necessary. One does not discover the conclusion of an argument by observing what one thinks but by thinking through the argument.... In the end, to conduct a thought experiment is not to experiment but to reason; it is an appeal, not to experimentation, but to reasoning.[25]

Indeed, the development of the complex concept of the state of nature, or the natural condition of mankind, is but the first of several "thought experiments" associated with the social contract approach in political theory. The idea of the social contract itself, together with its constituent laws of nature in the case of Hobbes, is undoubtedly the primary "thought experiment" utilized by Hobbes. It is the crucial stage in an overall form of argument that is conductive, for it "depends" upon what was stated before and after, and each phase of the argument is part of a lengthy process of creating a new paradigm of social and personal meaning. But the "elements" of the argument cannot be said logically to entail one another. That the laws of nature oblige *in foro interno* but not *in foro externo* does not logically necessitate Hobbes' "multitude" to give up their right to govern themselves to a sovereign "common power." On the other hand, it is not *prima facie* unreasonable within the Hobbesian context, where one phase of argumentation leads into another and all stages together lead forward into a new intellectual world, a new conceptual structure that as a whole gives meaning to a new view of civic order. Thus, what might seem to be an arbitrary definition or assumption when isolated and considered out of context might well be a reasonable and integral part of a coherent conductive argument, although not a logically necessary part.

Now it should be noted that Hobbes' language is descriptive. Men seek gain, safety and reputation and thus "are in that condition called war...of every man against every man." Hobbes obviously is not arguing that one man, whoever is the stronger, *should* seek control and impose order. Indeed, if men are roughly equal in strength and cunning, this cannot be a reasonable description of actual political life, as Thrasymachus held. If men are as Hobbes describes them—free, equal and dominated by the passions, especially by the fear of violent death at the hands of another person—then through this mental experiment the reasonable thing to do is recognize the validity of the terms of the contract and find security in the protection afforded by acceptance of the "laws of nature" and the "sword" that induces consistency of acceptance.

Now the point of this is not to review Hobbes' theory in its entirety, but to illustrate the process of conductive argument and to show how typical it is in political thought. Hobbes starts with epistemological postulates, touches on empirical knowledge, and assumes empirical speculative generalizations about the nature of man and the human condition.[26] From all these statements, various in both substance and form, Hobbes leads the reader directly into normative conclusions, the specific laws of nature. Although Hobbes' writing style appears deductive, the variety of the crucial elements that constitute his argument clearly indicate that he is *led toward* his conclusion, which ultimately involves a new way of looking at political relations, by the cumulative weight of various types of propositions—an example of conductive argument.

Roussseau. Rousseau suggests in the opening paragraph of the *Social Contract* that, while man is born free and now everywhere he is in chains, he might be able to explain how "to render legitimate" the movement from pristine liberty to the chains of the modern state. In developing his argument, Rousseau first undermines three criteria for legitimacy associated with three alternative models of society in an attempt to prepare the reader to accept a substitute.[27]

The first view of society is itself based upon an argument by analogy, an analogy between the oldest and only "natural" form of political association—the family—and the state. The result is a patriarchal, authoritarian model he associates with Grotius, Hobbes, and Aristotle. It is rejected by Rousseau on the ground that, while the helplessness of young children makes the authority of parents inevitable and natural, the mature person must pursue his own interests, and citizens are mature, not children. Rulers are not like fathers, nor citizens like children; thus, there is no "natural" obligation to obey the State.

Rousseau rejects the second criterion for legitimacy, a restatement of the "right of the strongest" to rule, on the basis of two types of argument, one "empirical" and the other "logical." The "empirical" argument is an historical generalization to the effect that the strongest man "is never strong enough to remain master always, unless he transforms his Might into Right..." What I am terming a "logical" argument begins with the assumption that some kind of "Right" based on Force does exist, and then claims that the only "deduction" that can be made from this assumption will be nonsensical. If the strongest is always right, "what validity can there be in a right which ceases to exist when Might changes hands?" The word "Right" adds nothing to the word "Might." Its use is meaningless.

Third, Rousseau refuses to accept the position of Grotius and Hobbes that legitimacy is established by agreement to a State which provides peace and security. Grotius had argued that an entire people, like an individual, may transfer or sell all their liberty to a ruler through some convention for the sake of peace and safety.

Again, Rousseau has recourse to two types of argument already familiar to us. First, he states an historical generalization to the effect that true peace cannot really be established this way because rulers with absolute power will embroil their nations in one war after another for their own glory and aggrandizement. Second, Rousseau argues that even if relative peace were established by a despot, civil peace would be a cause of wretchedness for his subjects. His argument is implicit in the statement that follows: "one can live peacefully enough in a dungeon, but such peace will hardly, of itself, ensure one's happiness." This statement appeals to the reader to make a basic assumption about human nature, namely, that the universal and ultimate value held by humans is liberty. An attempt to renounce his liberty "is incompatible with man's nature."[28] Are the speculative historical generalization and the assumption about human nature logically related? No. Neither can they, taken together, logically entail a conclusion.

All that can be said is that Rousseau's arguments combined constitute an attempt on his part to "falsify" or at least partially undermine competing views regarding the bases of legitimate authority—as a prelude to defending his own view of civil society. While it need not in any strict sense, in Rousseau's case such a defense initially involves two important assumptions that seem *prima facie* incompatible; first, that security of the type the State can provide is valued but, second, must be achieved in such a way that each associate "shall obey only himself and remain as free as before." This is a form of conduction in which we move with Rousseau from a partial undermining of alternative views, first to a proclaimed need for a type of association that will provide security and freedom, and finally to the conceptual clarification of key notions such as "moral liberty" and "General Will." Acceptance of the combination of these radically different arguments leads to a special type of political *praxis* involving full and free political participation in a process intended to lead to the discovery of rules of action for oneself as a member of the community, a *praxis* that provides the conditions for possible self-actualization. A political system that provides this deserves obedience because one will obey self-prescribed norms. We do not know that this will occur. But the argument persuasively leads to this point, a point where we might share Rousseau's vision of a new form of political activity that is vitally important—for it is only by filtering our wills through a special legislative process that we discover what is right for ourselves; and it is through our participating as citizens that we create legitimate authority.

There is no logical entailment between these types of argument, just as the later sections of *The Social Contract* contain a (logically) strange mixture of statements. Some seem to be attempts at conceptual clarification, as in Book II, where he discusses the concept of sovereignty as inalienable and indivisible. But in the very same context he makes empirical assumptions, as when he assumes that beneath the apparently diverse interests of individuals there is an identity of interests that makes his kind of social order possible.

And in arguing that sovereignty is indivisible, Rousseau also utilizes an *ad hominem* attack on Grotius' attempt to divide sovereignty between the king and the people. Rousseau claims that Grotius, living in France as a refugee, was trying to "win the favour of Louis XIII," and for this reason argued strenuously that the people had no "rights," only the king.[29] Desiring to separate sovereign power *for reasons of personal interest,* Grotius is led into confusion. Rousseau, of course, used this technique to bolster his belief in the inalienable unity and popular locus of sovereignty. The argument, an *ad hominem* one, may be said to be relevant, appropriate, and conducive to persuading the reader of the "truth" of Rousseau's position, but Rousseau's position is not logically entailed by the "confusion" allegedly produced by holding the opposite view of Grotius.

Marx. Another type of conductive argument that forms an important part of political reasoning is the process of "imagining things contrary to fact." Argument by induction has no part in this, although argument by deduction and especially by analogy would seem to be an integral part of this type of reasoning. An important thing to keep in mind in connection with this aspect of conduction is the close connection between social environment (technology, Western education, urbanization, e.g.) and the *capacity* for thinking in this manner.[30] Political theorizing is practical; that is, it ensues in the justification of actions as well as statements and beliefs. And at crucial junctures in history such theorizing may help to bring about a new paradigm of social meaning. It may create new ways of making sense out of, or interpreting, vital aspects of developing social systems. Hobbes' political theory is of this type, but Marx's is not only more relevant to our own times but more clearly indicative of the difference between what Wellman calls the "thought experiment," of which all social contract theories are examples, and the "contrary to fact" argument that is essential to Marxism.

Much of Marx's argument is to the effect that there are "forces" or "contradictions" within capitalist society that are thrusting that

society toward a specific kind of radical change. Now the existence
of private ownership of the means of production, distribution and
exchange in Western industrialized market economies, coupled with
socialized production in the Marxist sense, are specifiable and
demonstrable facts. The forces of production and the relations of
production are specifiable and their interaction capable of empirical
and historical study. But to claim that a certain type of socialism
will necessarily develop out of the contradiction between the latter is
counter to fact. Few if any historical situations have fit the pattern
and, in addition, cause is non-necessary. The vision of ideal
communism is also counter to fact, but nevertheless is a dialectical[31]
element in a certain type of conductive argument developed by Marx
as the most valid approach to analyzing the defects of modern
society.

A concept vitally important to Marxism, alienation, points to
the significance and utility of another type of counter-factual
argumentation.

Any complete, normative ethic must give some attention to
personal ideals of moral excellence, problems that receive little
attention in non-self-realizationist theories. We need to ask, not only
what ought I to do now—choose x or y—but what should I strive to
become? "What should I make of my life and how should I live in a
non-alienated, non-self-estranged way?"[32] Thus, if there can be seen
to be an alienated self on the basis of historical, economic research,
there must be some concept of a true, or unalienated, self. As Nielsen
argues, despite the weaknesses of self-realizationist ethics, notions
of "a fully human life" imply a conception of self-realization.[33]
Nielsen's essay does not focus on Marx inasmuch as his intention is
to explore the problems of the concept of self-realization.
Nevertheless, he concludes that despite the weaknesses and
ambiguities of self-realization and related concepts, this vague
"family of notions"

all the same signifies something, we know not clearly what, that we quite
unequivocally take as precious. An account of morality and the moral life which
ignores these features of morality is plainly thereby impoverished.[34]

The point that is important for my argument is that, aside from
unsolved problems with the concepts of alienation and self-
realization, it is an important *type of argumentation* in political
theories such as Marx's to document the features of what is denoted
by a certain concept, such as alienation, by means of empirical or
historical research and to argue or assume that such an actual state

of affairs can, and should, be overcome. In other words, there may be little specific attention given to analyzing the nature of what can be imagined as contrary to fact—of what some would term utopian speculation—but a great deal of attention might be given instead to empirical studies of the given-as-evil (alienating), of the given-as-what-must-be-overcome. And there is no way at all that the "solution" can be said to be entailed or necessitated by a given state of affairs, even if the analysis of that state is accurate. It can only be said to lead to the conclusion, probably with the support of other types of argument, and only to the person making the argument or to others who find the substance of the argument sound as well as its form or forms. In the case of Marxism, the substance of the argument would be in part the assumptions of a more human mode of life that human beings, the distinctively productive animals, could create by first developing changes in how they produce and ultimately achieving a transformation of human nature.[35] The reality of alienation implies a counter-factual understanding of human potential that cannot be "proved," only justified in a new social paradigm and in historical achievement.

D. Conclusions

The core problem I have dealt with has been *how* to develop normative or justificatory political argument, in as explicit terms as possible, in order to better understand how one might *do* political theory rather than talk about past political theories. In other terms, what specific modes of argument may be employed legitimately in theorizing about politics? Doing political theory does involve, as Spragens suggests, perception of social disorders, diagnosis, and prescription. It also usually requires a "model" or "vision" of a new or at least more adequate society to structure one's criticism and undergird one's prescriptions, as Berlin, Wolin, Miller and others suggest. But precisely *how* does one articulate one's perceptions and models, give reasons for one's diagnoses, and argue for one's values or prescriptions? All of these problems have been talked *about,* usually though not always in quite general terms, but there has been no attempt to explicate as thoroughly as possible the actual types of argumentation that may be used in developing a political theory. This I have tried to initiate, both by analyzing certain widely, though not universally, accepted interpretations of normative reasoning—such as the good reasons approach, conduction, and especially self-referential argument—and by briefly examining some types of argument utilized by selected major theorists of the past. I would like to claim completeness, but I am sure other specific ways of arguing can be articulated, especially through a more wide-ranging study of the "logic(s)-in-use" in past theories.

I have suggested, through an analysis particularly of the good reasons approach in ethics, that deductive inference cannot be utilized in "vindication" or "pragmatic justification." Nor do the latter exhaust the kinds of argumentation that structure a political theory. "Vindication" is founded upon a choice of a "way of life" that is "rationally chosen." "Rational choice" of a "way of life" is thus also a crucial part of normative argument, and its meaning is the ultimate question for the political theorist who endeavors to understand what he can do.

If one does not restrict "rational choice" to the merely instrumental or efficient, to a choice of the most effective way of achieving given goals, it is clear that any attempt to specify how a choice can be "rational" will always end in the specification of actual or existential conditions. It will be recalled that Taylor suggested that a choice is rational to the extent it is made under conditions of freedom, enlightenment, and impartiality—all rather carefully defined. Others, like Wellman and David Miller, also end with existential factors under which a decision is made.

I believe, however, that many who have reached this conclusion in the context of a discussion of ethics have not realized that while a moralist might rest comfortable merely defending, or giving reasons for, his position, the situation of the citizen and therefore the political theorist is quite different. The political theorist is always and necessarily confronted by constitutional (foundational or constitutive) and policy differences that are directly grounded in fundamentally opposed ways of life. The political theorist cannot avoid the problem of what is meant by making a "rational choice" *across* ways of life. And for this "instrumental rationality" is manifestly inadequate.

A political theory is a paradigm of social meaning, and in giving specific meaning to the political, and the many implications that flow from that, the paradigm also *creates* a definite type of rationality in conduct or reasonableness. The fact that political theories are constitutive of both politics and rationality indicates a relationship between reason and practice that goes beyond deductive reasoning. The normative reasoning process does involve deduction, but also induction and conduction. More important, conductive arguments are always nonformal; that is to say, the substance or subject matter affects the validity. In any form of practical reasoning, logical consistency is not enough. It is not *logically* inconsistent to will an end and not will any possible means to achieve it. However, one can argue in a *substantive* sense that to do that would be "contradictory" or "irrational."

I have tried to show in some detail just what is involved in this non-formal, normative reasoning, by distinguishing political theory from philosophical analysis of concepts important to political discourse. Political theory takes place in practice, grows out of practice, and is reflection upon practice. The close relationship between theory and practice for the political theorist has been stressed frequently, of course, in several schools of thought, but what this specifically implies for *how one argues* in developing theories of politics has not been made explicit. This cannot be seen from within the perspective of any single philosophy. The nature of argument in political theories can be seen by analogy with the kind of argument that is only rarely attempted between proponents of fundamentally opposed philosophical perspectives. In this form of argument—*across* ways of life and philosophical perspectives rather than from within one way of life or philosophy—the assessment of effectiveness of argument must be made on non-demonstrative, but not necessarily non-rational or unreasonable grounds.

A fundamental non-deductive ground is, indeed, a type of political relation; a bilateral power relation, as Johnstone terms it, for one can possess it only by granting it to others. "For there is no dispute at all unless each party to it is willing to be corrected by precisely the same principles he uses to correct the others." In my judgment, that kind of reciprocal acceptance undergirds, though it does not constitute, normal "logical compulsion" as well as normal processes of scientific inquiry. But the norms of logical analysis and empirical inquiry, while not irrelevant to true controversy, do not allow communication or persuasion between either fundamentally opposed philosophies or political ways of life.

Only what Johnstone calls internal polemic, or arguments that are intended to show that a philosophy defeats its *own* purpose, or contradicts the *motives* that had given rise to the position in the first place, would clearly be accepted as a defect by that position's proponents. Sound uses of various kinds of *argumentum ad hominem,* each a type of "internal polemic," can be distinguished, and they in turn point directly to requisite psychological and social conditions of existence. Although philosophers seldom function at this level of discourse, the work of political theorists must necessarily be done at this level of argumentation across ways of life. This is the case, for example, whether one considers traditional natural law, offered as a bridge for political associaton between

Christian and non-Christian, or moves to the present to Habermas' notion of "communicative action" through which the inter-subjective validity of norms is agreed upon. The basis of the former is transcendental metaphysics, and of the latter consensus developed through discourse, but the point for our purposes is that the political theorist—as compared with, say, either the philosopher or the theologian—*must* endeavor to speak across ways of life. This is the primal political problem for the theorist and the statesman. They seek to speak across ways of life by transforming symbolic expression in inventing a vision of a new way of life, a paradigmatic polity.

Way of life controversies can be eliminated through means other than politics, but those involve annihilation or domination of opponents. Political argument falls between the extremes of logical proof and war; it does not involve logical demonstration, but it can be reasonable, rational or cognitive in the broad sense of being sound or unsound—but like scientific argument always contingently, always more or less so.

Notes

Notes to Chapter One

[1]Mulford Q. Sibley, *Political Ideas and Ideologies* (New York: Harper and Row, 1970), p. 1.

[2]Mulford Q. Sibley, *Nature and Civilization: Some Implications for Politics* (Itasca, Illinois: F.E. Peacock, 1977), p. 28.

[3]*Political Ideas and Ideologies*, p. 79.

[4]See Mulford Q. Sibley, "The Limitations of Behavioralism," in *Contemporary Political Analysis*, ed. James C. Charlesworth (New York: The Free Press, 1967), pp. 51-71.

[5]Mulford Q. Sibley, "Apology for Utopia: II," *Journal of Politics* 2 (1940), p. 187.

[6]*Ibid.*, p. 188.

[7]*Nature and Civilization*, p. 151.

[8]*Ibid.*, p. 141.

[9]*Ibid.*, pp. 292-293.

[10]"Apology for Utopia: II," p. 185.

[11]*Political Ideas and Ideologies*, p. 594.

Notes to Chapter Two

[1]Mulford Q. Sibley, *Nature and Civilization* (Itasca, Ill.: F.E. Peacock Publishers, 1977), p. 145. See also his "The Morality of War," *Natural Law Forum* 12 (1967), pp. 209-225.

[2]Reinhold Niebuhr, *An Interpretation of Christian Ethics* (New York: Harper and Row, 1935), p. 189.

[3]Reinhold Niebuhr, *Leaves From the Notebook of a Tamed Cynic* (New York: Willett, Clark and Colby, 1929), p. 47.

[4]Niebuhr, "Intellectual Autobiography of Reinhold Niebuhr," in *Reinhold Niebuhr: His Religious, Social, and Political Thought,* ed. Charles Kegley and Robert Bretall (New York: The Macmillan Co., 1961), p. 8. The article referred to is "A Critique of Pacifism," *Atlantic Monthly,* May, 1927.

[5]Niebuhr, *Moral Man and Immoral Society* (New York: Charles Scribner's Sons, 1932; Paperback Edition, 1960), chs. 6, 7, 8.

[6]Niebuhr, *Love and Justice,* ed. D.B. Robertson (Cleveland and New York: World Publishing Co., 1957; Meredian, 1967), p. 256.

[7]Niebuhr, *Christianity and Power Politics* (New York: Charles Scribner's Sons, 1940), p. 7. See also pp. 5, 6, 20. Also see Niebuhr, *Reinhold Niebuhr on Politics,* ed. Harry Davis and Robert Good (New York: Charles Scribner's Sons, 1960), ch. 2.

[8]*Ibid.*, p. 2.

[9]Niebuhr, *Nature and Destiny of Man,* 2 vols. (New York: Charles Scribner's Sons, 1941, 1943, 1949), 1: 150, 179-80.

[10]Niebuhr, *Love and Justice,* pp. 268-269; *Power Politics,* ch. 1.

[11]Niebuhr, *Love and Justice,* p. 270.

[12]Niebuhr, *Nature and Destiny,* 2: 247.

[13]Niebuhr, *Power Politics,* pp. 9, 21-22; *Love and Justice,* p. 276.

[14]Niebuhr, *Power Politics,* p. 10.

[15]Niebuhr, *Moral Man and Immoral Society,* pp. 178-79.

[16]Davis and Good, *Reinhold Niebuhr,* pp. 140-141.

[17]Niebuhr, *Nature and Destiny,* 2: 244; *Interpretation,* ch. 4; *Power Politics,* p. 3.

[18]Niebuhr, *Nature and Destiny,* 2: 246. Chapter seven is a good summary of Niebuhr's views on the relationship of love and justice.

[19]Niebuhr, *Moral Man,* p. xi. See also Davis and Good, *Reinhold Niebuhr,* p. 161.

[20]Niebuhr, *Nature and Destiny,* 2: 88; see also Davis and Good, *Reinhold Niebuhr,* p. 142.

[21]Davis and Good, *Reinhold Niebuhr,* p. 143.

[22]*Ibid.,* pp. 139, 144-145; see also his *Love and Justice,* p. 278.

[23]*Ibid.,* p. 144. Also see his *Moral Man,* pp. 233-235, 229; *Love and Justice,* p. 279; "Christian Faith and the World Crisis," *Christianity and Crisis,* February 10, 1941.

[24]Niebuhr, *Love and Justice,* p. 283.

[25]*Ibid.,* p. 301; Davis and Good, *Reinhold Niebuhr,* pp. 144-146.

[26]Davis and Good, *Reinhold Niebuhr,* p. 147.

[27]Niebuhr, *Power Politics,* pp. 11-12.

[28]Davis and Good, *Reinhold Niebuhr,* p. 140.

[29]Niebuhr, *Power Politics,* p. 31.

[30]Davis and Good, *Reinhold Niebuhr,* p. 149.

[31]*Ibid.,* p. 150, emphasis added.

[32]Mulford Sibley, *The Political Theories of Modern Pacifism,* Revised. (Philadelphia: Pacifist Research Bureau, 1970), pp. 49, 53-54.

[33]See Sibley, *Nature and Civilization,* chs. 3, 4; Reinhold Niebuhr, *Children of Light and Children of Darkness* (New York: Charles Scribner's Sons, 1944), ch. 2; Niebuhr, *Nature and Destiny,* 2: ch. 7.

[34]Sibley, *Modern Pacifism,* p. 49. Two other pacifist critiques of Niebuhr are C.H.C. MacGregor, *The Relevance of the Impossible Ideal* (London: Fellowship of Reconciliation, 1960) and John Yoder, "Reinhold Niebuhr and Christian Pacifism," *Mennonite Quarterly* 29 (April, 1955): 101-117.

[35]*Ibid.,* pp. 27-54.

[36]*Ibid.,* pp. 62, 54.

[37]Sibley, *Nature and Civilization,* p. 17.

[38]*Ibid.,* p. 13.

[39]*Ibid.,* p. 16.

[40]Mulford Sibley, "Political Theories of Modern Religious Pacifism," *American Political Science Review* 49 (June, 1943): 454.

[41]Sibley, *Modern Pacifism,* p. 53.

[42]Sibley, *Nature and Civilization,* p. 99; also see *Modern Pacifism,* p. 52; M. Sibley *et. al., Conflict in the Social Order* (Minneapolis: Centennial Lecture Series, 1951).

[43]*Ibid.,* p. 288; Mulford Q. Sibley, *The Obligation to Disobey* (New York: Council on Religion and International Affairs, 1970), p. 74.

[44]Sibley, *Modern Pacifism,* pp. 47, 53-54.

[45]*Ibid.,* p. 18.

[46]*Ibid.,* pp. 8-12. See also Mulford Q. Sibley, *Political Ideas and Ideologies* (New York: Harper and Row, 1970), ch. 8.

[47]*Ibid.,* p. 11.

[48]*Ibid.,* p. 25.

[49]*Ibid.,* p. 50.

[50]Sibley, *Nature and Civilization,* p. 67.

[51]Sibley, *Modern Pacifism,* pp. 31-32; see also *Nature and Civilization,* p. 68.

[52]*Ibid.*

[53]Sibley, *Nature and Civilization,* p. 142; *Modern Pacifism,* p. 28.

[54]Sibley, *Nature and Civilization,* p. 145.

[55]Mulford Sibley, *Revolution and Violence* (London: Housemans, 1969), p. 4.

[56]Sibley, *Modern Pacifism*, pp. 29-30; Sibley, *Obligation to Disobey*, p. 113.

[57]Sibley, *Modern Pacifism*, p. 48; *Nature and Civilzation*, p. 149.

[58]Sibley, *Modern Pacifism*, p. 48.

[59]Sibley, *Nature and Civilization*, pp. 149-50; *Obligation to Disobey*, pp. 21-23, 54; *Modern Pacifism*, p. 26; Sibley, "On Political Obligation and Civil Disobedience," *Journal of Minnesota Academy of Science*, 33 (1965): 16-24.

[60]Mulford Sibley, ed., *The Quiet Battle* (Boston: Beacon Press Paperback, 1968), 371; also see *Modern Pacifism*, pp. 49, 55.

[61]Sibley, *Modern Pacifism*, pp. 36-39.

[62]*Ibid.*, pp. 45, 37.

[63]Sibley, *Nature and Civilization*, pp. 150-151.

[64]*Ibid.*, pp. 25, 45; *Obligation to Disobey*, pp. 88-89; *International Encyclopedia of the Social Sciences*, s.v. "Pacifism" by Mulford Sibley.

[65]Sibley, *Nature and Civilization*, p. 152.

[66]Reinhold Niebuhr, "Response to *Speak Truth to Power*," *Progressive* 19 (Oct., 1955): 14. However, Sibley also recognizes the problem of making decisions that affect others adversely. See his *Modern Pacifism*, p. 36.

[67]Sibley, *Nature and Civilization*, p. 95; see also p. 284.

[68]American Friends Service Committee, *In Place of War* (New York: Grossman, 1967), p. 28.

[69]Sibley, *Modern Pacifism*, p. 55.

[70]Sibley, "Pacifism," pp. 356-57.

[71]Sibley, *Modern Pacifism*, p. 29.

[72]Sibley, *Nature and Civilization*, pp. 145-146.

[73]Sibley, *Quiet Battle*, pp. 205, 369-371; *Modern Pacifism*, pp. 38-39, 60; *Political Ideas*, pp. 371-372.

[74]Sibley, *Modern Pacifism*, p. 49.

[75]*Ibid.*, pp. 51-53. For a summary of the kind of society Sibley envisions, the reader is referred to *The Quiet Battle*, pp. 359-365, and *Nature and Civilization*, chs. 5, 6, 7.

[76]*Ibid.*, pp. 50-53.

[77]Niebuhr, *Love and Justice*, p. 268.

[78]Davis and Good, *Reinhold Niebuhr*, p. 142.

[79]Sibley, *Nature and Civilization*, p. 146.

[80]*Ibid.*, p. 147.

[81]Mulford Sibley, "Unilateral Disarmament," in *America Armed*, ed. Robert Goldwin (Chicago: Rand McNally, 1963), pp. 112-140.

[82]Niebuhr, *Love and Justice*, p. 233. See Dan Epp-Tiessen, "Realism in the Nuclear Age," *Christian Century*, March 3, 1982, pp. 231-232.

[83]*Ibid.*, p. 237.

[84]Quoted in John Bennett, "Niebuhr's Ethic: The Later Years," *Christianity and Crisis*, April 12, 1982, pp. 93-94.

[85]Sibley, "Anonymity, Dissent and Individual Integrity in America," *Annals*, 378 (July, 1968), pp. 52-53.

Notes to Chapter Three

[1]See Immanuel Kant, *Groundwork of the Metaphysics of Morals*, trans. H.J. Paton (New York: Harper Torchbooks, 1964), esp. pp. 8-14.

[2]The two *loci classici* of the "good reasons" view of ethics are Stephen Toulmin, *An Examination of the Place of Reason in Ethics* (first publ. 1950; Cambridge: Cambridge University Press, 1968), Part III, and Kurt Baier, *The Moral Point of View* (first publ. 1958; abr. edn. New York: Random House, 1965). A forceful restatement and defense can be found in Alan Gewirth, *Reason and Morality* (Chicago: University of Chicago Press, 1978).

³The view that philosophical theses and theories are "criticizable" though not definitively "refutable" is defended by Sir Karl Popper, *Conjectures and Refutations* (New York: Harper Torchbooks, 1968), pp. 193-200.

⁴A.J. Ayer, *Language, Truth and Logic* (New York: Dover Books, n.d. [1936]), esp. pp. 107-112. Somewhat more sophisticated versions of emotivism were subsequently formulated and defended by Charles L. Stevenson in his *Ethics and Language* (New Haven: Yale University Press, 1944), and Paul Edwards, *The Logic of Moral Discourse* (Glencoe, Ill.: Free Press, 1969). For an excellent overview and critique of emotivism, see J.O. Urmson, *The Emotive Theory of Ethics* (New York: Oxford University Press, 1969).

⁵Said, not in celebration but despairing resignation, by Peter Laslett in his Introduction to *Philosophy, Politics, and Society,* first series (Oxford: Blackwell, 1956), p. vii. In the interim his optimism has grown, as can be seen from his introductions to four successive additions to that series.

⁶"Logical Positivism and Its Legacy: Dialogue with A.J. Ayer," in *Men of Ideas,* ed. Bryan Magee (New York: Viking, 1978), p. 131.

⁷See—for one example among many—Sibley's contribution to the *Sibley-Kendall Debate: War and the Use of Force,* ed. Kent Lloyd *et. al.* (Denver: Swallow Press, 1959), pp. 15-29.

⁸John Dewey, *Democracy and Education* (New York: Macmillan, 1916), pp. 4-5.

⁹Bertrand De Jouvenel, *Sovereignty: An Inquiry Into the Political Good* (Chicago: University of Chicago Press, 1963), p. 304.

¹⁰See Pericles' Funeral Oration in Thucydides, *History of the Peloponnesian War,* trans. Crawley (New York: Modern Library, 1951), p. 79.

¹¹See, e.g., Jürgen Habermas, "On Systematically Distorted Communication," *Inquiry,* 13 (1970), pp. 205-218, and "Hannah Arendt's Communications Concept of Power," *Social Research,* 44 (1977), pp. 3-24.

¹²In schematically reconstructing Professor Sibley's position, and the arguments advanced in support of it, I have relied not only upon his voluminous writings but also upon personal conversations and upon the position he staked out in a public "disputation" between us, sponsored in the Spring 1980 term by the Undergraduate Political Science Association at the University of Minnesota. I am most grateful to the Association for suggesting and sponsoring this encounter, which gave me a good deal to think about. Some of my subsequent thoughts are to be found in sections III and IV of the present essay.

¹³Mulford Q. Sibley, "Pacifism," *International Encyclopedia of the Social Sciences* (New York: Macmillan, 1968), pp. 353-357, at 353.

¹⁴*Ibid.,* p. 355.

¹⁵See my *Civil Disobedience and Civil Deviance* (Beverly Hills and London: Sage Publications, 1973), ch. 3.

¹⁶Henry David Thoreau, *Civil Disobedience,* in *Writings* (Boston: Houghton Mifflin, 1893), Vol. IV, p. 361.

¹⁷Thoreau, *Slavery in Massachusetts, Writings,* Vol. IV, p. 402.

¹⁸Thoreau,*Civil Disobedience,* p. 362.

¹⁹See Sibley, *The Obligation to Disobey: Conscience and the Law* (New York: Council on Religion and International Affairs, 1970).

²⁰Thoreau, *Slavery in Massachusetts,* p. 40.

²¹Mulford Q. Sibley, *Nature and Civilization* (Itasca, Ill.: F.E. Peacock Publishers, 1977), pp. 67-68, 142-152.

²²*Ibid.,* p. 67.

²³*Ibid.*

²⁴G.W.F. Hegel, *Philosophy of Right,* trans. T.M. Knox (New York: Oxford University Press, 1967), Sec. 118 (p. 80). Hegel, of course, believed it possible to "sublate"—i.e., negate, preserve and transcend—both the deontological and consequentialist "moments" described here. This sublation was not to be the work of abstract understanding but of actual human history. But in the end he appears to

embrace a rather queer species of utilitarianism, inasmuch as actions are to be judged, not by the agents' imperfect and short-sighted intentions but by their utterly unintended world-historical *consequences.* Thus Hegel's ethical theory is subordinated to his philosophy of history. Much the same can also be said of Marx's implicit theory of ethics. In this sense, at least, Marx remained a thoroughgoing Hegelian.

25Ferdinand Lasalle, *Franz von Sickingen,* Act II, scene 5, lines 93-97.

26Sibley, *Nature and Civilization,* p. 142.

27See Alasdair MacIntyre, *After Virtue* (Notre Dame: University of Notre Dame Press, 1981), chs. 1-3.

28J.S. Mill, in *The Amberly Papers,* second edition, eds. Bertrand and Patricia Russell (London: Macmillan, 1966), Vol. II, p. 373.

Notes to Chapter Four

1This notion of definition approximates the "pragmatic-contextual" approach elaborated by Raziel Abelson, "Definition," *The Encyclopedia of Philosophy,* Vol. 2, (New York: Macmillan, 1967), pp. 314-324.

2Samuel DuBois Cook, "Coercion and Social Change," in *Coercion* (Nomos XIV), ed. J. Roland Pennock and John W. Chapman (Chicago: Aldine, Atherton, 1972), p. 115.

3*Ibid.,* p. 116.

4Christian Bay, *The Structure of Freedom* (Stanford, Calif.: Stanford University Press, 1958), p. 93.

5*Ibid.,* p. 92.

6Cook, p. 126.

7Mulford Q. Sibley, for example, uses coercion in this broad fashion when he writes of "the coercions by Nature." See Sibley, *Nature and Civilization* (Itasca, Ill.: F.E. Peacock, 1977), p. 141.

8Again, I think Sibley uses the term too broadly even when he moves from "Natural" to human coercions. See *Ibid.,* p. 150.

9See, for example, Virginia Held, "Coercion and Coercive Offers" in Pennock and Chapman, pp. 49-62.

10For an elaboration of this point, see Bernard Gert, "Coercion and Freedom," in Pennock and Chapman, pp. 30-48.

11Michael D. Bayles, "A Concept of Coercion," in Pennock and Chapman, p. 19.

12For a provocative discussion of a response theory of meaning, see Morse Peckham, *Explanation and Power: The Control of Human Behavior* (New York: Seabury Press, 1979).

13John Locke, *Second Treatise of Government,* section 6.

14If one accepts an organic view of the state, then an analogous argument might be developed: The individual may be lost for the benefit of the whole. In an extreme organic state, the individual would have no entitlements to anything. Harm could only be done to the collective. The individual might still be protected, but only because it is in the interests of the organic community to do so.

15This interesting notion is developed by Michael A. Weinstein, "Coercion, Space, and the Modes of Human Domination," in Pennock and Chapman, pp. 63-80.

16For more extensive discussions of the hermeneutical approach see *Interpretive Social Science,* ed. Paul Rabinow and William M. Sullivan (Berkeley: University of California Press, 1979). See also Morse Peckham, "The Problem of Interpretation" *College Literature* 6 (1979-80), pp. 1-17.

17I think this constitutes a reasonable clarification of Max Weber's well known definition involving the state's "monopoly" of the use of force. Actually, at one point Weber states that "the use of force is regarded as legitimate only so far as it is either permitted by the state or prescribed by it." Max Weber, *Economy and Society*, ed. G. Roth and C. Wittich (Berkeley: University of California Press, 1978), p. 56.

[18]Cook, p. 113.

[19]Sibley, pp. 143-149.

[20]Robert Paul Wolff, "Is Coercion Ethically Neutral?" in Pennock and Chapman, pp. 144-147.

[21]Richard L. Rubenstein, *The Cunning of History: The Holocaust and the American Future* (New York: Harper Colophon, 1978), esp. Ch. 6.

[22]*Ibid.*, passim.

[23]B. F. Skinner, *Beyond Freedom and Dignity* (New York: Bantam, 1971). See also B. F. Skinner *Walden Two* (New York: Macmillan, 1970).

[24]Morse Peckham, *Art and Pornography* (New York: Harper and Row, 1971), p. 141.

[25]Peckham refers to this as the "delta effect;" see *Explanation and Power*, pp. 164-166.

[26]Sibley, pp. 148-149.

[27]Walter Kaufmann, *Without Guilt and Justice* (New York: Peter H. Wyden, 1973), esp. Chs. 2 and 3.

[28]Gene Sharp, *The Politics of Nonviolent Action* (Boston: Porter Sargent, 1973), pp. 72-73. Sharp's impressive study does much to dispell the "myth of inefficiency" surrounding nonviolent action.

[29]Friedrich Nietzsche, *The Twilight of the Idols* in *The Portable Nietzsche,* trans. and ed. Walter Kaufman (Baltimore: Penguin/Viking 1976), p. 479.

[30]Noble lies, however, may have their uses. See, for example H. Vaihinger, *The Philosophy of "As if,"* trans. by C. K. Ogden (New York: Barnes and Noble, 1924).

Notes to Chapter Five

[1]The relevant documents are contained in Department of the Army Pamphlet 27-1, *Treaties Governing Land Warfare,* December, 1956.

[2]See the author's *The Forgotten Victim: A History of the Civilian* (Chicago: Precedent Publishing, Inc., 1982).

[3]In Germany, the two movements are traditionally referred to as *Gottesfrieden,* with no special attempt to distinguish them, which in fact were only distinct for about one hundred years. See Ludwig Quidde, "Histoire de la Paix Publique in Allemagne au Moyen Age," *Recueil des Cours,* Tome 28 (Paris: Librairie Hachette, 1930).

[4]Ernest Semichon, *La paix et la treve de Dieu,* 2 vols. (Paris: Albanel, 1869). Scholarly studies of the Peace and Truce are rare and of limited value. The best and most recent work in English is by Dolorosa Kennelly, *The Peace and Truce of God: Fact or Fiction?* (Unpublished Ph. D. dissertation, University of California, Berkeley, 1963).

[5]The canons and decrees here may be found in *Sacrorum Conciliorum nova et amplissima collectio,* ed. J. Mansi (Venice: 1774), hereafter cited as "Mansi," with the appropriate volume and column. Decrees of the General Church Councils (though not those of local synods) may be found in English in M.F. Schroeder, *Disciplinary Decrees of the General Councils* (St. Louis: Herder, 1937). Schroeder's commentary on those texts pertaining to the Peace and Truce are most often naive and misleading.

[6]Loren C. MacKinney, "The People and Public Opinion in the Eleventh-Century Peace Movement," *Speculum,* V (1930), p. 184.

[7]No canons of this council are extant, but Mansi provides commentary. See Mansi, volume XIX, col. 103.

[8]The peace movement spread to Catalonia by means of the peace councils of Narbonne which the Catalonian bishops had attended. See Robert E. McNally, *The Peace Movement in Catalonia During the Eleventh Century* (unpublished master's thesis, Catholic University, Washington, D.C., 1953).

[9]Mansi, cols. 483-84.

[10]*Ibid.,* cols. 829-32.

[11]*Ibid.,* col. 827.

[12]*Ibid.,* cols. 912-14.

[13]MacKinney, p. 204.

[14]See Marie R. Madden, *Political Theory and Law in Medieval Spain* (New York: Fordham University Press, 1930), pp. 58 and 62.

[15]Sidney Painter, *Feudalism and Liberty*, (Baltimore: Johns Hopkins Press, 1962), p. 91.

[16]The story is told that King John of France, captured at Poiters, was released from his English prison in exchange for a number of hostages. When one of the hostages escaped, the King voluntarily returned to prison in Long. Similar accounts demonstrating the worth of a knight's word are related in *The Chronicles of Froissart,* trans. Lord Derners, the Harvard Classics (New York: Collier, 1910), vol. 35.

[17]Canon XIV, Second Lateran Council, translated by Schroeder, p. 204.

[18]Canon XXIX.

[19]It is true that among the Moslem jurists there was a common agreement that noncombatants among the enemy should be left alone. Women, children, monks and hermits, the old, the blind and the insane were in this category, and some jurists also included peasants and merchants. These general rules were qualified by so many factors, however, that the jihadists, those taking part in a Holy War, could consider themselves most often excused from compliance with them. For Moslem sources and commentary, consult Majid Khadduri, *War and Peace in the Law of Islam* (Baltimore: Johns Hopkins Press, 1955).

[20]The general lack of mercy which Christians and Saracens showed to each other may be seen from an event which occurred during the great siege of Malta by the Ottoman Turks in 1565. See Ernie Bradford, *The Great Siege* (New York: Harcourt, Brace, 1962), p. 127.

Notes to Chapter Six

[1]Harold N. Lee, "Time and Continuity," *Southern Journal of Philosophy,* 10 (Fall, 1972), p. 298.

[2]William James, *Essays in Radical Empiricism and a Pluralistic Universe,* (New York: E.P. Dutton and Co., 1971), p. 141.

[3]Henri Bergson, *Time and Free Will,* (London: George Allen and Unwin, 1910), p. 104.

[4]Alfred Schutz, *The Phenomenology of the Social World,* (Northwestern University Press, 1967), p. 45.

[5]The quotations in this paragraph are taken, in order, from James, p. 120; p. 17; p. 46.

[6]Bergson, p. 98; p. 99.

[7]Bertrand Russell, *The ABC of Relativity,* (New York: New American Library, 1959), *passim.*

[8]Schutz, p. 86.

[9]James V. Schall, "Possibilities and Madness: A Note on the Scope of Political Theory," *Review of Politics* (April, 1975), pp. 161-174.

[10]Albert Camus, *The Rebel,* (New York: Alfred A. Knopf, 1956), p. 255; p. 284; p. 285.

[11]Camus, *Resistance, Rebellion and Death,* (New York: Vintage Books, 1974), p. 7.

[12]I would like to thank Dr. Michael Weinstein, Department of Political Science, Purdue University, for pointing out to me the importance of this distinction between the ontological and moral dualisms in revolutionary practice.

[13]Camus, *The Rebel,* p. 282.

[14]In "On Being Conservative," Michael Oakeshott makes a persuasive case for the virtues of familiarity in collective life. See *Rationalism In Politics,* (New York: Barnes and Noble, 1974).

[15]For a sample of the sources that either elucidate typological distinctions or summarize the existing literature on typologies, see: Carl J. Frederick, ed., *Revolution, (Nomos,* VIII) (New York: Atherton Press, 1966); Elbaki Hermassi, "Toward a Comparative Study of Revolutions," *Comparative Studies in Society and History,* 18 (April 1976), pp. 211-235; Samuel Huntington, *Political Order in Changing Societies,* (New York: Yale University Press, 1968); Stanley Kochanek, "Perspectives on the Study of Revolutions," *Comparative Politics,* 5 (April, 1973), pp. 313-320; Issac Kramnick, "Reflections on Revolution: Definition and Explanation in Recent Scholarship," *History and Theory* 11 (1972), pp. 26-63; Barrington Moore, *The Social Origins of Dictatorship and Democracy,* (Boston: Beacon Press, 1966); Kai Nielson, "On the Choice Between Reform and Revolution," *Inquiry,* 14 (Autumn, 1971), pp. 271-295; Lawrence Stone, "Theories of Revolution," *World Politics,* 18 January, 1966), pp. 159-176; R. Tantor and M. Midlarsky, "A Theory of Revolution," *Journal of Conflict Resolution,* 11 (September, 1967), pp. 264-280; Claude E. Welch Jr. and Mavis Bunker Taintor, *Revolution and Political Change,* (Belmont, California: Wadsworth Publishing Co., 1972); Perez Zagorin, "Theories of Revolution in Contemporary Historiography," *Political Science Quarterly,* 88 (March, 1973), pp. 23-52.

[16]Barbara Salert, *Revolutions and Revolutionaries,* (New York: Elsevier Scientific Publishing Co., 1976), p. 5.

[17]In *Utopia and Revolution* (Chicago: University of Chicago Press, 1976), Melvin Lasky argues that the word and concept of revolution came to Northern Europe in the 1600s from Italy after two centuries of political and social upheavals (p. 242). He rejects R.G. Collingwood's contention in *The New Leviathan* that the word came from French literary criticism. Hannah Arendt, in *On Revolution* (New York: Viking Press, 1965) rejects both arguments and claims that the word was first used in the conversation between King Louis XVI and the Duc de La Rochefoucauld-Liancourt (pp. 40-41).

[18]Ernst Vollbrath, "Rosa Luxemburg's Theory of Revolution," *Social Research* 40 (Spring, 1973), p. 83.

[19]See David and Marina Ottoway, *Algeria: The Politics of a Socialist Revolution,* (Berkeley: University of California Press, 1970), for an excellent analysis of the failure of Ben Bella's government to establish viable institutional channels for participatory government, especially at the local level.

[20]Camus, *The Rebel,* p. 249.

[21]E.V. Wolfenstein, *The Revolutionary Personaltiy,* (Princeton, New Jersey: Princeton University Press, 1967).

[22]Eric Hoffer, *The True Believer,* (New York: Harper and Brothers, 1951).

[23]Lucian Pye, "Personality and Communism in Malaya," cited in Welch and Taintor, p. 172.

[24]For a related discussion of the psychological distinctions between reformers and revolutionaries, see Lasky, *passim.*

[25]William T. Daly, *The Revolutionary: A Review and Synthesis,* (London: Sage Publications, 1972), p. 7; p. 18; pp. 27-34.

[26]Peter Suedfeld and A.D. Rank, "Revolutionary Leaders: Long Term Success as a Function of Changes in Conceptual Complexity," *Journal of Personality and Social Psychology* 34 (August, 1976), p. 172; p. 173. The differences between agitators and administrators is also discussed in H.D. Lasswell, *Psychopathology and Politics,* (New York: Viking Press, 1960); in Robert Blackney and Clifford T. Paynton, *Revolution and the Revolutionary Ideal,* (Cambridge, Massachusetts: Schenkman Publishing Co., 1976); and in Arendt, p. 278, *passim.*

[27]Paul Avrich, *Kronstadt 1921,* (New York: W. W. Norton, 1970), p. 58.

[28]J.P. Nettl, *Rosa Luxemburg,* (London: Oxford University Press, 1966).

[29]Emma Goldman, *Living My Life,* I and II, (New York: Dover Publications, Inc., 1970); and *My Disillusionment in Russia*, (New York: Thomas Y. Crowell, Co., 1970).

[30]Lasky, p. 394.

[31]Arendt, p. 156.

[32]This point is made in Crane Brinton's classic work *Anatomy of Revolution*, (New York: Vintage Books, 1938).

[33]Arendt, p. 160.

[34]Camus, *The Rebel,* p. 122.

[35]Max Stirner, *The Ego and Its Own,* (London: The Trinity Press, 1971), p. 122.

[36]Lasky, p. 584.

Notes to Chapter Seven

[1]See his "Concluding Remarks," in *The Quiet Battle,* ed. Mulford Q. Sibley (Garden City, New York: Anchor, 1963), pp. 359-377, at p. 361.

[2]See "President Warns of Marxist 'Virus', " as reported by Steven R. Weisman from Bridgetown, Barbados, *New York Times,* April 9, 1982, p. 4.

[3]See, for example, Peter Bachrach, *The Theory of Democratic Elitism* (Boston: Little Brown, 1967); C. Wright Mills, *The Power Elite* (New York: Oxford University Press, 1957); G. William Domhoff, *Who Rules America?* (Englewood Cliffs, New Jersey: Prentice-Hall, 1967).

[4]Ralph Nader has repeatedly called for "open books" as an elementary requirement for all corporations engaged in manufacturing—taking materials from the environment and releasing other materials. The open books should reveal not only all fiscal but all material dispositions as well. When corporations violate the public interest under their habitual cloak of secrecy Nader encourages their employees to become "whistle blowers." See *Whistle Blowing,* ed. Ralph Nader, *et. al.* (New York: Bantam, 1982).

[5]See Daniel Ellsberg, "Call to Mutiny," in *Protest and Survive,* ed. E.P. Thompson and Dan Smith (New York: Monthly Review Press, 1981).

[6]See *ibid.*, and Robert C. Aldridge, *The Counterforce Syndrome* (Washington: Institute for Policy Studies, 1979 ed.), pp. 66-68.

[7]Even some leading proponents of earlier phases of the Cold War, men who were in the top echelon among American policy makers, in a recently published paper, now concede that there never was a Soviet superiority in nuclear weaponry; moreover, they assert that even in conventional weaponry there is now, as before, no significant Soviet lead. On the basis of this and other considerations they argue that it is in the urgent interest of our survival, both in the West and in the East bloc nations, that Washington now consider the merits of the United States going along with the Soviet Union in renouncing any first use of nuclear weapons. See McGeorge Bundy, George F. Kennan, Robert S. McNamara, and Gerard Smith, "Nuclear Weapons and the Atlantic Alliance," *Foreign Affairs,* 60 (Spring, 1982), pp. 753-768. Also see Herman Kahn, "Thinking About Nuclear Morality," *New York Times Magazine,* June 13, 1982, pp. 42-50 and 56-66.

[8]Ronald Inglehart, *The Silent Revolution* (Princeton: Princeton University Press, 1977).

[9]Ronald Inglehart, "Post-Materialism in an Environment of Insecurity," *American Political Science Review,* 75 (December, 1981), pp. 880-900.

[10]Her "Dictatorships and Double Standards" first appeared in *Commentary,* 68 (November, 1979), pp. 34-45. Now also in her *Dictatorships and Double Standards* (New York: Simon and Schuster, 1982), pp. 23-52.

[11]On these issues I am indebted most of all to John R. Seeley. See, for example, his "Quo Warranto: The Berkeley Issue" and "The 'Berkeley Issue' in Time and Place," in *The University Game,* ed. Howard Adelman and Dennis Lee (Toronto: Anansi, 1968), pp. 125-145.

¹²See his *The Sociological Imagination* (New York: Grove Press, 1961).

¹³See my "Politics and Pseudopolitics," in *Behavioralism in Political Science,* ed. Heinz Eulau (New York: Atherton, 1969), ch. 5; also Walter Berns, "Voting Studies," in *Essays on the Scientific Study of Politics,* ed. Herbert J. Storing (New York: Holt, Rinehart and Winston, 1962), ch. 1.

¹⁴See both his *Democratic Theory: Essays in Retrieval* (Oxford: Clarendon, 1973), and *The Life and Times of Liberal Democracy* (Oxford: Oxford University Press, 1977).

¹⁵See his *A Theory of Justice* (Cambridge: Harvard Uiversity Press, 1971), and my *Strategies of Political Emancipation* (Notre Dame: Notre Dame University Press, 1981), chs. 1 and 6.

¹⁶Mulford Sibley, *Nature and Civilization* (Itasca, Ill.: F. E. Peacock, 1977), pp. 253 and 254.

Notes to Chapter Eight

¹See Mulford Q. Sibley, "Apology for Utopia: I. An Examination of Professor Sait's Excogitated Ideas," *Journal of Politics* 2 (February, 1940), pp. 57-74; "Apology for Utopia: II. Utopia and Politics," *Journal of Politics* 2 (April, 1940), pp. 165-188; "Nature, Civilization and the Problem of Utopia," in his *Nature and Civilization: Some Implications for Politics* (Itasca, Ill.: F.E. Peacock, 1977), pp. 251-303; and *Technology and Utopian Thought* (Minneapolis: Burgess Publishing Co., 1971).

²On definitional questions, see Lyman Tower Sargent, "Utopia: The Problem of Definition," *Extrapolation* 16 (May, 1975), pp. 127-48; Darko Suvin, "Defining the Literary Genre of Utopia," *Studies in the Literary Imagination* 6 (Fall, 1973), pp. 121-45; Paul Sawada, "Toward the Definition of Utopia," *Moreana* Nos. 31-32 (November, 1971), pp. 135-46; and Renato Poggioli, *Definizione dell'utopia,* No. 46 of *Saggi di Varia Unamita* ([Pisa:] Nistri-Lischi, [1964]). For bibliography see Lyman Tower Sargent, *British and American Utopian Literature 1516-1975* (Boston: G. K. Hall, 1979); and Glenn Negley, *Utopian Literature* (Lawrence, Kans.: Regents Press of Kansas, 1977).

³I say "apparently" because the bibliography of works outside the Anglo-American tradition has not yet received the attention it probably deserves.

⁴As far as I can tell this subject has only been discussed once before, in a short article limited to a few 17th- and 18th- century French utopias. See Jean Meral, "Heurs et malheurs du mariage en pays d'Utopie," *Annales de la Faculté des Lettres de Toulouse* 16 (1969), pp. 39-49.

⁵For contrasting viewpoints see Lynda Lange, "The Function of Equal Education in Plato's *Republic* and *Laws,*" in *The Sexism of Social and Political Theory,* ed. Lorenne M. G. Clark and Lynda Lange (Toronto: University of Toronto Press, 1979), pp. 3-15; Susan Moller Okin, *Women in Western Political Thought* (Princeton: Princeton University Press, 1979), pp. 15-70; and Arlene W. Saxonhouse, "The Philosopher and the Female in the Political Thought of Plato," *Political Theory* 4 (May, 1976), pp. 195-212.

⁶Diod. Sic. 58.1 trans. and ed. Ernest Barker, *From Alexander to Constantine* (Oxford: Clarendon Press, 1956), p. 63. See Amédée Polet, "Deux utopies hellenistiques; La Panchaie d'Euhémère et la cité du soleil de Jambule," *Bulletin of the Faculty of Arts, Fouad I University* 9 (1947), pp. 47-62; David Winston, "Iambulus' *Islands of the Sun* and Hellenistic Literary Utopias," *Science-Fiction Studies* 3 (November, 1976), pp. 219-27, and Winston, "Iambulus: A Literary Study in Greek Utopianism," (Dissertation, Columbia University, 1956).

⁷See Anton-Herman Chroust, "The Ideal Polity of the Early Stoics: Zeno's *Republic,*" *Review of Politics* 27 (April, 1965), pp. 173-83; and H. D. Baldry, "Zeno's Ideal State," *Journal of Hellenic Studies* 79 (1959), pp. 3-15.

⁸For further material see John Ferguson, *Utopias of the Classical World*

(London: Thames and Hudson, 1975), pp. 19-21.

⁹For a survey of the public-private relationship in political thought see Jean Bethke Elshtain, *Public Man, Private Woman* (Princeton: Princeton University Press, 1981).

¹⁰Thomas More, *Utopia,* ed. Edward Surtz, S.J. (New Haven: Yale University Press, 1964), p. 77.

¹¹*Ibid.,* p. 143. For a different view of More's patriarchalism, see Elisabeth Mann Borgese, *Ascent of Woman* (New York: George Braziller, 1963), p. 127. For an altogether more positive view of More's attitude to women, see Lee Cullen Khanna, "No Less Real Than Ideal: Images of Women in More's Work," *Moreana,* 14 (December, 1977), pp. 35-51.

¹²*Ibid.,* p. 75.

¹³*Ibid.,* p. 76.

¹⁴*Ibid.*

¹⁵*Ibid.,* p. 67.

¹⁶*Ibid.,* p. 112.

¹⁷*Ibid.,* p. 109.

¹⁸The English utopias of this period all fit this pattern. They are *A Pleasant Dialogue between a Lady called Listra and a Pilgrim* [Signed] T.N. London: John Charlewood, 1579; *The second part of the painefull Jorney of the poore Pylgrime into Asia, and the straynge woonders that he sawe* [Signed] T. N. (London: John Charlewood, 1579); [Thomas Lupton] *Siuqila. Too good, to be true* (London: Henrie Bynemann, 1580); and Lupton, *The Second part and Knitting up the Boke entitled Too good, to be true* (London: Henry Binnemann, 1581).

¹⁹[Lupton] *Siuqila,* p. 37.

²⁰*Ibid.,* pp. 37-38.

²¹*Ibid.*

²²*Ibid.,* pp. 39-40.

²³Johann Valentin Andreae, *Christianopolis,* trans. and ed. Felix Emil Held (New York: Oxford University Press, 1916), p. 258.

²⁴*Ibid.,* p. 258-9.

²⁵*Ibid.,* p. 208.

²⁶See, for example, *An Essay Concerning Adepts* by a Philadept (pseud.) (London: Printed by J. Majors, 1698); *Annus Sophiae Jubilaeus, The Sophick Constitution* (London: Printed for A. Baldwin, 1700); and Denis Vairasse d'Allais, *Histoire des Sevrambes* (Amsterdam: E. Roger, 1702. Part First Published in English 1675; first French edition 1677-79).

²⁷See Andreae, p. 261, and d'Allais, trans. by Frank E. Manuel and Fritzie P. Manuel in *French Utopias: An Anthology of Ideal Societies,* ed. Manuel and Manuel (New York: Free Press, 1966), p. 57.

²⁸[Edward Howard], *The Six Days Adventure, or the New Utopia* (London: Theo. Dring, 1671), p. 27.

²⁹See, for example, William Hodgson, *The Commonwealth of Reason* (London: Author, 1795), p. 79.

³⁰See, for example, Hodgson, p. 73; and [Thomas Northmore], *Memoirs of Planetes, or a Sketch of the Laws and Manners of Makar,* by Phileleutherus Devoniensis (pseud.) (London: Printed by Vaughan Griffiths, 1795), pp. 101-102.

³¹See, for example [Simon Berington], *The Memoirs of Sigr Guadentio di Lucca* (pseud.) (London: Printed for T. Cooper, 1737); [James Burgh]; *An Account of the First Settlement, Laws, Form of Government, and Police of the Cessares, a People of South America: In Nine Letters, from Mr. Vander Neck* (pseud.) (London: Printed for J. Payne, 1764); [Francis Gentlemen], *A Trip to the Moon,* by Sir Humphrey Lunatic (pseud.) (York: Printed by A. Ward, 1764); and *A True and Faithful Account of the Island of Veritas,* by Jasper Richardson (pseud). (London: Printed for C. Stalker [1709?].

³²Burgh, p. 78.

³³*Ibid.,* p. 66.

[34]See, for example, Louis Sebastien Mercier, *L'An deux mille quatre cent quarante* (London: np. 1771).

[35]Denis Diderot, *Supplement to Bougainville's Voyage* (1772) (Geneve: Librairie Droz, 1955); Morelly, *Naufrage des Isles Flottantes, ou Basiliade du celebre Pilpai* (Paris: Une Société de Librairie, 1775-83); Morelly, *Code de la nature* (1755) (Paris: Raymond Cavruiel, 1950); and Nicolas Rétif de la Bretonne, *Les Gynographes* (The Hague: Grosse et Pinet, 1777).

[36]*The Swiss Family Robinson* has an odd publishing history. I have used the standard Kingston version of 1849 which combines parts of the original Wyss version and the first volume of the Montholieu version of 1824-26.

[37]See, for example [Jane Sophia Appleton], "Sequel to the Vision of Bangor in the Twentieth Century," *Voices from the Kenduskeag* (1848) in Arthur O. Lewis, Jr. (ed.) *American Utopias* (New York: Arno Press and *The New York Times*, 1971); *New Britain. A Narrative of a Journey, by Mr. Ellis* (pseud.?) (London: L. Simpkin and R. Marshall, 1820); and [John Macnie], *The Diothas or a Far Look Ahead*, by Ismar Thiusen (pseud.) (New York: G.P. Putnam's Sons, 1883). This is, of course, also true of Bellamy and most of his immediate followers. For this period see also Christopher Yelverton, *Oneiros or Some Questions of the Day* (London: Kegan Paul, Trench Co., 1889); John Petzler, *Life in Utopia* (London: Author's Cooperative Pub. Co., 1890); [Charles Wicksteed Armstrong], *The Yorl of the Northmen* (London: Reeves & Turner, 1892); and John Munro, *A Trip to Venus* (London: Jarrold [1897]).

[38]See, for example, Ferdinand IV. King of the Two Sicilies [King of Naples] *Origin and History of St. Leucio* [c1800]. Trans. into French by Abbe Louis Antoine Clemaron de S. Maurice and then into English by Adam Clarke in Adam Clarke, *The Miscellaneous Works* (London: T. Tegg, 1837), vol. II, pp. 97-160; and [Benjamin Lumley], *Another World; or, Fragments from the Star City Montalluyah*, by Hermes (pseud.) 3rd ed. (London: Samuel Tinsley, 1873). In the post-Bellamy period see, for example, Petzler, op. cit.; and Fayette Stratton Giles, *Shadows Before or a Century Onward*, No. 57 of *The Twentieth-Century Library* (New York: Humboldt Pub. Co., 1893).

[39][Thomas Low Nichols] *Esperanza; My Journey Thither and What I Found There* (Cincinnati: Valentine Nicholson, 1860), p. 139. See also, *Equality; [or,] A History of Lithconia* [by James Reynolds?] (Philadelphia: The Prime Press, 1947). Originally published 1802; and John Minter Morgan, *The Revolt of the Bees* (London: Longmans, Rees, Orme, Brown, and Green, 1826). In the post-Bellamy period see, in particular, the works of Henry Olerich, such as *A Cityless and Countryless World; An Outline of Co-operative Individualism* (Holstein, Ia.: Gilmore & Olerich, 1893).

[40]See, for example, *New Britain*, and Lewis Masquerier, *Sociology: or, The Reconstruction of Society, Government, and Property* (New York: The Author, 1877).

[41]See, for example, Charles Fourier, *Le Nouveau monde amoureaux*, ed. Simone Debout-Oleskiewicz, vol. VII of *Ouevres complete de Charles Fourier*, 12 vols. (Paris: Editions Anthropos, 1967); James Lawrence, *The Empire of the Nairs; or, The Rights of Women* 4 vols. in 2 (London: Printed for T. Hookham, Jun. & E. T. Hookham, 1811); [Calvin Blanchard], *The Art of Real Pleasure* (New York: Calvin Blanchard, 1864); [H. C. M. Watson], *Erchomenon; or, The Republic of Materialism* (London: Sampson Low, Marston, Searle, & Rivington, 1879); and two works presenting and defending the system of "complex marriage" as practiced at the Oneida Community, George Noyes Miller, *The Strike of a Sex* (London: William Reeves [1890]), and Miller, *After the Strike of a Sex or, Zugassent's Discovery* (London: William Reeves [1891]).

[42]See, for example, Percy Greg. *Across the Zodiac; The Story of a Wrecked Record*, 2 vols. (London: Trubner, 1880); Mrs. George Corbett, *New Amazonia; A Foretaste of the Future* (London: Tower [1889]); Byron A [Iden] Brooks, *Earth Revisited* (Boston: Arena, 1893), Solomon Schindler, *Young West* (Boston: Arena, 1894); Frederic Condé Williams (ed.), [written by] *"Utopia." The Story of a Strange Experience* (Cambridge: Metcalfe & Co., 1895), *The Cambridge Christmas Annual 1895*; and D. L. Stump. *From World to World* (Asbury, Mo.: World to World Pub. Co., 1896).

[43]See, for example, Joanna Russ, "Nobody's Home," in *New Dimensions II*, ed. Robert Silverberg (Garden City: Doubleday, 1972), pp. 1-20. Reprinted: *Women of*

Wonder; Science Fiction by and about Women, ed. Pamela Sargent (New York: Vintage, 1974), pp. 235-256.
⁴⁴See, for example, James Cooke Brown, *The Troika Incident* (Garden City: Doubleday, 1970).

Notes to Chapter Nine

¹George Sabine, ed., *The Works of Gerrard Winstanley* (Ithaca: Cornell University Press, 1941), p. 5.
²Parenthetical references in the text are to Sabine's edition of Winstanley's works *(ibid.).* I also follow Sabine in leaving Winstanley's seventeenth century English in its original form.
³The best full-length study of Winstanley is by David Petegorsky, *Left-Wing Democracy in the English Civil War* (London: Victor Gollanz, 1940). Besides a number of articles (some of which are cited below), Sabine's introduction is particularly important, as is Christopher Hill's to his edition of Winstanley's works, *The Law of Freedom and Other Essays* (Middlesex: Harmondsworth, 1973). Also see Hill's *The World Turned Upside Down* (New York: Viking Press, 1972), ch. 7. Histories of political thought often fail to deal with Winstanley and the Diggers. The exceptions are important: Perez Zagorin, *A History of Political Thought in the English Revolution* (London: Routledge and Kegan Paul, 1954); and Mulford Sibley, *Political Ideas and Ideologies* (New York: Harper and Row, 1970).
⁴Mulford Sibley, *Technology and Utopian Thought* (Minneapolis: Burgess, 1971); and *Nature and Civilization: Some Implications for Politics* (Itasca: F. E. Peacock, 1977).
⁵*Nature and Civilization,* pp. 171ff.
⁶For areas of Digger influence see Keith Thomas "Another Digger Broadside," *Past and Present,* 42 (1969). With the discovery of this pamphlet those areas proved to be greater than previously thought.
⁷Thomas, p. 58, has suggested the broader background against which to understand the Diggers of 1649: "The whole Digger movement can plausibly be regarded as the culmination of a century of unauthorized encroachment upon the forests and wastes by squatters and local commoners, pushed on by land shortage and the pressure of population."
⁸*Nature and Civilization,* p. 254.
⁹For a longer discussion of the importance of this feature of Winstanley's program see J.C. Davis, "Gerrard Winstanley and the Restoration of True Magistracy," *Past and Present,* 70 (1976).
¹⁰*Political Ideas and Ideologies,* p. 369.
¹¹*Technology and Utopian Thought,* p. 20.
¹²*Nature and Civilization,* p. 171.
¹³The ideological connection between Winstanley's ideas and the early Quakers has frequently been noted. Some have sought a more material connection between them, suggesting that Winstanley once was a Quaker, or became one sometime after 1652. See the articles by R.T. Vann, "From Radicalism to Quakerism: Gerrard Winstanley and Friends," *Friends Historical Society Journal,* XLIX (1959); "Diggers and Friends—A Further Note," *ibid,* L (1961); and "The Later Life of Gerrard Winstanley," *Journal of the History of Ideas,* XXVI (1965).
¹⁴Nell Eurich, *Science in Utopia* (Cambridge: Harvard University Press, 1967), p. 314.
¹⁵Hill, *The Law of Freedom and Other Essays,* p. 46.
¹⁶Bacon in *Ideal Commonwealths,* edited by Henry Morley (New York: The Colonial Press, 1901), p. 129.
¹⁷R.L. Greaves, "Gerrard Winstanley and Educational Reform in Puritan England," *British Journal of Educational Studies,* XVII (1969), p. 169.
¹⁸*Nature and Civilization,* p. 273.
¹⁹See discussion in *ibid,* p. 183.

Notes to Chapter Ten

[1]See especially "Social Order and Human Ends," in *Political Theory and Social Change*, ed. David Spitz (New York: Atherton, 1967), pp. 221-255, and *Nature and Civilization* (Itasca, Ill.: F. E. Peacock, 1977), *passim*.

[2]James C. Miller III, "A Program for Direct and Proxy Voting in the Legislative Process," *Public Choice*, 7 (Fall 1969), 107-113; Martin Shubik, "On Homo Politicus and the Instant Referendum," *Public Choice*, 9 (Fall 1970), 79-84; Robert Paul Wolff, *In Defense of Anarchism* (New York: Harper and Row, 1970), pp. 34-37; Peter Singer, *Democracy and Disobedience* (Oxford: Oxford University Press, 1973), pp. 106-107; Ithiel de Sola Pool, "Citizen Feedback in Political Philosophy," in *Talking Back: Citizen Feedback and Cable Technology,* ed. Pool (Cambridge, Ma.: MIT Press, 1973), pp. 237-246; Kenneth Laudon, *Communications Technology and Democratic Participation* (New York: Praeger, 1977), chs. 1-3; Keith Graham, "Democracy, Paradox and the Real World," *Proceedings of the Aristotelian Society,* 76 (1975/1976), p. 242; and C. B. Macpherson, *The Life and Times of Liberal Democracy* (Oxford: Oxford University Press, 1977), pp. 94-98.

[3]I am indebted to Nannerl O. Keohane for impressing the importance of this objection on me.

[4]I refer to Wolff; see section III, *infra*.

[5]Those who think this too fanciful should read John Wicklein, "Wired City, U.S.A.: The Charms and Dangers of Two-Way TV," *The Atlantic Monthly,* 243 (February 1979), 35-42.

[6]Michael Margolis, *Viable Democracy* (Harmondsworth: Penguin Books, 1979), p. 130.

[7]Graham, p. 242.

[8]For the first suggestion see Singer, p. 107; for the second see Wolff, p. 35.

[9]Dennis Mueller, *Public Choice* (Cambridge: Cambridge University Press, 1979), p. 66.

[10]George Kateb, "The Moral Distinctiveness of Representative Democracy," *Ethics,* 91 (April 1981), p. 373.

[11]This point is made by Bernard Grofman, "Fair and Equal Representation," *Ethics,* 91 (April 1981), p. 484. See also Jane Mansbridge's essay in the same volume, "Living with Conflict: Representation in the Theory of Adversary Democracy," p. 475, note 15.

[12]*Participation in America: Democracy and Social Equality* (New York: Harper and Row, 1972), pp. 79-80.

[13]Macpherson, pp. 95-96.

[14]Wolff, pp. 36-37.

[15]In "The Selfish-Voter Paradox and the Thrown-Away Vote Argument," *American Political Science Review,* 71 (March 1977), Paul Meehl concludes (p. 11) that his chances of casting the vote which determines the winner of a presidential election "are of about the same order of magnitude as my chances of being killed driving to the polls..."

[16]Here I draw upon my "Metropolis, Memory, and Citizenship," *American Journal of Political Science,* 25 (November 1981), esp. pp. 716-719.

[17]*The Politics,* trans. T. A. Sinclair (Baltimore: Penguin Books, 1967), Book III, Ch. 1, p. 103; also Book III, Ch. 13, pp. 131-132, where Aristotle defines a citizen "in general" as "one who has a share both in ruling and in being ruled; this will not be identical in every kind of constitution, but in the best constitution it means one who is able and who chooses to rule and to be ruled with a view of life that is in accordance with goodness."

[18]In addition to the sources cited in the next two notes, see Robert Dahl and Edward Tufte, *Size and Democracy* (Stanford: Stanford University Press, 1973); Jane Mansbridge, *Beyond Adversary Democracy* (New York: Basic Books, 1980), esp. ch. 20; and Warren Miller and R. Kenneth Godwin, *Psyche and Demos: Individual Psychology and the Issues of Population* (New York: Oxford University Press, 1977), pp. 151-152, 203.

[19]*The Spirit of the Laws,* Book VIII, Ch. XVI, in Melvin Richter, *The Political Theory of Montesquieu* (Cambridge: Cambridge University Press, 1977), p. 233.

[20]Mancur Olson, *The Logic of Collective Action* (New York: Schocken Books, 1971), esp. ch. 2, and Michael Taylor, *Anarchy and Cooperation* (London: John Wiley and Sons, 1976), esp. 7.2.

[21]Cf. Mansbridge, *Beyond Adversary Democracy,* p. 301: "Most Americans experience democracy only in the voting booth. Citizens file into a curtained box, mark a preference, and file out. In special circumstances, if a big-city political machine is at work or if the community is small, they may see someone they know on the way in and out of the box, smile, and exchange a triviality. Most voters see no one they know. They sit in their homes; they consume information; they determine a preference; they go to the polling place; they register the preference; they return to their homes. Small wonder that the preferences so conceived and so expressed should tend toward the private and the selfish."

[22]Mansbridge makes a case for direct democracy in town meetings and in the workplace in *Beyond Adversary Democracy.* For similar arguments, see Carole Pateman, *Participation and Democratic Theory* (Cambridge: Cambridge University Press, 1970), and Sibley, *Nature and Civilization,* esp. ch. 7.

[23]For a provocative example, see Miller.

Notes to Chapter Eleven

[1]Mulford Q. Sibley, *Nature and Civilization* (Itasca, Illinois: F. E. Peacock, 1977), p. 96. The sketch is presented in Chapter Seven, and discussions of authority and freedom appear both in that Chapter (at pp. 267-268, 284-290) and in Chapter Two.

[2]Also *ibid.,* pp. 65-69, 267-268.

[3]Sibley articulates the same position in his *The Obligation to Disobey* (New York: Council on Religion and International Affairs, 1970), pp. 36-42, 50-55, 116-117.

[4]This argument is elaborated by the Thomist Yves Simon in *A General Theory of Authority* (Notre Dame: University of Notre Dame Press, 1962), esp. Ch. II.

[5]For the same reason there is in utopia no political parties; see *Nature and Civilization,* pp. 287-288.

[6]Additional conditions are described here (at *ibid.,* p. 285) and on p. 267.

[7]The larger units are briefly described at *ibid.,* p. 268.

[8]*Ibid.,* p. 80: "Any polity which . . . [denies] scope for . . . uniqueness is by definition unjust."

[9]See esp. *ibid.,* p. 97, where negative freedom is described as a means, positive freedom an intrinsic good.

[10]See also *ibid.,* pp. 288-289 and 90.

[11]Cf. *The Obligation to Disobey,* esp. pp. 57-70, 84, 116-117.

[12]Stephen Holmes, "Two Concepts of Legitimacy," *Political Theory* 10 (1982), p. 181.

[13]See on this esp. Richard B. Friedman, "On the Concept of Authority in Political Philosophy," in *Concepts in Social and Political Philosophy,* ed. Richard Flathman (New York: Macmillan, 1973), pp. 121-145.

[14]Richard Flathman, "Citizenship and Authority: A Chastened View of Citizenship," *NEWS* (Washington, D.C.: American Political Science Association), Summer 1981, p. 17. See also and more generally Flathman's *The Practice of Political Authority* (Chicago: University of Chicago Press, 1980), esp. chs. 11-13.

[15]*The Obligation to Disobey,* p. 46.

[16]*Ibid.,* p. 75.

[17]*Ibid.,* pp. 98, 99.

Notes to Chapter Twelve

[1]See further David Spitz, "Politics and the Critical Imagination," *Review of*

Politics XXXII (1970), pp. 419-435.

[2]See Marvin Fox, "Moral Facts and Moral Theory," in *Perspectives in Philosophy* (Columbus, Ohio: The Ohio State University, 1953), p. 111.

[3]Francis Bacon, *The Great Instauration* (1620), preface, in *The Enlightenment*, ed. Peter Gay (New York: Simon and Schuster, 1973), p. 47.

[4]Fox, p. 124.

[5]Cf. Shlomo Avineri, *The Social and Political Thought of Karl Marx* (Cambridge: Cambridge University Press, 1968), pp. 124-134; Ernst Bloch, *On Karl Marx*, trans. J. Maxwell (New York: Herder and Herder, 1971), pp. 84f.; Nicholas Lobkowicz, *Theory and Practice: History of a Concept from Aristotle to Marx* (Notre Dame: University of Notre Dame Press, 1967), ch. 13 and *passim;* and David McLellan, *The Young Hegelians and Karl Marx* (London: Macmillan, 1969), pp. 9ff.

[6]See, for example, Bloch, pp. 93-98.

[7]George Lichtheim, *Marxism: An Historical and Critical Study* (London: Routledge and Kegan Paul, 1961), p. 236; see also Eugene Kamenka, *The Ethical Foundations of Marxism* (London: Routledge and Kegan Paul, 1962), p. 20.

[8]Ludwig Feuerbach, *The Fiery Brook: Selected Writings,* trans. Zawar Hanfi (Garden City, New York: Doubleday Anchor, 1972), pp. 253f., 297.

[9]Marx, "A Contribution to the Critique...Introduction," in *Critique of Hegel's 'Philosophy of Right,'* ed. Joseph O'Malley (Cambridge: Cambridge University Press, 1970), p. 136. See also Avineri, pp. 136f.; Lichtheim, pp. 44, 53ff.; and Nathan Rotenstreich, *Basic Problems of Marx's Philosophy* (Indianapolis: Bobbs-Merrill, 1965), pp. 91-104, 110-124.

[10]Marx and Engels, *The German Ideology,* trans. S. Ryazanskaya (Moscow: Progress Publishers, 1964), pp. 254ff.

[11]Cf. *ibid.,* pp. 86f., 91-95.

[12]Which Bertell Ollman, following Engels, tells us "Marx is reputed to have had in great abundance." Ollman, *Alienation: Marx's Conception of Man in Capitalist Society* (Cambridge: Cambridge University Press, 1971), p. 64.

[13]Marx, *Economic and Philosophic Manuscripts of 1844,* trans. M. Milligan (Moscow: Foreign Languages Publishing House, 1959), pp. 67-83, esp. pp. 70, 79; and see Kamenka, chs. 7, 14; Lobkowicz, chs. 20-23; and Ollman, chs. 19-22.

[14]Marx and Engels, *Collected Works* (New York: International Publishers, 1975), IV, p. 35; italics added.

[15]*The German Ideology,* p. 50.

[16]*Ibid.* See further Marx's *The Eighteenth Brumaire of Louis Bonaparte* (1852), in *Selected Works* (Moscow: Foreign Languages Publishing House, 1951), I, p. 225, where he writes: "Men make their own history, but they do not make it just as they please; they do not make it under circumstances chosen by themselves, but under circumstances directly encountered, given and transmitted from the past."

[17]*Economic and Philosophic Manuscripts of 1844,* p. 104.

[18]*The German Ideology,* p. 193.

[19]But see Ollman, ch. 3 and Appendix. Part II of this work, constituting an elaborate effort to describe Marx's theory of human nature, includes the following ascription: "Man's activities are always purposive, but in communism the plan setting is more conscious, more creatively enjoyable, and the plan itself grander than ever before. Furthermore, the communist man will be able to concentrate harder, if not longer, than any of his predecessors.... To achieve this degree of success at transforming nature, communist man must be extraordinarily good at whatever he undertakes. *All physical and mental work is done with the ease of an expert.* Thus, the activity of this Jack-of-all-trades, *who is also master of them all,* is always skillful. This new found ascendancy over objects may also be attributed to man's heightened rationality in this period. *In his knowledge, he has at last gotten beneath appearances to essences."* *Ibid.,* pp. 116f.; italics added. See further his argument on pp. 124-127. Here, of course, Ollman but embellishes Engels' panegyric on communist man in his October 1847 draft of what was later to become *The Communist Manifesto.* See Engels, *Principles of Communism,* trans. Paul M. Sweezy (New York:

Monthly Review, 1952), Question 20, pp. 16ff.

To which Alexander Gray acidly retorts: "That each individual should have the opportunity of developing *all* his faculties, physical *and* mental, in *all* directions, is a dream which will cheer the vision only of the simple-minded, oblivious of the restrictions imposed by the narrow limits of human life. For life is a series of acts of choice, and each choice is at the same time a renunciation and an act of abdication.... Even the inhabitant of Engels' future fairyland will have to decide sooner or later whether he wishes to be Archbishop of Canterbury or First Sea Lord, whether he should seek to excel as a violinist or as a pugilist, whether he should elect to know all about Chinese literature or about the hidden pages in the life of the mackeral." Gray, *The Socialist Tradition* (London: Longmans, Green and Co., 1946), p. 328.

For other, and somewhat disparate, views of Marx's idea of human nature, see Erich Fromm, *Marx's Concept of Man* (New York: Frederick Ungar Publishing Co., 1961), and Vernon Venable, *Human Nature: The Marxian View* (Cleveland: Meridian Books ed., 1966). Cf. also Kamenka, pp. 152-160

[20]The same question and inadequate response plague other forms of determinism as well, e.g., that of B. F. Skinner. See David Spitz, "The Higher Reaches of the Lower Orders," *Dissent* XX (1973), pp. 243-269.

[21]Istvan Meszaros, *Marx's Theory of Alienation* (New York: Harper Torchbooks, 1972), pp. 180-184.

[22]Lichtheim, p. 252; Sidney Hook, *From Hegel to Marx* (New York: Humanities Press, 1950), pp. 286-290; also Meszaros, p. 189 and ch. 10.

[23]Their exchange of letters, discreetly omitted from the *Selected Correspondence*, may be found in Otto Ruhle, *Karl Marx: His Life and Work,* trans. E. and C. Paul (New York: New Home Library, 1943), pp. 225f.

[24]On Marx and Bakunin, see Franz Mehring, *Karl Marx,* trans. E. Fitzgerald (New York: Covici, Friede, 1935), pp. 426-455, 520-524, and *passim*; Ruhle, esp. pp. 274-292; and Leopold Schwarzschild, *The Red Prussian: The Life and Legend of Karl Marx,* trans. M. Wing (New York: Scribner's, 1947), ch. 16 and *passim.* This last (somewhat intemperate) work details any number of incidents in which Marx and Engels engaged in rather shoddy practices. On Marx and Lassalle, see David McLellan, *Karl Marx: His Life and Thought* (London: MacMillan, 1973), pp. 315-325; Mehring, pp. 332-341 and *passim*; Ruhle, pp. 228-238; and Schwarzschild, esp. pp. 248-251, 275ff., and 303ff.; also, for a more sympathetic portrayal of Marx's role in this relationship, Isaiah Berlin, *Karl Marx: His Life and Environment* (London: Oxford University Press, 1948), pp. 194-202, and David Footman, *Ferdinand Lassalle: Romantic Revolutionary* (New Haven: Yale University Press, 1947), *passim.*

[25]*Economic and Philosophic Manuscripts of 1844,* pp. 73-76.

[26]For one such demonstration, see Lichtheim, Part V, ch. 8, and Part VI, chs. 1-2.

[27]Bloch, p. 124. But cf. Maurice Merleau-Ponty, *Adventures of the Dialectic,* trans. Joseph Bien (Evanston, Ill.: Northwestern University Press, 1973), p. 207, who notes: "There is no dialectic without opposition or freedom..."

[28]Avineri, Kamenka, and Lichtheim, among others, insist on distinguishing Marx from Engels, especially with respect to Engels' later writings and what Plekhanov termed his "dialectical materialism;" see also Irving Fetscher, *Marx and Marxism* (New York: Herder and Herder, 1971), pp. 162-172 and *passim*, and (with respect to the economic base and literature) Peter Demetz, *Marx, Engels, and the Poets,* trans. J. L. Sammons (Chicago: University of Chicago Press, 1967), pp. 127-151. But see contra Althusser, Ollman, p. 52 and *passim,* and Adam Schaff, "Studies of the Young Marx: A Rejoinder," in *Revisionism,* ed. Leopold Labedz (London, 1962), pp. 188-194. Cf. also A.J. Gregor's argument in *A Survey of Marxism* (New York: Random House, 1965), pp. 38f., 71f., 285ff., and ch. 5: while "the philosophy revealed in the works of Engels is a strange bedfellow to the positive Humanism of the youthful Marx," Engels is "the philosopher of classical Marxism." For a critique of Engels' idea of the dialectic, see Sidney Hook, *Reason, Social Myths, and Democracy* (New York: John Day, 1940), ch. 9.

[29]This is cautiously conceded by Avineri, pp. 251, 258, despite his insistence that

Marx must be rescued from his disciples. See also Kamenka, pp. 143, 165ff., 197f.

[30]Letter of January 28, 1872; quoted in Ruhle, p. 291.

[31]*Selected Works,* I, p. 51 (italics added); and see Avineri, pp. 91-95.

[32]On differentiation, between individuals and within economic classes, see John Plamenatz, *German Marxism and Russian Communism* (New York: Harper Torchbooks, 1965), pp. 315ff., and G.D.H. Cole, *The Meaning of Marxism* (London: Victor Gollancz, 1948), chs. 4-6; and cf. more generally David Spitz, *Democracy and the Challenge of Power* (New York: Columbia Unviersity Press, 1958), ch. 5.

[33]*The German Ideology,* p. 47. But cf. Robert C. Tucker, *Philosophy and Myth in Karl Marx* (Cambridge: Cambridge University Press, 1961), pp. 234ff.

[34]While Marx often asserted that the transformation from a capitalist to a socialist society could be effected only through the use of force, he also said (in a speech in Amsterdam in September 1872) that because of the special conditions—i.e., democracy—which prevailed in England and the United States, and possibly also in Holland, it was conceivable that this transformation could be brought about in those countries by peaceful and legal means. Engels, in his preface to the 1895 edition of Marx's *Class Struggles in France,* went even further, asserting that a duly elected socialist majority was not only an attainable goal but the surest guarantee of victory. Lenin, however, later rejected this thesis on the ground that conditions in "bourgeois democracy" had changed. See Spitz, *Democracy and the Challenge of Power,* pp. 36-39, 186ff.; Avineri, pp. 202-220; Lichtheim, p. 230 and *passim.*

[35]"A Contribution to the Critique...Introduction," p. 140.

[36]David Spitz, "Four Fragments on Politics," *Dissent* XVIII (1971), pp. 580ff. It is doubtless unbecoming to quote one's self, but I do not think I can say better now what I said then.

[37]*Capital,* trans. S. Moore and E. Aveling, ed. F. Engels, (Moscow: Foreign Languages Publishing House, 1959), I, p. 17.

[38]*Selected Works,* II, p. 30.

[39]But for a sophisticated interpretation of Marx on this issue, see Avineri, ch. 8; also Cole, ch. 7; and David McLellan, *The Thought of Karl Marx* (London: Macmillan, 1971), Part II, ch. 8.

[40]Lenin, *Selected Works,* II, Part 1, pp. 291-294; italics in the original.

[41]"...in a revolution opposition and freedom do not last for long. It is no accident that all known revolutions have degenerated: it is because as established regimes they can never be what they were as movements; precisely because it succeeded and ended up as an institution, the historical movement is no longer itself: it 'betrays' and 'disfigures' itself in accomplishing itself. Revolutions are true as movements and false as regimes." Merleau-Ponty, p. 207; also pp. 209, 216.

[42]In a letter to August Bebel (March 1875), Engels declared that "The whole talk about the state should be dropped.... Marx's book against Proudhon [*The Poverty of Philosophy* (1847)] and later the *Communist Manifesto* directly declare that with the introduction of the socialist order of society the state will dissolve of itself and disappear. As, therefore, the state is only a transitional institution which is used in the struggle, in the revolution, in order to hold down one's adversaries by force, it is pure nonsense to talk of a free people's state: so long as the proleteriat still *uses* the state, it does not use it in the interests of freedom but in order to hold down its adversaries, and as soon as it becomes possible to speak of freedom the state as such ceases to exist." *Selected Works,* II, p. 39. See further Engels' *Anti Duhring,* pp. 306f., where Engels (but not Marx) said: "The state is not 'abolished,' it *withers away.*" For a disdainful treatment of Engels on the state, see Plamenatz, pp. 135-144, 152-155, 164-167. For a defense, see Nicos Poulantzsas, *Political Power and Social Classes,* trans. Timothy O'Hagan (London: New Left Books and Sheed and Ward, 1973).

[43]*The German Ideology,* pp. 44f.

[44]See Michael Walzer, "A Day in the Life of a Socialist Citizen," in his *Obligations: Essays on Disobedience, War, and Citizenship* (Harvard: Harvard University Press, 1970), ch. 11.

[45]For example, in 1844-1847, as Lichtheim, p. 52, notes, "Marx was occupied with the problem of fitting the imminent German revolution into the conceptual

framework he had just elaborated."

[46]Avineri, p. 92.

[47]Cf. *ibid.,* pp. 140-149.

[48]*Collected Works,* IV, p. 37; italics in the original.

[49]Kautsky's remarks, published in the *Neue Zeit* (1901-1902), are quoted by Lenin in his *What Is To Be Done?* (1917), along with Lenin's elaboration of this theme. See Lenin, *Selected Works,* I, Part 1, pp. 233f., 242f. In *The Communist Manifesto* Marx and Engels did, to be sure, call upon the Communist Party to serve a tutorial function vis-a-vis the working class *(Selected Works,* I, pp. 44, 61). They even anticipated that "a portion of the bourgeois ideologists, who have raised themselves to the level of comprehending theoretically the historical movement as a whole," would desert the ruling class and join the proletariat; but this would occur, they painstakingly pointed out, only "in times when the class struggle nears the decisive hour" *(ibid.,* pp. 42, 41). Thus the class struggle, which is always (in Marx's view) a political struggle, had to come into being before the bourgeois intelligentsia could fashion the proletariat into such a class-conscious and revolutionary party. And it was precisely the failure of such a class and party to emerge that led Kautsky to formulate, and Lenin to approve, a new and revisionist doctrine.

Notes to Chapter Thirteen

[1]See for example, Harold D. Lasswell and Abraham Kaplan, *Power and Society* (New Haven: Yale University Press, 1950), p. xi.

[2]Leo Strauss, "An Epilogue," in *Essays on the Scientific Study of Politics,* ed. Herbert Storing (New York: Holt, Rinehart and Winston, 1962), p. 327.

[3]Two particularly important essays are "The Place of Classical Political Theory in the Study of Politics: The Legitimate Spell of Plato," in *Approaches to the Study of Politics,* ed. Roland Young (Evanston, Illinois: Northwestern University Press, 1958), pp. 125-148; and "The Limitations of Behavioralism," in *Contemporary Political Analysis,* ed. James C. Charlesworth (New York: The Free Press, 1967), pp. 51-71.

[4]These conceptualizations are also important for the normative dimensions of political theory. For a discussion see my "Values and Political Theory," *Journal of Politics* 39 (1977), pp. 877-903.

[5]G.W.F. Hegel, *The Philosophy of Right,* trans. T.M. Knox (Oxford: Oxford University Press, 1952), p. 11.

[6]Quentin Skinner, "Meaning and Understanding in the History of Ideas," *History and Theory* 8 (1969), pp. 3-53. Parenthetical references in this section are to this article.

[7]Quentin Skinner, " 'Social Meaning' and the Explanation of Social Action," in *Philosophy, Politics and Society,* 4th Series, ed. P. Laslett, W.G. Runciman, and Q. Skinner (Oxford: Basil Blackwell, 1972), p. 142.

[8]Mulford Sibley, *Political Ideas and Ideologies* (New York: Harper and Row, 1970), p. 5.

[9]Paul Ricoeur, *Interpretation Theory* (Fort Worth, Texas: Texas Christian University Press, 1976), pp. 29-30.

[10]Peter Winch, "Understanding a Primitive Society," in *Rationality,* ed. Bryan Wilson (New York: Harper and Row, 1970), p. 107.

[11]Felix Oppenheim, *Moral Principles in Political Philosophy* (New York: Random House, 1968), pp. 15-16.

[12]A. James Gregor, *An Introduction to Metapolitics* (New York: The Free Press, 1971), pp. 346-347.

[13]Felix Oppenheim, "The Language of Political Inquiry," in *Handbook of Political Science,* ed. F. I. Greenstein and N. Polsby (Reading, Mass.: Addison-Wesley, 1975), p. 283.

[14]Cf. Gregor, p. 27ff. and pp. 119-159.

[15]Israel Scheffler, *Science and Subjectivity* (Indianapolis, Indiana: Bobbs-

Merrill, 1967), p. 114.

¹⁶In the remainder of this section I follow the argument presented by Lakatos very closely. See Imre Lakatos, "Falsification and the Methodology of Scientific Research Programs," in *Criticism and the Growth of Knoweldge,* ed. Lakatos and A. Musgrave (Cambridge: Cambridge University Press, 1970).

¹⁷Lakatos's concept of a research program and Kuhn's concept of a paradigm are, I believe, closely related, and so I have been using them interchangeably. Perhaps Lakatos's term is preferable, since it is not subject to the many ambiguities which plague Kuhn's usage of "paradigm," but Kuhn's terminology has the advantage of familiarity. Kuhn argues the similarity between these concepts in his "Notes on Lakatos," *Boston Studies in the Philosophy of Science,* Vol. VIII, ed. Roger C. Buck and Robert S. Cohen (New York: Humanities Press, 1971), pp. 137-146.

¹⁸Thomas Hobbes, *Leviathan* (Oxford: Oxford University Press, 1909). Parenthetical references in this section are to the pagination of the 1651 edition.

¹⁹Anthony Downs, "An Economic Theory of Political Action in a Democracy," *Journal of Political Economy* 65 (1957), pp. 135-138.

Notes to Chapter Fourteen

¹Benjamin F. Wright, "The Federalist on the Nature of Political Man," *Ethics,* LIX (1949), Part II, p. 1.

²Merle Curti, "Woodrow Wilson's Concept of Human Nature," *Midwest Journal of Political Science,* I (1957), p. 3.

³See Sibley's *Political Ideas and Ideologies: A History of Political Thought* (New York: Harper and Row, 1970), *passim;* and *Nature and Civilization* (Itasca, Ill.: F. E. Peacock, 1977), esp. chs. 1-3.

⁴G.P. Gooch, "Forward" to Stanton Coit's *The One Sure Foundation of Democracy* (London: Watts, 1937), p. v.

⁵See H. Shelton Smith, *Changing Conceptions of Original Sin* (New York: Charles Scribner's Sons, 1955), and N. P. Williams, *The Ideas of the Fall and Original Sin* (London: Longman's Green and Co., Ltd., 1927).

⁶This threefold classification is not exhaustive. Belief in original sin seems as compatible with the absence of the state as it is with positions considered here. An excellent example is provided by the Eastern Catholic (Russian Orthodox) Nicolas Berdyaev, whose belief in original sin did not prevent him from expounding an essentially anarchist position. For his political and social thought see, e.g., *The Destiny of Man,* trans. Natalie Duddington (London: Geoffrey Bles, Ltd., 1937), pp. 195-212; *The Fate of Man in the Modern World,* trans. D. A. Lowrie (New York: Morehouse, 1935), chs. 2-4; *Christianity and Class War,* trans. D. Attwater (London: Sheed and Ward, 1933), chs. 2-5; *The End of Our Time,* trans. D. Attwater (London: Sheed and Ward, 1933), chs. 2 and 4; and *Towards A New Epoch,* trans. O. F. Clark (London: Geoffey Bles, Ltd., 1949), pp. 1-52, 76-80.

⁷Reinhold Niebuhr, *The Nature and Destiny of Man* (New York: Charles Scribner's Sons, 1941), I, p. 221. Also see his *Reflections on the End of an Era* (New York: Charles Scribner's Sons, 1934), esp. pp. 217-222.

⁸See in particular Luther's "To the Nobility of the German Nation," "On Secular Authority," and "On Good Works."

⁹Since "the temporal power has been ordained by God for the punishment of the bad, and the protection of the good, therefore we must let it do its duty throughout the whole Christian body, without respect of persons: whether it strikes popes, bishops, priests, monks, or nuns." "Address to the Christian Nobility of the German Nation," in *First Principles of the Reformation or the Ninety-Five Theses and the Three Works of Dr. Martin Luther,* trans. and ed. Henry Wace and C. A. Buchheim (Philadelphia: Lutheran Publication Society, 1885), p. 23. For a sympathetic treatment of Luther under the pressure of events, see Arthur C. McGiffert, *Martin Luther: The Man and*

His Work (New York: The Century Co., 1910).

¹⁰See, e.g., John T. McNeill, "Natural Law in the Thought of Luther," *Church History,* IX (1941), pp. 211-228, and his "Reformation Sources" in *Foundations of Democracy,* ed. F. Ernest Johnson (New York: Harper and Brothers, 1947).

¹¹A. D. Lindsay, *The Churches and Democracy* (London: The Epworth Press, 1934), p. 8. Also see Walter Rauschenbusch, *Christianity and the Social Crisis* (New York: Macmillan, 1907), pp. 187, 325, 334.

¹²On Calvin's alleged contribution to democracy, see G. Harkness,"Calvin and his Tradition," in *Protestantism: A Symposium,* ed. W. K. Anderson (Nashville: Commisison on Courses of Study, the Methodist Church, 1944).

¹³See Emil Brunner, *The Divine Imperative,* trans. Olive Wyon (New York: Macmillan, 1937), n. 7, pp. 680-682.

¹⁴Walter Rauschenbush, *Christianizing the Social Order* (New York: Macmillan, 1916), p. 86.

¹⁵See Smith, ch. 1, and Perry Miller, *The New England Mind* (New York: Macmillan, 1939), esp. pp. 21-25, 36-37.

¹⁶R. B. Perry, *Puritanism and Democracy* (New York: Vanguard Press, 1944); James H. Nichols, *Democracy and the Churches* (Philadelphia: Westminister Press, 1951), esp. ch. 1; Lindsay, pp. 5-39, and also Lindsay's *The Modern Democratic State* (New York: Oxford University Press, 1941), I, pp. 58-63, 75-77, 85-89, 115-278, and *The Essentials of Democracy* (Philadelphia: University of Pennsylvania Press, 1929), Lectures I and II.

¹⁷Johnson, "Introduction Depicting the Crisis in Modern Democracy," in Johnson.

¹⁸See, e.g., Walter Johnson, "Religion and Democracy in Colonial America," *Journal of Liberal Religion,* VI (1944), pp. 14-25; and Ernest S. Bates, *American Faith* (New York: W. W. Norton and Co., 1940), esp. chs. 8 and 11.

¹⁹*Ibid.*

²⁰Bates, p. 124.

²¹Walter Johnson, p. 15.

²²See Bates, p. 168; also Walter Johnson, pp. 15-18.

²³V. L. Parrington, *Main Currents in American Thought* (New York: Harcourt, Brace and Co., 1927-30), I, Bk. I; Perry Miller, *Orthodoxy in Massachusetts* (Cambridge: Harvard University Press, 1933); *The Puritans,* ed. Perry Miller and Thomas H. Johnson (New York: American Book Co., 1938), ch. 2, esp. pp. 181-194; Thomas J. Wertenbaker, *The Puritan Oligarchy* (New York: Charles Scribner's Sons, 1947); and James T. Adams, *The Founding of New England* (Boston: The Atlantic Monthly Press, 1921), chs. 7 and 11.

²⁴Quoted in Parrington, p. 20.

²⁵See, e.g., S. Paul Schilling, "The Christian Bases of Rights, Freedoms, and Responsibilities," in *The Church and Social Responsibility,* ed. J. R. Spann (New York: Abingdon-Cokesbury Press, 1953), pp. 17-78.

²⁶James Bryce, *The American Commonwealth* (London: Macmillan, 1888), I, p. 299.

²⁷See, e.g., William W. Sweet, *American Culture and Religion* (Dallas: Southern Methodist University Press, 1951), pp. 53-63; Moorhouse F. X. Millar, "The Founding Fathers," in F. Ernest Johsnon; Robert C. Hartnett, S. J., "The Religion of the Founding Fathers," in *Wellspring of the American Spirit* (New York: Harper and Brothers, 1948); and Theodore Maynard, *The Story of American Catholicism* (New York: Doubleday and Co., 1960), pp. 118-124, 149-158.

²⁸Norman Cousins, in his edited *In God We Trust* (New York: Harper and Brothers, 1958), p. 12. See further, Ralph H. Gabriel, *The Course of American Democratic Thought* (New York: Ronald Press Co., 1956 ed.), p. 12.

²⁹Richard Hofstadter, *The American Political Tradition* (New York: Alfred A. Knopf, 1948), p. 3.

³⁰See Wright, pp. 1-31; Ralph L. Ketcham, "James Madison and the Nature of Man," *Journal of the History of Ideas,* XIX (1958), pp. 62-76; and Louis Hartz, *The*

Liberal Tradition in America (New York: Harcourt, Brace and World, 1955), pp. 39-50.

[31]The literature on this point is staggering indeed. But those who contend that the "Fathers" were basically enemies of democracy generally follow, in various degrees, the broad framework laid down by Charles A. Beard, *An Economic Interpretation of the Constitution of the United States* (New York: Macmillan Co., 1935 rev. ed.), and J. Allen Smith, *The Spirit of American Government* (New York: Macmillan, 1911). Beard and Smith, it is true, have been severely criticized. But when all the peripheral points against them have been counted and their excesses corrected, the heart of their enterprises lingers with persuasive eloquence.

[32]Hofstadter, p. 3. Also see Hartz, pp. 39-50, and Arthur O. Lovejoy, *Reflections on Human Nature* (Baltimore: The Johns Hopkins Press, 1961), Lecture 2.

[33]Charles Frankel, *The Case for Modern Man* (New York: Harper and Brothers, 1955), p. 109.

[34]I have in mind those conservatives who emphasize traditionalism, inequality, hierarchy, privilege, aristocracy, nostalgia for old ways and ancient institutions as well as pessimism about man, opposition to social change, and contempt for the ideal of "progress." Typical representatives of the New (now not so new) Conservatism are Russell Kirk, Peter Viereck, Willmore Kendall, Francis G. Wilson, Frank S. Meyer, and William F. Buckley, Jr.

[35]Willard L. Sperry, *Jesus Then and Now* (New York: Harper and Brothers, 1949), p. 178.

[36]See Barth's *Against the Stream,* ed. Ronald G. Smith (New York: Philosophical Library, 1954), pp. 21, 25, 44, and *Church and State,* trans. G. Ronald Howe (London: Student Christian Movement Press, 1939), ch. 4, esp. pp. 71, 83. Also *The Church and the Political Problem of Our Day* (New York: Charles Scribner's Sons, 1939), esp. pp. 38-69, and *The Knowledge of God and the Service of God,* trans. J. L. M. Haire and Ian Henderson (London: Charles Scribner's Sons, 1938), pp. 230-232.

[37]*Church and State,* p. 80, and *Against the Stream,* p. 44.

[38]*Against the Stream,* p. 25.

[39]*Ibid.,* p. 44.

[40]See *Church and State,* esp. pp. 71, 83, and *The Church and the Political Problem of Our Day,* esp. pp. 38-41.

[41]The Lutheran Church, Lindsay observes, "has always preached the other worldliness of religion and submission to the powers that be..." *The Churches and Democracy,* p. 38.

[42]However, Brunner extols the virtues of federalism and finds it to be the safeguard against totalitarianism. The burning issue of the day, according to him, is federalism or totalitarianism, not democracy or totalitarianism. See *Justice and the Social Order,* trans. Mary Hottinger (London: Harper and Brothers, 1945), pp. 71-72, 79, 120, 125-126, 183.

[43]*The Divine Imperative,* pp. 445-446, 466.

[44]*Justice and the Social Order,* p. 178.

[45]*Ibid.,* pp. 70, 125, and 189.

[46]Throughout Brunner's social and political writings is a haunting emphasis on the virtues of order *per se.* See *ibid.,* pp. 69-70, 93, 98-101, 107, 124, 174-179, and *The Divine Imperative,* esp. pp. 466-467.

[47]*Justice and the Social Order,* p. 178.

[48]With his customary ontological bearings, Tillich has sought to discover the "ultimate" foundations of power and justice and has virtually ignored the concrete problems of political existence. See *Love, Justice, and Power* (New York: Oxford University Press, 1954), esp. pp. 1-71, 91-106, and *The Interpretation of History,* trans. N. A. Rasetzki and Elsa L. Talmey (New York: Charles Scribner's Sons, 1936), Part III.

In spite of Tillich's persistent stress on religious socialism, he has given little consideration to its political bases, particularly the problem of how to control power and prevent abuses.

[49]See Tillich's "The World Situation," in *The Christian Answer,* ed. Henry P. Van

Dusen (New York: Charles Scribner's Sons, 1946), pp. 22-24.

⁵⁰*Ibid.*

⁵¹*Ibid.*, p. 24. "Religious socialism," Tillich maintains, "if it is to keep any meaning and power, must not become another ideological justification of present democracies..." *The Protestant Era,* trans. with concluding essay by James Luther Adams (Chicago: University of Chicago Press, 1948), p. 260.

⁵²*The Interpretation of History,* pp. 184-185.

⁵³See *The Protestant Era,* including Adams' concluding essay.

⁵⁴"The most important contribution of Protestantism to the world in the past, present, and future is the principle of prophetic protest against every power which claims divine character for itself—whether it be church or state, party or leader." *Ibid.,* p. 230.

⁵⁵For this reason I have exempted from this essay the influential Anglican cleric, the late Archbishop William Temple. In spite of his emphasis on both the universality of sin and the desirability of democracy, he justified democracy from the standpoint of its affirmation of the sacredness of personality which is, in his view, derived from the Fatherhood of God. See his *Essays in Christian Politics and Kindred Subjects* (London: Longmans, Green and Co., Ltd., 1927), pp. 52-55. For his account of original sin, see, e.g., *Christianity and the Social Order* (Aylesbury: Penguin Books, Inc., 1956), pp. 52-55, 58-59.

⁵⁶See Niebuhr's *Children of Light and the Children of Darkness* (New York: Charles Scribner's Sons, 1944), *Christian Realism and Political Problems* (London: Charles Scribner's Sons, 1954), ch. 7, *The Nature and Destiny of Man,* II, pp. 265-284, and *Reflections on the End of an Era,* chs. 15-17.

⁵⁷*Christian Realism and Political Problems,* p. 121.

Notes to Chapter Fifteen

¹Morris R. Cohen and Ernest Nagel, *An Introduction to Logic and Scientific Method* (New York: Harcourt, Brace and Company, 1934), Preface.

²See Mulford Q. Sibley, "The Limitations of Behavioralism," *Annals of the American Academy of Political and Social Science* (October, 1962), pp. 68-93. A political theory is not the same thing as a philosophy of politics. Whether one interprets philosophy as based on a method of linguistic analysis, or merely recognizes that conceptual analysis is important in the development of a political theory, it must be recognized that there is more to a political theory than conceptual clarification or the attempt to link political analysis to, for example, epistemological positions or arguments, or other "traditional" concerns of philosophers. At the very least, one must admit that empirical evidence is relevant in considering the theorist's understanding of how current society functions and regarding the feasibility of prescribed alternatives. In this respect see W.G. Runciman, "Sociological Evidence and Political Theory," in P. Laslett and W.G. Runciman (eds.), *Philosophy, Politics and Society;* and *Social Science and Political Theory* (Cambridge, 1969). There is also the prescriptive role and ideological function of the theorist. David Miller, in his *Social Justice,* briefly sketches some relationships among these aspects of political theories (Oxford, 1976). Miller's work is interesting also in that in attempting to clarify three alternative views of social justice as they are grounded in three views of society he utilizes three clear-cut proponents; Hume, a "good" philosopher, Spencer, a "mediocre" philosopher, and Kropotkin, who was not a philosopher at all. Philosophers may write about politics; but not all significant political theorists are philosophers.

³Hannah Arendt, *Between Past and Future* (New York: The Viking Press, 1961), p. 146.

⁴Henry W. Johnstone, "The Nature of Philosopshical Controversy," *The Journal of Philosophy,* LI (1954), p. 295; John R. Searle, "How to Derive 'Ought' from 'Is,' " *Philosophical Review.* LXXIII (January, 1964), pp. 43-58.

[5]*Ibid,* pp. 295-96.

[6]*Ibid,* p. 296. "A philosophy is a systematic point of view; it is a theory embracing a totality in which there are no surprises. For example, no atheist is moved by the announcement that there is design in nature; for such design is not even an intelligible idea on his outlook. Thus it does not fall within the range of possible facts."

[7]*Ibid,* p. 297.

[8]*Ibid,* p. 298.

[9]*Ibid,* p. 299. This theme is elaborated upon in Henry W. Johnstone, "Philosophy and *Argumentum ad Hominem,*" *The Journal of Philosophy,* IL (1952), pp. 489-98. Compare this view with Wellman's complex proposal that justification can go beyond defending a statement with good reasons, and that the several forms of challenges to an ethical or normative position involve "contradictions" between the motives of a thinker and the consequences of his views. Carl Wellman, *Challenge and Response: Justification in Ethics* (Carbondale: Southern Illinois Press, 1971), pp. 167-276.

[10]Johnstone, "Philosophy and *Argumentum ad Hominem*" p. 493.

[11]*Ibid,* p. 495.

[12]*Ibid,* p. 498. In a later article, "The Methods of Philosophical Polemic," Johnstone analyzes seven ways in which a philosophy might be impugned as undermining its own purposes. *Methodos,* V (1953), pp. 131-40.

[13]Conal Condren, "The Quest for a Concept of Needs," in Ross Fitzgerald, ed., *Human Needs and Politics* (New York: Pergamon, 1977), p. 257.

[14]Arthur L. Kalleberg, "The Logic of Political Theory," unpublished manuscript.

[15]Stephen E. Toulmin, Richard Rieke, and Allen Janik, *An Introduction to Reasoning* (New York: Macmillan Publishing Co., 1979), p. 77.

[16]*Ibid,* pp. 47-49.

[17]See Arthur L. Kalleberg and Larry Preston, "Normative Political Analysis and the Problem of Justification: The Cognitive Status of Basic Political Norms, *The Journal of Politics,* XXXVII (1975), pp. 650-84.

[18]Toulmin, *et. al.,* p. 282. For a discussion of politics as essentially a matter of conscious or rational control, see Mulford Q. Sibley, *Nature and Civilization* (Itasca, Ill.: Peacock, 1977), pp. 28, 33-73.

[19]*Ibid,* p. 332.

[20]See Sheldon Wolin, "Political Theory as a Vocation," *American Political Science Review,* LXIII, No. 4 (December, 1979), p. 29.

[21]The phrase is from Michael Walzer, "On the Role of Symbolism in Political Thought," *Political Science Quarterly,* LXXXII, No. 2 (June, 1967), p. 199.

[22]Wellman, p. 57.

[23]*Ibid,* p. 44.

[24]*Ibid,* p. 70.

[25]*Ibid,* p. 42.

[26]Hobbes, *Leviathan* (Indianapolis: Bobbs-Merrill, 1958), pp. 25, 47, 52, 86, 104-106.

[27]Ernest Barker, Introd., *Social Contract* (New York: Oxford University Press, 1960), pp. 170-78.

[28]*Ibid,* pp. 174-75.

[29]*Ibid,* p. 193.

[30]Counter-factual thought reveals a high level of political self-consciousness. As Robert E. Lane pointed out recently in an interesting discussion of the effects of the market economy on political personality, "cross-cultural research reveals that the primary cognitive difference between diverse samples of traditional societies, compared to samples of advanced societies, is their lower capacities for imagining things contrary to fact, for 'shuffling things around in their heads.' " "Autonomy, Felicity, Futility: The Effects of the Market Economy on Political Personality," *The Journal of Politics,* XL, No. 1 (February, 1978), p. 13, with subquote from Jacqueline Goodnow, "Cultural Variation in Cognitive Skills," in Jerome Hellmuth, ed.,

Cognitive Studies, I (New York: Bruner/Mazel, 1970), pp. 242-57.

³¹Johnstone contends that an interpretation of dialectic can be developed that meets the objections of Hume, Kant and the logical positivists and which remains effective in the criticism of philosophical ideas. Construed in this manner, dialectic is synthetic, necessary, and non-definite. As such, it does not obligate every possible mind; "it obligates only that actual mind which, in its striving to maintain its own identity, has been driven by reflective thought from thesis to antithesis." Of course, if point of view is irrelevant to logic, then dialectic is more psychological than strictly logical, although leading to a kind of knowledge. Henry W. Johnstone, "Cause, Implication, and Dialectic," *Philosophy and Phenomenological Research,* XIV (1945), pp. 400-404.

³²Kai Nielsen, "Alienation and Self-Realization," *Philosophy,* XLVIII (January, 1973), pp. 21-35. Although Nielsen is largely concerned with pointing out the mistakes involved in self-realizationist ethics, he argues that the concept of alienation essential to Marxism does imply counter-factual assumptions concerning human nature and its potential.

³³*Ibid.* p. 32.

³⁴*Ibid.,* p. 33.

³⁵Allen W. Wood, "The Marxian Critique of Justice," *Philosophy and Public Affairs,* I, No. 3 (Spring, 1972), p. 249.

Mulford Q. Sibley:
A Selected Bibliography
Compiled by Marjorie Sibley and Dan Sabia
Books and Shorter Monographs

1944.   *The Political Theories of Modern Pacifism: An Analysis and Criticism.* Philadelphia: Pacifist Research Bureau, 1944. (Reprinted, with a new Introduction, in the Garland Library of War and Peace, 1972.)

1945.   *Conscientious Objectors in Prison.* With Ada Wardlaw. Philadelphia: Pacifist Research Bureau, 1945.

1952.   *Conscription of Conscience.* With Philip E. Jacob. Ithaca, New York: Cornell University Press, 1952.

1953.   *Introduction to Social Science: Personality, Work, Community.* Editor and contributor, with D. Calhoun, A. Naftalin, B. Nelson, and A. Papandreou. Philadelphia: J. B. Lippincott, 1953. (New edition, 1957; third edition, 1961.)

1962.   *Unilateral Initiatives and Disarmament.* Philadelphia: American Friends Service Committee, 1962.

1963.   *The Quiet Battle: Writings in the Theory and Practice of Non-Violent Resistance.* Editor and contributor. Chicago: Quandrangle Books, 1963. (Also published by Bharatiya Vidya Bhavan, Bombay, 1965; and by Beacon Press, Boston, 1968.)

1970.   *Political Ideas and Ideologies: A History of Political Thought.* New York: Harper and Row, 1970.

1970.   *The Obligation to Disobey: Conscience and the Law.* New York: Council on Religion and International Affairs, 1970.

1971.   *Technology and Utopian Thought.* Minneapolis: Burgess, 1971.

1975.   *Life After Death?* Minneapolis: Dillon, 1975.

1977.   *Nature and Civilization: Some Implications for Politics.* Itasca, Illinois: F. E. Peacock, 1977.

Forthcoming.   Professor Sibley's *Pacifism, Socialism, and Anarchism* is soon to be published by A. J. Muste Institute. In addition, Professor Sibley is currently working with Arthur L. Kalleberg on a book entitled *The Logic of Political Theory*; with Marjorie Sibley on a book entitled *Introduction to Political Sociology;* and on a utopian fictional work, tentatively entitled *Sitnalta.*

Major Essays and Articles

1940.   "Apology for Utopia: I." *Journal of Politics.* 2: 57-74.

1940.   "Apology for Utopia: II." *Journal of Politics.* 2: 165-188.

1943.   "The Political Theories of Modern Religious Pacifism." *American Political Science Review.* 37: 439-454.

1946.   "Modern Universalism." *Twentieth Century Political Thought,* ed. Joseph S. Roucek. New York: Philosophical Library, pp. 439-454.

1948.   "Can Foreign Policy Be Democratic?" *American Perspective.* 2: 155-162. (Reprinted in *Readings in World Politics,* ed. Robert A. Goldwin. New York: Oxford University Press, 1959, pp. 151-158.)

1949.   "Conscientious Objectors." *Colliers Encyclopedia.* 5: 611-613.

1950.   "The Traditional Doctrine of Freedom of Thought and Speech." *American Quarterly.* 2: 133-143.

1950.   "The American Alternatives." *American Perspectives.* 4: 11-17.

1951.   "The Problem of Might and Right." *Conflict in the Social Order, Series I.* Minneapolis: Centennial Lecture Series, University of Minnesota, pp. 10-17.

1955.   "Soviet Power and Soviet Ideology." *How Strong Is the U.S.S.R.?,* ed. Philip Siegelman. Minneapolis: Center for International Relations and Area Studies, University of Minnesota, pp. 1-15.

1957.   "Soviet Ideology Since the Death of Stalin." *The Post-Stalin Era.* Proceedings of a Symposium held at the University of Minnesota. Minneapolis: Center for International Relations and Area Studies, University of Minnesota, pp. 6-17.

1958.   "The Place of Classical Political Theory in the Study of Politics: The Legitimate Spell of Plato." *Approaches to the Study of Politics,* ed. Roland Young. Evanston, Illinois: Northwestern University Press, pp. 125-148.

1959.   "Force and War." *The Sibley-Kendall Debate: War and the Use of Force,* ed. Kent Lloyd, *et. al.* Denver: Swallow Press, pp. 15-29.

1960.   "Oneida's Challenge to American Culture." *Studies in American Culture,* ed. Joseph J. Kwiat and Mary Turpie. Minneapolis: University of Minnesota Press, pp. 41-62.

1961.   "Ideas and Attitudes at the Turn of the Decade, 1959-1961." *American Government Annual, 1961-1962,* ed. Ivan Hinderaker. New York: Holt, Rinehart and Winston, pp. 1-28.

1961.   "Socialism and Technology." *New Politics.* 1: 202-214.

1961.   "The Role of Political Theory in Political Education." With Ralph Miva and J. Hauptmann. *Problems of Political Theory.* Columbia,

Missouri: Bureau of Governmental Research, University of Missouri, pp. 38-57.

1962.   "The Limitations of Behavioralism." *The Limits of Behavioralism in Politial Science,* ed. James C. Charlesworth. Philadelphia: American Academy of Political and Social Science, pp. 68-93. (Reprinted in *Contemporary Political Analysis,* ed. James C. Charlesworth. New York: Free Press, 1967, pp. 51-71.)

1962.   "American Socialism and Thermonuclear War: A Symposium." *New Politics.* 1: 46-52.

1963.   "Unilateral Disarmament." *America Armed: Essays on United States Military Policy,* ed. Robert A. Goldwin. Chicago: Rand McNally, pp. 112-140.

1963.   "War Crimes, Morals, and Civilization." *The Minnesota Review.* 3: 142-153.

1964.   "The Nature of Academic Freedom." *Liberation.* March: 26-28.

1964.   "Agrarian;" "Anarchism." *Dictionary of the Social Sciences,* ed. Julius Gould and William Kolb. New York: Free Press, pp. 18-19; 25.

1965.   "Direct Action and the Struggle for Integration." *Hastings Law Journal.* 16: 351-400.

1965.   "On Political Obligation and Civil Disobedience." *Journal of the Minnesota Academy of Science.* 33: 67-72. (Reprinted in *Political Obligation and Civil Disobedience,* ed. Michael P. Smith and K. L. Deutsch. New York: Thomas Crowell, 1972, pp. 21-34.)

1966.   "Ethics and the Professional Patriots." *Annals of the American Academy of Political and Social Science,* 363: 126-136.

1966.   "Academic Freedom, It's Nature, and Some Implications." *Minnesota Teacher.* 8: 6-9.

1966.   "Development for What? Civilization, Technology, and Democracy." *Empathy and Ideology: Aspects of Administrative Innovation,* ed. Charles Press and Alan Arian. Chicago: Rand McNally, pp. 226-251.

1966.   "Time and the Significance of Politics." *Man vs. Time,* ed. Sally Pratt. Minneapolis: Graduate School Research Center, University of Minnesota, pp. 175-189.

1967.   "Social Order and Human Ends: Some Central Issues in the Modern Problem." *Political Theory and Social Change,* ed. David Spitz. New York: Atherton, pp. 221-255.

1967.   "Aspects of Nonviolence in American Culture." *Gandhi: His Relevance for Our Times,* ed. G. Ramachandran and T. K. Mahadevan. Bombay: Gandhi Peace Foundation, Bharatiya Vidya Bhavan, pp. 222-235.

1967.   "The Morality of War: The Case of Vietnam." *Natural Law Forum.* 12: 209-225.

1967.   "Why the U. S. Should Quit Vietnam." *The Torch.* 40: 48-54.

1968.   "Anonymity, Dissent, and Individual Integrity in America." *Annals of the American Academy of Political and Social Science.* 378: 45-57.

1968.   "The Need for a Radical Ethic." *New Left Forum.* 1: 7-18.

1968.   "Pacifism." *International Encyclopedia of the Social Sciences,* ed. David L. Sills. New York: Macmillan and the Free Press. 11: 353-357.

1968.   "Dissent: The Tradition and Its Implications." *A Conflict of Loyalties,* ed. James Finn. New York: Pegasus, pp. 103-139.

1968.   "Martin Luther King and Nonviolent Revolution." *Gandhi Marg* (New Delhi). July: 240-245.

1968.   "The President as Monarch." *Ivory Tower.* 16: 12-17.

1969.   *Revolution and Violence.* London: A *Peace News* Reprint; Housmans.

1969.   "Gandhi, the Technological Problem, and the Economic Order." *Khadigramodyog* (Bombay). June: 631-642.

1969.   "American Pacifism: The Problems and the Promise." *Worldview.* 12: 8-12.

1970.   "Conscience, Law, and the Obligation to Obey." *The Monist.* 54: 556-586.

1970.   "The Greater the Violence, the Less the Revolution." *Violence and Political Change.* Springfield, Missouri: Proceedings of the Sixth Annual Conference on Contemporary Issues, pp. 16-26.

1971.   "Violence, Non-violence, and Political Strategy." *Worldview.* 14: 5-9.

1972.   *Proceedings: Death and Attitudes Toward Death,* ed. Stacey B. Day. A Symposium with others. Minneapolis: Bell Museum of Pathology, University of Minnesota Medical School.

1973.   *Proceedings: Ethics in Medicine in a Changing Society,* ed. Stacey B. Day. A Symposium with others. Minneapolis: Bell Museum of Pathobiology, University of Minnesota Medical School.

1973.   "The Nature of Radical Man." *Political Science Reviewer.* 3: 85-108

1973.   "Utopian Thought and Technology." *American Journal of Political Science.* 17: 255-281.

1973.   "A Pacifist View of Peacemaking." *Society.* 10: 68-75.

1973.   "The Relevance of Classical Political Theory for Economy, Technology, and Ecology." *Alternatives: Perspectives on Society and Environment.* 2: 14-35.

1974.   "Regionalism and Industrial Society: Some Political and Administrative Dilemmas." *Perspectives on Regionalism,* ed. Ahmed
El-Afandi. Winona, Minnesota, pp. 74-83.

1975.   "Coercion of States and World Peace." *Foundations of Peace and
Freedom,* ed. Ted Dunn. Swansea, Wales: Christopher Davies,
pp. 316-324.

1976.   "Anarchists;" "Socialist Labor Party;" "Socialist Movement."
Dictionary of American History. New York: Charles Scribner's
Sons, 1: 116-117; 6:325-326.

1976.   "Law Day, May 1: On Law in Human Life." *Preachings on Natonal
Holidays,* ed. Alton M. Motter. Philadelphia: Fortress Press, pp.
25-31.

1976.   "Some Issues of Paranormal Communications." With J. Feola. *Bio-
sciences Communications.* 2: 157-169.

1977.   "Social Welfare and Some Implications of Non-Violence." *Journal
of Sociology and Social Welfare.* 4: 611-625.

1978.   "Political Theory, Peace, and the Problem of World Order." *From
Contract to Community,* ed. Fred R. Dallmayr. New York: Marcel
Dekker, pp. 127-165.

1978.   "Some Reflections on Life After Death." *Vital Statistics.* Fall:
64-82.

1978.   "The Time Is Now: The Case for Unilateral Disarmament." *Fellowship.* 44: 7-10.

1978.   "The Quest for Distributive Justice and the Liberal Outlook."
Liberalism and the Modern Polity, ed. Michael J. McGrath. New
York: Marcel Dekker, pp. 145-175.

1979.   "Intellectual Freedom, Suppression, and Obscenity." *Intellectual
Freedom in Minnesota: The Continuing Problem of Obscenity,* ed.
Nancy K. Herther. Minneapolis: Library Association, pp. 7-17.

1979.   "Political Science, Moses, and Ancient Hebrew Thought." *Western
Political Quarterly.* 32: 148-149.

1980.   "Ideological Factors in War." *Reconciliation Quarterly.* March: 24-
31.

1981.   "The Future of Peace and the Peace of the Future." *Futurics.* 5: 309-
322.

Forthcoming.   "The Problem of Coercion." *The Ethical Dimension of Political Life:
Essays in Honor of John H. Hallowell,* ed. Francis Canavan.
Durham: Duke University Press.
"Modernity in Politics and Political Theory." *Canadian Journal of
Political and Social Theory.*

Contributors

Terence Ball: Associate Professor of Political Science, University of Minnesota. Ph. D., University of California, Berkeley. Professor Ball is the author of *Civil Disobedience and Civil Deviance,* and editor of *Political Theory and Praxis;* his articles, reviews, and translations have appeared in a number of anthologies and in such journals as *Political Theory, American Political Science Review, The Review of Politics,* and *Philosophy of the Social Sciences.*

Christian Bay: Professor of Political Science, University of Toronto. Ph. D., University of Oslo. Professor Bay, who has published in many journals and anthologies, is the author of *The Structure of Freedom* and, most recently, of *Strategies of Political Emancipation.*

Samuel DuBois Cook: President, Dillard University. Ph. D., Ohio State University. President Cook is the author of numerous articles appearing in such journals as the *American Political Science Review, Journal of Politics,* and *Journal of Religious Thought.*

Richard Dagger: Assistant Professor of Political Science, Arizona State University. Ph. D., University of Minnesota. Professor Dagger has published articles in anthologies as well as in such journals as the *American Political Science Review, American Journal of Political Science,* and *Western Political Quarterly.*

James Farr: Assistant Professor of Political Science, Ohio State University. Ph. D., University of Minnsota. Professor Farr is coeditor of *After Marx,* and has published essays in *History and Theory, American Journal of Political Science, Inquiry,* and *Philosophy of the Social Sciences.*

Kathy E. Ferguson: Associate Professor of Political Science, Siena College. Ph. D., University of Minnesota. Professor Ferguson is the author of *Self, Society and Womankind* and of articles appearing in such journals as the *Review of Politics, Administration and Society,* and *Idealistic Studies.*

Richard Shelly Hartigan: Professor of Political Science and Adjunct Professor, Classics, Loyola University of Chicago. Ph. D., Georgetown University. Professor Hartigan's most recent books include *The Forgotten Victim: A History of the Civilian, Francis Lieber and the Law of War* and *The Future Remembered: Biology, Politics and Man.*

Arthur L. Kalleberg: Professor of Political Science, University of Missouri-Columbia. Ph.D., University of Minnesota. Professor Kalleberg, currently completing a book with Mulford Sibley on *The Logic of Political Theory,* has published articles in the *American Political Science Review, Journal of Politics, Polity, World Politics,* and other journals.

278   Dissent and Affirmation

J. Donald Moon: Associate Professor of Government, Wesleyan University. Ph. D., University of Minnesota. Professor Moon has contributed articles to many anthologies and to such journals as *American Journal of Political Science, Political Theory, Philosophy of the Social Sciences,* and *Journal of Politics.*

Daniel R. Sabia, Jr.: Assistant Professor of Political Science, University of South Carolina. Ph. D., University of Minnesota. Professor Sabia, who has coedited and contributed to *Changing Social Science: Critical Theory and Other Critical Perspectives,* is the author of numerous reviews and of an article in *Journal of Political Science.*

Lyman Tower Sargent: Professor of Political Science, University of Missouri-St. Louis. Ph. D., University of Minnesota. Professor Sargent, author of numerous journal and anthology articles, is also the author of *Contemporary Political Ideologies, New Left Thought,* and *British and American Utopian Literature 1516-1975;* coauthor of *Techniques of Political Analysis;* and editor of *Consent: Concept, Capacity, Conditions, Constraints.*

Peter C. Sederberg: Professor of Political Science, University of South Carolina. Ph. D., Johns Hopkins University. Professor Sederberg is the author of *Interpreting Politics,* coeditor of and contributor to *Vigilante Politics,* and the author of many articles and essays.

L. Earl Shaw: Associate Professor of Political Science, University of Minnesota. Ph. D., University of North Carolina. Professor Shaw is the coauthor of *United States Congress in Comparative Perspective,* coeditor of *Readings on the American Political System,* editor of *Modern Competing Ideologies,* and author of articles in *Policy Studies Journal* and *Political Science Reviewer.*

David Spitz: Professor of Political Science, Hunter College and Graduate Center, CUNY. Ph. D., Columbia University. Professor Spitz taught for many years at Ohio State University and also at Kenyon College, University of California at Berkeley, Johns Hopkins Bologna Center, and Cornell University. He contributed essays to many journals, served as an editor for *Dissent,* and was the author of *Patterns of Anti-Democratic Thought, Democracy and the Challenge of Power, The Liberal Idea of Freedom,* and *The Real World of Liberalism.*